Sheila Macqueen's

Complete Flower Arranging

Line drawings by Leslie Greenwood

Cymbidium hybrid 'Leslie Greenwood'

Sheila Macqueen's
Complete Flower Arranging

Times
BOOKS

To
Henry, William and Charlotte

Published by Times Books, a division
of Quadrangle/The New York Times Book Co., Inc.
Three Park Avenue, New York, N.Y. 10016

Published simultaneously in Canada by
Fitzhenry and Whiteside, Ltd., Toronto.

Published in Great Britain in 1979 by
Ward Lock Limited, London, a Pentos Company.

Printed in Italy

Library of Congress Cataloging in Publication Data
 Macqueen, Sheila
 Sheila Macqueen's complete Flower Arranging.
 Includes Index.
 1. Flower Arrangement. I. Title II. Title:
Flower Arranging.
SB449.M314 745.92 79-17939
 ISBN 0-8129-0866-X

Contents

Acknowledgments

I would like to express my sincere thanks to all those who have made this book possible. To Leslie Greenwood for his exquisite line drawings; they have added so much interest and will, I know, delight all those who read the book. To Caroline Mackinlay, not only for her invaluable help, but for her patience and good humour. To Roy Smith for his really lovely photographs, his immaculate attention to detail, and his bounding enthusiasm which makes these hard working days a pleasure. The black and white photographs are from the Harry Smith Photographic Collection.

Again I am most grateful to Ward Lock and their staff, several of them new since my last book, but they have fallen in cheerfully with all the welcoming help I experienced before, and a very special thank you to Suzanne Kendall.

This is the second Hyperion Book I have been privileged to write for Peter Crawley and his kindness, encouragement and understanding never cease to amaze me.

Sheila Macqueen

Introduction

It is nearly fifteen years since I wrote *Encyclopaedia of Flower Arranging* (now out of print for a number of years) and a great deal has happened in the flower world since then. A considerable number of people in England, the United States and other parts of the world have become interested in both arranging and growing flowers, and flower arranging clubs are flourishing everywhere.

One of the effects of this upsurge of interest is that standards are constantly rising and this is encouraging people to experiment not only with unusual materials and combinations of flowers for textures and colour, but also with their conditioning and preserving. Also plants which have been known to you for years suddenly take on a new interest as you find yourself seeing them through different eyes and using a leaf or a seed head you were not conscious of before. So even after many years, when you might think you ought, perhaps, to know it all you are amazed to find you are still learning.

I have often been told that the encyclopedia style of my first large book was invaluable for looking up information and I have, therefore, used this method again. I do hope I have succeeded in providing the helpful reference book you have been looking for.

Sheila Macqueen

Athyrium filix-femina

Part One
Equipment and how to use it

Equipment and methods

All flower arrangers need some equipment, and a place to keep it, whether your flower arranging is a hobby or a part-time job, as it is for many people nowadays. I have a small room in which I like to keep all of my flower arranging equipment and apart from it being less likely that things will be lost or borrowed, it saves me so much time to have everything I need to hand. I have found it most helpful to have a number of polythene bags of different sizes – they are invaluable for keeping vases in – and if you are fortunate enough to have brass or silver vases they will remain clean for much longer by being stored in polythene bags. Vases should be well washed and the netting scalded in hot water. The netting may then be put back into the vase and it is all ready for use on a later occasion. You will probably find that there are some vases you use only at particular times of the year, and it is better to keep them stored away, clean and ready for use. If you have only open shelves for storage the polythene bags become even more valuable.

Scissors and secateurs For years I have recommended flower arrangers to have a pair of small stub scissors of the type used by florists. They are invaluable as they cut not only stems but wire as well. Easy to handle, they can be kept in a pocket and will cut practically everything, apart from thick branches.

Secateurs are most useful. The small ones brought out by Wilkinson, called Flower Cutters, are excellent and I can thoroughly recommend these; they are compact and light, they will cut the thickest stems, and I carry mine about everywhere. There is a long-arm kind made by the French firm Talabot Pradines; this they name Cueille-Fleurs. It has a light clipper on a 60cm (2ft) handle – so convenient for the odd high spray and good for dead-heading roses, as you can use it with one hand and it saves treading all over the beds.

Stripper This is another small gadget I have found most useful; it is shaped like a pair of sugar tongs, with a V cut out of each end. You place it about 6cm (2½in) up the stem, depending on the amount of green you want to remove, and pressing both ends together, pull firmly downwards. This removes any surplus leaves and thorns from the bottom of the stem. Most useful in the summer, and especially for prickly shrubs or roses.

Baskets, trugs and sheets A trug or shallow flower basket that allows flowers to lie flat is by far the best for picking. If you can pick straight into a basket it saves a great deal of time, apart from reducing the amount of handling the flowers get – try always to keep this to the minimum.

Flower arrangers are sometimes bothered by the problem of carrying flowers to another place, such as a church or a coffee morning where an arrangement has to be made. The answer to this is to use one of those versatile polythene bags I mentioned earlier. This is by far the most effective carrier. It is best, I have found, to condition the flowers and give them several hours in water. Then take the thorns off the roses and other prickly subjects and put them into the bag, the longest stems first. And, of course, head first! Incidentally, white flowers and those with delicate petals should be taken out of the bag as soon as possible. This does not apply to tougher plants, particularly those with tough, shiny leaves such as the ivies or decorative cabbage – they will remain happily in a bag for several days and come out looking as fresh as when they went in. Bluebells and other wild flowers will last much better if put quickly into a polythene bag as soon as they are picked. If this is not done they will wilt almost immediately and take a long time to recover. (And may not recover at all, as I'm sure many of you have discovered. I should add, perhaps, when thinking of picking wild flowers that you should be sure it is lawful to do so as restrictions on picking wild flowers apply in a number of countries.) If you have no polythene I suggest you wrap the flowers in newspaper or something which covers the heads. Florists always do this – it helps enormously to keep flowers fresh, particularly in unusually cold or hot weather.

One of the problems of flower arranging is the mess one makes, unavoidably, with petals and bits of unwanted stem and so on. A dust sheet is very useful and if you can get hold of a large sheet of polythene, the heavy variety, and sew a pleat down each side and slide canes into them you will have a most useful and easily stored appliance! When you are starting a new arrangement make sure the water is fresh and that the vase is in the position in which the arrangement is to be. It is important to be aware of the difference in height of similar pieces of furniture, for the way the light falls from a window can completely alter the effect of the colour of the flowers, so that often one needs extra foliage for backing or finds no need for quite so much after all. Whenever possible, spread out your dust sheet and work where the vase is going to remain.

Watering cans and buckets A watering can or bucket is necessary if you are working away from home. A lot of time can be wasted hunting for a can when one is in a strange house or church. Vases are easier to arrange when the water is in them – they are then better balanced. I fill them three-quarters of the way and top up at the end. For this you need a small can with a long spout, but a bottle or jug will do very well.

Positioning

Most people have their own method of holding flower stems in position. Some think wire net-

ting is the best, others prefer pin-holders – it doesn't really matter. What is important is that you should use what you find quickest and easiest.

Wire netting I strongly recommend you use 5cm (2in) mesh wire netting. Smaller mesh, once it is crumpled, does not allow enough space for the stems. A guide as to how much you need is that the length of the piece should be twice the width of the aperture at the top of the vase. For very small-stemmed flowers you will need a little more, and less for large stems, such as lupins. Large mesh is advisable in every way, and is much more pliable and easier to handle. Plastic-covered wire netting is excellent for precious vases.

Pin-holders (needle-point) Pin-holders have heavy bases of metal with a large number of small, upright pins mounted in them which impale any flower stem pressed on to the points. Always buy the most expensive pin-holder – it is well worth the extra cost. It is usually heavier and made in copper, which doesn't rust – and the heavier the holder, the easier to use. To hold the pin-holder firm, if you are using it alone, roll a piece of plasticine into a circle and fix it on to the base of the holder before placing it in the vase, making quite sure that the surface is dry. The Japanese have marvellous 'well' pin-holders – rather like a small pot made in metal with the needle-point pins in the bottom. I find these extremely useful. With a large vase I generally use an ordinary pin-holder at the bottom, then several layers of crushed-up wire netting. This gives the best results. The weight of the pin-holder secures heavy background branches, and the wire netting allows for easy placing of the smaller and horizontal stems.

Oasis This is a green synthetic brick and the one I find most useful. Take the brick and cut out a piece to fit the size of the vase, soak this really well and after that you can use it, the flowers lasting for at least twelve hours without additional water. Flowers stand in it easily and you can be certain they will not move. I like to use it in deep water, and with a piece of wire netting over the top to ensure that it will not break up easily. When it is under water, one knows that the flowers will last really well.

Mossette and Florapack Oasis has taken over from both of these products but I will still include their uses here, as there could be parts of the world where they are still very much in use. Both are better if they are crumbled first, then placed in a jug full of water with a weight on top, to get really soaked. After that put them in a polythene bag, fill it with water and immerse the whole in the vase. You may find it advisable to puncture the bag, and then secure it with a piece of wire netting over the top.

All of these water-absorbing materials are useful in vases sent on board ship or to a nursing home, where flowers may well stand out of water for some time. They are quite expensive and I rarely use them in my own home, because I can fill up the vases, but for a wedding or flowers for a special occasion then I think they are well worthwhile. Oasis is often covered, particularly in the United States, with a piece of foil paper and this method is ideal when used in a shallow container that does not hold much water.

Cones or tubes These cones are rarely found in tin today but mostly in plastic and even these are quite hard to come by. They are invaluable for raising a few short-stemmed flowers to give additional height and colour to a group. Using silver wire or adhesive tape, attach each cone to a cane or stick at the height you require; push a small piece of wire netting into the cone itself to prevent the stems from slipping about; secure the netting and fill the cones with water – they should hold enough to keep the flowers fresh for several hours. As it is difficult to fill them with water once the vase is crowded with flowers, remember to do this first. When the cones have been filled place the whole device in the vase, pushing the canes through the wire netting in the vase so that they go right to the bottom. I find this method useful for really large groups but I try to avoid using cones too often as they tend to give a slightly artificial effect. But they are invaluable sometimes for foliage, or some lilies perhaps, that you don't want to cut on too long a stem.

String or gardener's twist (green) Handy at any time and useful to tie round a vase to keep the wire netting in securely. Once the flowers are in place, they are balanced and the string can be cut; however, I never bother to do this unless the string actually shows in the finished arrangement.

Silver wire Even more useful, as it never shows. If you only want a little, then a card of fuse wire is all that you require, but the reels that are obtainable from a florist or local flower club are a good investment.

Sellotape (Scotch tape) Again something that can be used to hold the wire netting securely in the vase. It hardly shows and can be placed either just over the sides or right over the whole vase. Roll the adhesive tape that goes over the top of the vase, as it is inclined to take up too much stem space. I have found that the green tape like a form of Sellotape is wonderful for securing the Oasis or wire netting. I first bought mine in the United States but have since found that you can buy it in England. It has the advantage over Sellotape in that it is very much firmer, and also that it can be easily torn in half and the half is really all you need, except for a really large arrangement.

Elastic bands Also useful for keeping wire netting in place.

Florist's wires These are handy to have in the house and though I never advocate wiring any flower that goes into a vase, a broken stem can be splinted with a wire run up the inside. It can be quickly attached to a stem to keep it in position. Try to avoid wiring flowers that are in an arrangement as they immediately assume an unnatural angle. Only wire such flowers as are to be worn or carried.

Balancing

Plumber's lead Strips of lead can be used instead of string for securing wire netting in a vase. Make a loop round the wire netting with one end of the strip and let the other hang over the back of the vase; this helps to balance the weight of the flowers in the front. They can also be used to keep a heavy stem or branch in place. Take a strip of lead about 23cm (9in) long, cut it along the middle to about half way down, so that you have two arms and a trunk; insert the trunk part in the vase and wind the two arms round the branch; this will ensure that the stem is really steady – most important, as the stem carries most of the weight.

Gravel and sand I recommend you keep a little gravel or sand in a tin as it is extremely useful for stabilizing light vases or containers.

Stones of attractive colour or shape, are good for weighting or for concealing a pin-holder, and can also add charm to an arrangement. When you are in the country or near the sea, look out for chunks of stone from streams and well-coloured pebbles. (And, of course, for driftwood.)

Window-wedges are most useful for propping under a sloping vase. These are particularly good for a sloping window-ledge in a church. The thickness of the wedge depends on the slope you need to counteract. A shallow ovenware dish can be used on a sill with quite a steep slope and still be kept firm, and the water kept level, with one of these wedges.

Methods of arrangement

Of course it is necessary to give guidance for those who are fairly new to flower arranging, and strangely it is for me one of the most difficult things to write about. It is easier to teach by example, and watching demonstrations is probably one of the best ways to learn. However here are some guides that I hope will help. As I mentioned earlier, the aids that you use to hold your flower stems in place are a matter of personal choice. I think I use wire netting more generally, simply because it is what I started with, but I like to use pin-holders for shallow vases, and use the two combined for large groups.

To arrange the flowers where they are actually going to stand is one of the most important things to do, as I mentioned previously. It is so difficult to get the feeling of colour, shape,

height, light, and proportion if you arrange in the kitchen and then proceed through three swing doors to your final destination. For home or church I like to work with dust sheets, first removing all the dead flowers which can be thrown away so that you are not tramping on or through dead pieces. Then remove the vase and wash thoroughly, scalding the wire netting should it be unpleasant. Replace and fill the vase three-quarters full of water, having first fixed your half brick of damp oasis, or pin-holder, and several layers of 5cm (2in) mesh wire netting. I like about five layers of wire.

Decide on a container suitable for both the position in which you want to use it and the sort of material that you have available, at the time of year. If you have a large amount of flowers available then the container is not so important. A shallow dish will hold water and as it will not be seen is very adequate. If flowers are scarce then it is best to obtain a pretty little vase as the vase will be seen a lot and its attractiveness will play an important part in the final emphasis of the arrangement. Collect some tall spikes, either in foliage or flowers – gladiolus, delphinium, larkspur, verbascum, iris leaves; flowering branches in season – forsythia, plum, cherry; seed heads like lupin, foxglove; pointed foliage – beech, *Viburnum sterile opulus*, in autumn colour, or azalea. These are all needed according to season, for *light* background material. Light is important; the outline must be delicate in order not to spoil the finished arrangement.

Starting with a basic urn which calls for a fan-shaped arrangement, take your tallest stem and fix this firmly in the wire netting. This stem is of paramount importance, as if it starts to slip or move it can disarrange the whole vase and often end in tipping it over. The tallest stem must stand straight, not leaning forward or backwards, as strangely this stem decides whether the vase as a whole looks as if it is falling forward or

A collection of suitable containers for flower arrangements, many of which have been used in the photographs throughout this book.

backwards. The first stem must be vertical but it can be off centre. If you look at the photographs you will see that my topmost stem is either to right or left of the arrangement as I find in this way I can get a slight twist to the vase and prevent it looking too stiff. In short, fix the main stems firmly. Then get your general outline shape. For a fan-shaped arrangement this should be approximately one and a half to twice the height of the vase, and the overall width about the same. These are just approximations, and not rules. Use the lighter and more delicate spray-like material for the outline.

Having placed the central piece to give you the height, take two stems that are slightly shorter and place them one on either side; these should not be of identical height, or the whole vase will look too symmetrical. The next stems on either side can be shorter still; the next, almost the same height as the first, but placed at a slight angle to the horizontal to give you the fan shape; the next should be threaded through the wire netting horizontally, to curve over the sides of the bowl. Then carefully choose slightly curving pieces, to hang over the front. In order to get these to fall gracefully, the stems should be threaded again through the netting, almost horizontally. To ensure that these stems are well in water, it is essential to fill the vase right up to the top. Now fill in this outline with flowers: say, one or two stems of delphiniums, and larkspurs, gradually coming to the more solid flower heads. For the actual centre use the boldest and best flowers with a 'face', as we call them – flat-headed of many petals, such as an open rose, dahlias or chrysanthemums. Use an uneven number in the centre; this avoids forming straight lines. So take two or three roses for instance, and let these hang about 15–30cm (6–12in) over the front of the vase; then recess or tuck in one or two more right in the centre, and these will give the impact of colour to the arrangement. It is interesting to note that these central flowers dominate the colour of the vase, and if in a mixed vase you want blue to predominate, then the blue must go right in the centre. Recessing one or two flowers deep in the centre of the vase may seem a bit of a waste, but they are most valuable for this intensifying of the colour effect. Study the stems and the angle at

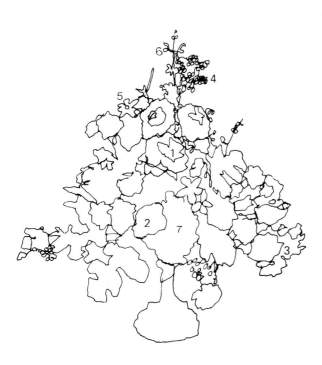

This strange pinky-mauve and brown arrangement was entirely built up round the unusual colours of the leaves that I found on a walk.

1 Rose 'Vesper'
2 Rose 'Magenta'
3 *Campanula lactiflora* 'Loddon Anna' (Bellflower)
4 Berries
5 *Nicotiana affinis* (Tobacco plant)
6 *Salvia sclarea* 'Turkestanica'
7 *Euphorbia polychroma*

which they have grown, so that you find a piece that will curve naturally to the right and one that will curve to the left. This can be achieved more easily with stems that fall gracefully, with a natural tendency to bend slightly in one direction or another. Stems of ivy, old man's beard, *Alchemilla mollis*, periwinkle, and so on, all give a natural down-sweeping effect. There is no need to push every flower stem right down to the bottom of the vase; some can well be tucked in horizontally provided a good part is under water and not exposed to the air.

The upright stem with which it is easiest to start all flower arrangements is the stem that must *always* be upright, firmly fixed through the layers of wire netting, and then impaled on the pin-holder if you use one. It is better not to shorten any stems until you are certain that this is essential. Before cutting the stem, hold your flower against the arrangement to get an idea where you are going to place it. If it seems a little too long always first try pushing it down well into the vase, then take it out again and cut it if necessary. Try to keep all stems as long as possible, as this takes away from an over-stiff and too formal effect. A natural effect is often hard to achieve and you can never add a piece on! In the final adjustment to the vase a stem is often better pulled forward a little, and this might not be possible if the stems have been cut too short. For large groups the conical tubes mentioned earlier can help to give added colour and height to bridge the gap between tall foliages and short flowers. The use of several large leaves tucked in at the base of the vase helps to add under-shadow and has the effect of 'cleaning up' the whole vase.

Now we come to the method for a shallow dish, often described as a line arrangement, and shown in the photograph on page 187. You will see this rather strange looking fungus, but the colour was so beautiful that it inspired me to pick up the colourings in the *iris peony*, 'Souvenir de Maxime Cornu' and sprig of cream honeysuckle; it made a most interesting arrangement in a shallow container fixed on a pin-holder in a small bowl sufficiently deep to hold the water. Fix the pin-holder firmly with a strip of plasticine. Roll the plasticine between your hands into a sausage, fit this round the base of

the pin-holder and press down on a dry surface. Take the tallest stem and fix it firmly on the pin points, allowing the beauty of the iris to show to advantage, and try and arrange the next two so that all three are seen as perfect flowers. I placed the fungus to cover the mechanics. You will see a similar type of arrangement with the chincherinchee on page 186. Here the base is virtually the vase, a round sliver of wood, and very effective.

The method for a small mass arrangement as seen for the spring flower vase is really the same method used as in the big arrangement. Place in the tall stems and then work from the outside in, but here the use of small bunches of one type of flower is important. This is what I term 'blocking', by which I mean working the flowers so that you have several together; even if not the same flower they should have the same colouring. In this way you avoid a spotty effect, and the arrangement is better defined. By placing single flowers, one here and one there, you lose much of the colour values.

Daffodils look well by themselves, with perhaps a branch of forsythia or the catkins of alder. My own favourite way is to fill a shallow container with needle-point and wire netting, cover the whole with a layer of nice green moss, fix your branch firmly on to the needle-point, and make small holes in the moss to place your daffodils. They look more natural if you have about three or four daffodils together and you achieve a less formal arrangement than if you place each stem in singly. What you get here is a feeling that the flowers are growing in woodland; see the arrangement on page 67.

When making a massed arrangement of all one kind of flower and its own foliage, choose a box with a lid, or an oblong china dish or a copper trough, depending on the length of stem, of the flowers. Fix in the wire netting firmly, then take your well-soaked flowers – whether honeysuckle, bluebells, jasmine, old-fashioned roses, or wallflowers – and with small bunches of a few stems together arrange them in a flowing and unrestricted way. The flowers that are chosen for such arrangements are generally the ones that smell sweet and are perhaps not very long-lasting in water, but closely packed like this they seem to live longer. Or it could be that the fallen petals are not so conspicuous!

The foliage arrangements, often called 'mixed greens', are very popular and are used throughout the year. They last well and one can rely on at least one vase almost always looking fresh – and this for a flower arranger is a big thing, as one feels that one should never be caught without a flower in the house! I love a background of lichened branches to a winter group of ivies, ferns and perhaps a stem of variegated camellia foliage. A vase of grey greens and a vase of yellow greens both make interesting subjects. When I set out to do mixed foliages, I like to avoid the rules and mix in seed pods in all the shades of green, and perhaps a few green flowers. These make really unusual vases. Of course if you are showing a group and the class says mixed foliage, then one cannot put in any flower or seed head, however green it may be. By the same token, one cannot put in yellow or greys for a class of green foliage. These variations are much more fun to do at home. Try to find unusual and varying shapes and forms: leaves that are stiff and upright, such as iris; feathery foliage, such as ferns; leaves and sprays that hang easily. All these make for more interest than leaves of just one shape. Although these foliage groups last longer than flower groups, they often take a little longer to pick and arrange and need a lot of thought beforehand. (For help in choosing material for foliage arrangements see the Foliage colour guide on page 112 which lists some lime-greens, yellows and greys.)

Having dealt with vases of flowers on their own, and then foliage alone, we come to the mixing of both, using flowers and unrelated foliage – such as sprays of reddish berberis with flowers in all the shades and tones of reds; pieces of different-coloured autumn foliage with orange-yellow dahlias or roses; grey foliages with pinks or mauves. Pink carnations are excellent mixed with greys, and a few tulips make an attractive group with a mixture of greens and dried seed heads. There are so many possible combinations.

The big group is one of the most difficult forms of arrangement, though nowadays, with the great interest in flower festivals, they are being done more than ever before by a wider range of people. What one notices so often at flower festivals is that there are far too many flowers in the big groups and they are desperately overcrowded. If you are doing flowers for a wedding or some important occasion, a pedestal vase is most important – aim to make this as bold and striking as you can. Choose good backing: flowering branches of cherry, stripped lime or autumn-coloured leaves. Next well-grown stems of gladioli, delphiniums, acanthus, lupins, and any flower that has a good flower spike. Lilies not only add quality to a big group, but have such good 'faces' that they show up well from any distance. Then concentrate on the focal point, with heads of hydrangeas, dahlias, roses, peonies or rhododendrons in the centre. I think it is a good maxim to go for quality rather than quantity, especially when you are working on a big vase. This prevents overcrowding, which can be caused by trying to create a startling effect, and in so doing, it is easy to lose the personality of each flower. Try to let each flower play its part and be seen as a whole flower, not overshadowed by another. Try to place each flower so that it is not obscured in any way. This is essential for flowers that form the focal point in the centre, for once this becomes overcrowded and messy the whole group is spoiled. Some of these central stems should be recessed to give a three-dimensional effect. Large groups that are seen from a distance need to be clear-cut with a tailored look. Bold leaves of arums, or saxifrage, and of course hosta, all play an important part at the base of a big group. They help to give it a feeling of tranquillity. These groups need design, and to be more than just the harmonious massing of colour.

I find flower arranging horribly contradictory, but perhaps because of this the interest never flags. You are forced to make continual reassessments – it is so easy to say that delicate flowers need delicate containers and be thinking of cosmos and columbines in dainty glass or porcelain vases. And yet what could be more lovely than an enormous earthenware bowl arranged with a mass of sweet peas in groups of individual colours? Flower arranging is like all other creative arts – do not allow yourself to be over burdened with rigid rules! Most of all, allow your own imagination and initiative every opportunity to express themselves – you will surprise yourself at the results you get.

Vases and containers

You will see a wide selection of containers throughout this book, and I have tried to vary the shapes and sizes as much as possible, hopeful that there is something here for everyone. If you buy a really nice container, be it old or new, your money will be well spent, because it is something you will use and enjoy for many years – long after the hat which could today cost about the same and is soon out of date and shape!

Some of the containers I love most dearly for flower arrangements have started life as something very different! Preserving pans and copper kettles are two examples but my tea urn has, perhaps, the oldest pedigree. The important thing is to have the widest possible selection, for so often there may be only one or two months each year when you can use something which, at the time, looks very dramatic. A really bright blue glass goblet for the side shoots of delphiniums, or some stems of gentian – then such a vase becomes of great importance in emphasizing the striking brilliance of the blue flowers. Similarly, red roses look superb in a pewter jug or dried grasses gathered, perhaps, from the side of a lane, seem absolutely right standing in an earthenware pot. You may very well, on occasion, not want to show a container you have adapted for an arrangement – the simple answer, if you have plenty of flowers, is to let them disguise it; I have wonderful effects using an ovenware dish.

But supposing you live in a town and have no garden to pick from, then the choice of container becomes particularly important; a small, fragile china vase can hold a bunch of primroses, or a spray of roses, which will look pretty just as it is without other foliage. If the size of the room demands a large vase, then it is often possible to buy one with a lid so that it can hold flowers when they are plentiful, and when they are scarce and expensive, you can always pop on the lid! The vase plays a far greater part in the house of the non-garden-owner than for the plant-grower.

When searching for a vase that you expect to use a lot, buy one in a neutral colour, say in white or grey, or a dusky pink, so that most of the mixtures of colourings can be used safely in it. Strikingly coloured containers can have their

drawbacks and you may find that you only use them at particular times of the year and with flowers of a certain colour. So buy a vase with care, though gradually as you become a flower arranger you will spend a lot of time (and possibly too much money!) in the pleasurable hunt for others. I spend many happy hours browsing around the antique shops, and in shops and markets at home and abroad, in search of something unusual; though naturally I still have my favourites, and these are used over and over again. Using a different vase in the same place in your room will change the whole effect, and the more often you can do this the better. And I must emphasize again, avoid using too many flower vases in the same room; one tall vase, perhaps, and something low – a pretty small vase on a coffee table – is all you need. It is much better to make one really attractive arrangement than to hurry through too many. For everyday use I would choose a vase that holds a lot of water. The shallow bowl-type need constant replenishment with water and are best kept for special occasions.

Some quite small rooms can take a pedestal arrangement well. The deciding factor is the amount of space you can allow for flowers. A large arrangement can take the place of a piece of furniture, and this is helpful for the young who are starting up a home. And a really large group which can be arranged with dried seed heads and preserved flowers in winter, and perhaps mixed foliage in the summer, will effectively fill a gap in a room until one knows what one wants to put there. A pedestal and vase are lovely for a party, showing up well and easily seen. This takes a lot of flowers, although good use can be made of inexpensive material. A good idea is to have a lamp, or decorative ornament, that can be placed on the top of the pedestal for everyday use or when there is not enough time for arranging flowers. These pedestals fill many a corner most effectively and, if used in a room with a high ceiling, help to fill the gap between floor and ceiling, having the effect of making a ceiling seem lower. They are of course ideal for using in a church for a wedding, or in a ballroom for a dance.

Wall vases, or wall pockets, have been in use for centuries and were quite common a few years ago. They are often seen at their best in restaurants where the flowers can be seen and admired without getting in anyone's way. They are also very useful for small entrance halls where space is at a premium – and what a splendid welcome they give! As they can look a little desolate when empty, I have found that a small dried flower arrangement can be kept in one of those ubiquitous polythene bags and popped into the wall vase when there are no fresh flowers on hand for it. Because of their often having a good, clear background they are not at all difficult to arrange and some excellent effects can be achieved.

Most people like to have some flowers on the table, and here one needs to be very careful in the choice of vase. Be guided by the amount of space that is to be used for the flowers themselves, remembering everything else that may have to go on the table, including fruit and candles and other decorative effects. Often a small rose on a shell, or a few flowers tucked into a bowl of fruit will give you the best results. Otherwise, my advice is take a smaller vase than you feel you will need and spread the flowers out well from the edge of the bowl. View from all sides, and keep the arrangement fairly low, or have it in a very tall vase, so that it will not obstruct the line of vision. When it is completed, always sit down and look at it, to make certain that no wire shows and that the rim of the vase is well concealed. There is of course a wide choice of containers, but sometimes it is nice to put the flowers in part of the dinner service, using perhaps a vegetable dish or sauce boat. Generally speaking, flower arrangements for the table must be all-round, or oval. Of course, if the table stands against the wall, the vase can be placed at the back, and face in one direction only.

Flowers are always welcoming in the guest's bedroom – preferably just a posy of something fragrant, placed on the dressing table or by the bed-side. Some of the pretty little Italian figurine vases are ideal; or one of the old-fashioned china hands, or other small pretty piece of china. Flowers on the breakfast tray, as a special luxury – primroses in an egg-cup look charming. Remember that a vase in the hall needs to be on a solid, stable base so that it is not likely to fall or be knocked over and that it is particularly carefully balanced. Gusts of wind when doors open can create havoc!

A jardinière is now very popular, with the ever-increasing interest in house plants. It is much more effective to collect several pot plants and put them together, rather than having them dotted about the house in odd corners. These indoor gardens are particularly suitable in a sun-room, or in the hall, and have the great advantage of needing very little maintenance.

Here is a list of various kinds of vases and containers that are all good to use.

Alabaster I have collected alabaster vases for more years than I care to mention. The delicate creamy colouring blends so well with all kinds of different colour combinations, from creams and yellows to brilliant reds; and almost all kinds of flowers are suitable, though I feel that some flowers look even better in it than others. I love roses in alabaster as much as I like a collection of cream and brown seed heads. Alabaster needs rather special care. Water roughens the surface after a time, and it is better to line the vase with a bowl to prevent this from happening. The acid from flower stems leaves deep marks – alabaster is a form of limestone, so it's hardly surprising – and if left near constant heat it loses a great deal of its translucence and becomes opaque. It should be treated with olive oil.

Baskets These are useful all the year round – a garden basket, baby trug, cornucopia – but avoid the gilded long-handled types. They can be bought quite inexpensively in every shape and size. If they are specially made to take flowers, they are supplied with a liner to hold the water; but should you see some other one that you like, it is quite easy to find a bowl or tin that will hold enough water for the flowers; pack this firmly round with newspaper to stop it moving about.

Brass This lacks the warm look of copper, but gives good highlights and is lovely with soft yellows, lime-greens, and autumn colourings. It is possible to find very nice brass bowls and boxes, though urns are a little more rare. Brass and copper both go well with dark oak furniture, and make a nice container for the hall.

Flowers last well in the coolness of metal containers.

Bronze has been used for many centuries for making beautiful vases. Chinese and Japanese flower arrangers have used it with exquisite effect for centuries and I can think of no better container than a really well-shaped bronze urn. As these vases are metal, flowers last so well in them and their dark colour will set off very varied material – for instance, the dramatic effect of a black and white group, done with perhaps black grapes or privet berries, and white dahlias or roses . . . but there are endless possibilities. If you are ever lucky enough to find a copy of the Warwick vase in bronze, it is one of the loveliest of all for a large, handsome arrangement.

China urns are becoming more popular all the time, for all types of flower arrangement. It is possible to buy them in different colours, and greys and mauvey-pink can make a pleasant change from the usual white, which I feel has become rather ordinary. However, as you can put almost any material into a white vase, this would be a good choice if you are going to use it continually.

Copper This is ideal for so many types of arrangements, especially for those with golds and reds – dahlias and chrysanthemums particularly. Copper jugs, bowls and tea-urns all make good containers. If you have a tea-urn, it is a good idea to have the tap expertly removed to be sure that it does not leak. The glow of a highly-polished copper surface will add warmth and reflections to any dark corner. The problem of constant cleaning has been largely overcome with 'long life' cleaner; or you can lacquer the surface, but be sure to remove all really bad stains beforehand – this can be done by rubbing on lemon and salt, or vinegar and salt, with a coarse cloth, and rinsing well with cold water before using a good metal polish.

Fibre glass It is possible to buy reproductions of some of the beautiful old lead vases, in pewter-grey fibre glass. The copies are extremely well finished and at first glance one could be taken in

by them. They are, however, as light as a feather. Even when they are filled with water, I think it is advisable to add additional weight, with a brick or a piece of lead, if you are going to use them to hold large branches. But I advise you to handle them with care as it is possible to knock bits off them fairly easily.

Glass The greatest disadvantages of glass vases are that the wire netting shows, and that the water must be kept scrupulously clean; a glass vase with dirty water looks most unattractive. They should be washed with soap and water as soon as they have been used. If in constant use, wash them as often as possible, as it becomes progressively more difficult to remove the water mark which forms on the rim. A piece of lemon dipped in salt will help to remove the stains and sediment from the base. Hydrochloric acid is a stronger but more drastic remedy which should be used with the greatest care as it can burn hands and clothes badly. Some modern vases are made in mottled glass which obscures the wire netting. I like to use glass when the vase is to stand against the light, giving a silhouette effect.

Marble Old marble is hard to find, but is lovely to use if you can get it, and much more durable than alabaster. It will hold water with no serious effects. A marble urn or bowl for summer flowers is ideal. The modern Italian marble, in various shapes and sizes, successfully reproduces some of the old designs, and though expensive can look enchanting in the right surroundings. Sometimes old-fashioned light-shades – the marble-bowl kind to hang from the ceiling on chains – are to be found and, once the chains are removed, are effective as a table bowl or to stand on a pedestal. As with copper and brass, flowers do particularly well through the temperature of the water remaining cool.

Ormolu This is generally made in France for compotes for fruit and flower vases. It is a mixture of metals: tin, copper and brass, with either a bronze or gilt finish. The ormolu vases and candlesticks that I have are some of my favourite flower containers. Their elegance and colour make them ideal for even a few flowers at any time of the year. A small bunch of grapes, and a few clematis or passion flowers, seem perfect in what is for some people a rather ornate vase.

Pewter When well-polished, pewter reflects the light well, though I am quite happy to have dull pewter to fill with lilacs and mauves, or even brilliant reds. There are many different pieces that are nice for flowers: mugs, teapots, bowls, shallow collecting-plates. A shallow pewter plate, with a pin-holder to support the flowers, can make a useful change for the dinner table. A full-blown rose on a shallow plate is another idea.

Porcelain Continental china or porcelains often take the form of a pretty little basket decorated with raised bunches of flowers, and when these are filled with either a few spring flowers or something sweet-smelling, they are ideal for a coffee table or the guest's bedroom. Delicate porcelain wall vases are most attractive also; when filled with trails of old-fashioned roses, or honeysuckle, they look very pretty. One house that I visit has beautiful Dresden china figures and these are grouped with a small vase hidden behind, in which a few sprays of flowers according to the season are placed so that they draw attention to the china and in no way obscure it. I was enchanted by the effect that this gave. Porcelain is usually precious and of course needs careful handling; the wire netting, if used, wants to be cut and shaped all ready before being put in the vase. Never press wire into the vases as it is so easy to break and scratch them. Wash carefully and store in a safe place. Because of the delicate nature of all porcelain containers, the flowers should be just as pretty and light as you can contrive: jasmine, sweet peas, roses, forget-me-nots, and any other pretty little bits. If the vase has a flower design on it, as they so often have, then try picking up the colours of the flowers, or possibly matching up the flowers themselves. Ginger jars are well worth looking out for – apart from being used as conventional containers they can make most effective hanging arrangements.

Pottery Many pottery urns and bowls are made today for flower arrangement. There is a wide range to choose from, including a great deal of Italian china in some of the prettiest designs and soft colours. Many of these are white or grey with a pink or blue lining; the inside is so attractive that it is a pity to hide it, and so I often do an arrangement that takes up only half the vase so that the delicate colour of the lining is revealed. White vases are available in every imaginable shape and size. Most of them are fairly well-proportioned and so are generally good to use for church flowers, but pure white is often distracting with the golds and wood of many churches, and I try to avoid it where possible. If necessary, the vase can be painted. Black paint mixed with silver gives a good 'pewter' finish. Gold paint with a little brown is also effective, and both of these seem to suit church decoration very much better than dazzling white. I find the aerosol tins of paint most useful for spraying vases. Pottery, unlike porcelain, is always replaceable, and so it generally makes the most practical of all the breakable vases.

Silver I still feel a really lovely silver bowl filled to overflowing with roses looks delightful. Silver flower vases are often in rather difficult shapes. A cone-shaped trumpet vase may look quite well when filled with gypsophila and sweet peas, but can be a headache to the modern flower arranger. Epergnes, if you can find one, are excellent for use with old shrub roses, which look particularly at home in the silver vases. The best silver 'vases' are of course the cups, entrée dishes, soup tureens, wine coolers, and any well-shaped cake basket, which make superb flower containers and fit into almost any home. Silver has the asset of highlights and looks best, I think, used with a profusion of flowers in high summer. I am never very fond of using it in the spring and prefer daffodils in something else. Silver vases need cleaning inside and out, as both flower stems and water leave a deposit which becomes most difficult to clear if left too long. Staining can be avoided by lining the container with thin plastic before inserting the wire netting. Clean all silver well and store in polythene bags, this keeps it beautifully for weeks. The new 'long life' cleaner is a great help for any silver that is in constant use. Plastic-coated wire netting is excellent to use in a silver container, as it prevents any possible chance of scratching. Try to avoid leaving metal pin-holders in silver vases for very long as this tends to stain them badly. A pin-holder used to hold a few stems of flowers in a shallow silver bowl, allowing the water to become part of the arrangement, is very effective and can make a charming table display.

Tin Ornamental Mexican tin is very decorative and there are some lovely flower vases made of this, but they are sometimes hard to find. So are some of the early French jardinières, which are usually hand-painted in charming soft colours – olive greens, pale blues and dull reds. They often have a floral design on one side, either in gold or in mixed colours. Oblong or oval shapes make them easy to arrange and most useful, but like all beautiful things they are expensive. The French use them for plants or for a mixture of plants and cut flowers. I love them used for a mixture like this, or just for cut flowers alone. Everyday kitchen tins have many good uses. As a lining to hold water in a vase or basket, a baking tin or bread tin is excellent. Or the tins can be painted with a coat or two of matt paint; in stone, white, cream or green they are unobtrusive and easy to camouflage with flowers or leaves – ideal for a party, for putting flowers on the mantelpiece, on the top of a cupboard, or on a window-sill. It is advisable to paint them inside and out to prevent rusting, and this will also act as a sealer for the joins. As tin is in itself very light, it is always advisable to weight it down with either a strip of lead or some clean pebbles or stones. I have seen round tin washing-up bowls effectively covered with a coat of plaster, roughed up and painted, and this makes a good pedestal vase.

Wood There are few wooden flower vases, but many good wooden containers that are both attractive and useful for flowers. Wooden tea-caddies or boxes, with a tin inside to hold the water, are most effective; these look lovely filled with simple marigolds, or daisies, or with a mixture of oranges and reds in the autumn, or daffodils in a bed of moss in spring. Knife boxes with their fittings removed, old salt boxes that will hang well on the wall, are other ideas for unusual vases. Wooden milk bowls are ideal for

making the most of homely flowers – nasturtiums, or daisies. The top of a carved pillar, or any decorative piece of wood, that can be hollowed out enough to hold a container for water is unusual, again, and handsome. Pieces like this look very nice if the wood is bleached; this can be done by using bleach and water and leaving out in the sun. If the wood has been painted, then of course the paint must be removed with some form of paint stripper before the bleaching. Lumps of driftwood, and twisted and gnarled roots or branches can be used to very good effect to house a small jar or bowl, which is then filled with some wild or simple flowers, and this also makes a very suitable container for some dried arrangements. Wooden platters and bases are part of the general pattern of modern flower decoration; I think this has stemmed from the Japanese, who use a base as part of the whole flower arrangement. I find them extremely useful – perhaps not quite as the Japanese use them, though I like them for certain types of arrangements, but they are also a great help for protecting furniture. On page 198 a branch of grape vine from France is used with a concealed 'well' pin-holder, forming an easy and economical type of flower vase. The old bible boxes were a great favourite with Constance Spry. These are difficult to find and quite expensive but it is a good substitute to make a wooden box that will hold a large roasting-tin; place it on a cheap whitewood stool and paint them both a pretty shade of green, and you will be able to have a large arrangement at knee-height, which makes a most welcome change. Shallow wooden boxes, either painted, or decorated with bark or shells, make an agreeable change for a dried group, and wonderful employment for the young on a wet day. Always well sandpaper any wood before painting – and matt paint is so much nicer.

Pedestal vases These can be used in the home, or in a hall for a wedding or party, or in church, to raise the flowers up to or well above eye-level. The type of pedestal should be entirely a matter of personal choice, and so should the vase or container that is used on it, provided that both are in proportion; a small urn on a tall pedestal looks quite out of place. Large urns of suitable material such as stone, lead, fibre glass, alabaster, bronze, copper, china, are satisfactory provided that they are the right size and hold plenty of water, and that they will stand the weight of heavy and often cascading flowers and foliage. Of course, vases on pedestals in your own home can be smaller and of more delicate material than those you would use in a church or hall. So be guided in your choice by how and where they are to be used. The use of pedestals has become much more general, and they are now considered the ideal answer for keeping flowers well out of the way and showing them off to the best advantage. I well remember the days when it was quite unheard-of to use flowers on a pedestal in a church, and only banks of pot plants and palms were the vogue. I use an old-fashioned wash-hand bowl on my church pedestal more often than not. These bowls are deep enough to hold plenty of water and shallow enough for the bowl itself to be easily concealed from view, with foliage or leaves.

Pedestals These can be bought, or they can be made from a wide choice of materials by a local craftsman. I am lucky in that I have a very beautiful pair – made for me in wood, and painted cream with a little gold decoration. They can be in alabaster, though these are expensive and rare. Pedestals from plywood nailed on to a framework of battens are simple to make and inexpensive, also light and easy to move about. It is best to make these straight-sided, or slightly tapered, but they can be in varying heights, and finished with matt paint, or rough cast distemper. The decorators of Winchester Cathedral finished theirs most effectively; to make them look like stone, they painted them and then covered them with coarse sand. Marble pedestals were used a great deal some years ago and are still to be found. You get such lovely colours in old marble – soft greens, creams, grey. However, if you are doing a lot of church work or decorating for various functions, I feel it is more practical to have pedestals made in a light material, easier to handle. It is quite possible to have wood painted to look like marble, and very effective it is. There are also many self-adhesive plastic coverings with wood and marble patterning which are simplicity itself to stick on. Stone pedestals as a rule are really only suitable for churches, or perhaps for use in a garden room. As they are so heavy, it is better to have these only if they can remain in one position. Many of the old pedestals were made of wood, some very ornate and others severely plain. They come in all kinds of woods, from oak to mahogany, some painted and others stripped and the wood bleached, which can look very pleasing. It is quite simple to paint them the colour of the walls of the room. Should you want to strip off any old paint to get a limed effect, use any paint stripper and then paint the surface with bleach; finish by covering with lime and water and brush it off when it is dry. In this way some of the white stays in the cracks and looks very effective. Old wrought iron standard lamps can sometimes be converted to use as pedestals, though many blacksmiths can make wrought iron pedestals to order. If you are having one made, be sure that the container on the top is large enough to hold plenty of water; a small one is often a disadvantage. They can be designed in many ways and be painted in any colours, though they are usually black or white.

I personally prefer to use dull finishes on both vases and pedestals, so a matt paint is what I would recommend. Gold paint mixed with a little brown gives a good effect. The aerosol sprays in gold and silver, particularly when used in combination, give an unusual and attractive finish to plinth or vase. A mixture of black and aluminium gives a pewter finish, and this surprisingly enough is one of the best for a base, to show off flowers really well.

Home-made containers The container covered in shells (on page 13) was made by a friend who has found that by covering a cheap wine glass, or some other rather unattractive container, you produce a new look and I think they are most effective. At the Brighton Festival in 1978 one of the most beautiful containers was a home-made one – a glass goblet covered with dried honesty seeds. It was quite lovely. You can also cover a small wooden box or shallow cigar box, and fill this with Oasis Sec, and you need no water. Should you want to put the flowers into water there is always some small plastic margarine or food container that will fit in quite well. Sadly nowadays it is hard to get the cylindrical biscuit tins that I used so much years ago. Should you find a well-shaped tin, if you cover it with a Japanese rush wallpaper, it makes an ideal container for a line arrangement for a few flowers.

Bases made of wood can take the place of a vase and are something that I find most useful, particularly for dried flowers, and at Christmas time.

Rules to remember in flower arranging

The moment one strikes a match to light the fire the whole room suddenly comes to life and for me the same thing happens when you place in the room a big bunch of flowers. You do not have to know how to arrange flowers to enjoy them. As in cooking you make a better cake if you read the instructions, and perhaps blend the butter and sugar a little longer, and so on. So with flowers you find that with some instructions you will perhaps make a more pleasing bouquet, but in neither case is it essential. The amount of time you can give to your flower arranging is of course up to the individual. If you have civic interests, or enjoy golf, tennis or any sport, then you would perhaps feel that your time could be better spent than messing around with flowers.

On the other hand, to take a bunch of flowers and arrange them well to fit in with your own surroundings, to get the satisfaction of blending colours and mixing different textures, to make the most of light and shade and depth and quality, is something we can experience today. The art of flower arrangement is not only an absorbing hobby for many people but is also a valuable form of relaxation that for many of us reduces the tensions of modern living. It gives us a new view of our other activities, particularly in gardening – we consciously grow out-of-the-ordinary plants for the sake of their flowers or foliage in our arrangements. And the garden benefits too!

By making different sorts of flower arrangement and discovering new places for them you will find you are taking a more critical view of your own home. You suddenly see a room needs rearranging in a way which makes it look excitingly different. Your judgement about fabrics and colours becomes much sharper and will make itself felt the next time you choose soft furnishings. Instead of choosing only for durability you will be choosing something particularly attractive *and* durable! More thought is given to plans for redecorating – different paint or paper which will provide a more effective background for flowers. It is surprising how the character of rooms can be altered.

And to turn to containers for a moment. Even though nowadays the competition for finding out-of-the-way containers in antique shops is severe, it is still great fun none the less, and makes a shopping expedition really exciting.

Flower arranging has become an international hobby. There are flourishing flower clubs in almost every town in England. Their membership has often multiplied since I wrote my first book and this amazes me as I felt it might be just a transitory interest. Not at all, the National Federation of Flower Arrangement Societies has well over 100,000 members up and down the land. The local education authorities have available many facilities for the flower arranger, so for those who really want to learn there is ample opportunity. And on every visit I am becoming more conscious of the ever-increasing interest in the United States. On the other hand, some people feel that flowers arrange themselves; though they like to see well arranged vases, they have no desire to learn. Some of you have little time, and some prefer not to learn in case of becoming copyists and losing their own way of expressing themselves. All I would say is that the approach does not matter one bit, as long as you enjoy flowers for their own sake and like to see them growing and to have them about you indoors; how you arrange them is of course your own affair.

Personally I still feel very strongly that one must consider surroundings first and always arrange the flowers to fit in with them, picking up colours and textures. It is a mistake to work for a perfect vase regardless as to whether this will look right in your home. It is so much more satisfying if someone says how lovely your flowers look with your curtains, carpet or chair-covers than how clever you have been to do a vase of such-and-such a shape. It is important also not to overdo arrangements! It is very easy to over-decorate a room with flowers, giving a tiresome sense of one group after another. I think one really good vase in a room is all that is needed, or perhaps a large one and a very small one. A surfeit of flowers seems self-conscious and tasteless.

I like to pick and start arranging the flowers in my hand as I walk round my garden. It is quite easy to decide what vase to use before you begin, for at that point you may be thinking about some special flower that is at its best just at that moment. It might be that three apricot tulips could be spared; knowing that none would be more than 23cm (9in) after cutting to allow the lower leaves and a small part of the stem to go on feeding the bulb for next year, makes one consider that maybe a gold urn about 30cm (12in) would be a suitable container. You pick accordingly, remembering that the outline material usually requires something light and feathery for a backing; this could be a blossom of some sort, or a branch of foliage in good contrast and just tall enough to be an inch or so above the main flower. Then, possibly, additional flowers or foliage; perhaps a stem of rhubarb in flower or the dark leaves of begonia or tiarella, and so you build up your picture.

The size of the container in proportion to the flowers is important, yet there can be no set rule. It is a matter of trial and error. Of course, it is obvious that delphiniums 1m (3–4ft) long look wrong in a tiny vase, also that long-stemmed flowers cut down to fit a particular vase can often look unhappy and out of place. Never cut a stem more than is necessary, but at the same time don't feel restricted about removing pieces once the flower has been picked. The moment to consider the length you would like is before you actually cut from the plant or shrub; this is not such a problem with herbaceous plants or annuals: it applies mainly to shrubs and trees. I find then that picking, from young bushes especially, becomes a major decision and a lot of time can be spent on trying to choose which branch can be taken, so as not to spoil the shape of the tree but as far as possible to improve it.

You need to take into account not only furniture when you are deciding how many flowers you can put in a room. There are all the other personal treasures – photographs, curios, ornaments and so on, all of which affect the appearance of an arrangement. The placing of flowers in each room includes practical problems: not in direct sunlight or over central heating; out of a draught, and away from a door or window or other danger spot where a vase could easily be knocked over or spilled. Then come questions of background – a plain wall for preference. If you have flowers against a patterned wallpaper, especially if the pattern is fussy, the effect looks confused: you get neither a good outline nor any feeling of colour. Against the window is another place to avoid if possible, as flowers seen against the light lose all their colour-value and just take on an outline or silhouette. This particular difficulty can be met, with a good deal of thought about the right choice of flowers and container; the flowers that look best are those with an airy effect – old man's beard, gypsophila – anything feathery or light.

Good lighting is most important, and artificial light, if it is needed, should come from above. Only the outline shows if light shines on to the flowers from below; colour-values are again lost and only a silhouette results. For hotels or shops, this can be an advantage and a few flowers, even though half dead, can look quite attractive in a subdued light shining up from a lower level; but this gives a false effect and should be avoided, I feel, in your own home. Flowers in pale shades are mandatory for panelled walls in dark wood, and yellows, whites or pale pinks show up best of all. Avoid deep reds or blues; blues can appear to have turned black by artificial light, but will show through well if used with another colour, such as pale pink or white.

I would always move furniture to try to avoid having a large 'all-round' vase, because this takes so many flowers and needs constant attention. Of course, there are times when it cannot be helped, and then I find the bowl type of container on a pedestal stand is perhaps the most generally useful.

One of the nicest things, I think, about having flowers in the house is that they make it seem lived-in and give a feeling of welcome. I like, if possible, to have a vase that gives an evident welcome and can be noticed at once by anyone entering the room. The mantelpiece is a focal point in most rooms and an ideal place for flowers; a small vase for everyday and a large long one, if you have it, for a party.

You can get a striking effect by arranging flowers under a picture so that they pick up its principal colours. It draws attention discreetly to the painting as well as to the flowers.

Halls, too, need flowers to make home-coming really nice. On a pedestal, for example, or if space is precious then on the wall. A wall vase is most helpful in a small narrow hall, perhaps in a flat or a cottage. A trough of house plants can be attractive and needs little attention; it can be watered and cared for once a week except in very hot weather. In modern flats it is possible to have them built in, and the plants can be quite happy over a radiator although they will need more watering because of the heat.

The dining-room needs table flowers and these are often quite enough, depending on the size of the room and the amount of furniture. Table flowers should not be matched to the general colour scheme of the room but linked positively to what is actually on the table. The colours in the porcelain or the table linen should give plenty of scope. If you have a sufficiently large dinner service and are able to use part of the service for flowers, this can be most effective. A vegetable dish or a soup tureen, gravy boat or a meat dish, make excellent containers which can be varied according to whether the flowers are long-stemmed or short.

Flowers in the guest's room are especially welcoming and pleasure-giving and usually I try to choose something fragrant. I have stayed in only one house where I had the luxury of flowers on the breakfast tray, but I still remember the pleasure it gave me.

I love flowers in my own room and usually manage to get a few all the year round, but I think the best of all are the sweetly scented ones: honeysuckle, pinks and jasmine.

The bathroom has come into its own in this age of house plants. Ivies, begonias and others enjoy the warm steamy atmosphere and they can look charming. Many of the variegated ivies are very decorative and can easily be trained to grow up trellis work, or just to cascade from a hanging container. Similarly, a sun room is another place where house plants look well and thrive in the warmth and sunlight.

Some people will ask, why arrange flowers at all when they are so lovely growing, and I find I am constantly in the position where I want them in both places at once! I do find however that often I leave a plant so that friends can come and see my treasure for themselves, and sure enough down comes the rain and no one has seen it at all. Few people ever want to walk over half an acre of wet grass to see anything, so it is often wonderful just to pick and arrange, then sit back by a warm fire and share with friends the delight of a spray of winter flowering shrub or early spring flowering bulbs.

Part Two
Encyclopedia of plants

At the end of each entry there is, where applicable, advice on conditioning and preserving the plant. For practical details of the various methods suggested see the entry under 'C' for Conditioning and Maintaining and under 'D' for Drying and Preserving.

Encyclopedia of plants

Abelia grandiflora

Not a very hardy shrub. I grow it not for the small pink bell-shaped flowers but for the delightful browny, copper calices which are left after the flowers have fallen. The arching form of the branches makes these sprays invaluable for an autumn flower arrangement giving a lovely outline to any vase you place them in. Their copper colour adds immensely to an apricot vase of the last of the apricot roses and dahlias. In fact, last autumn I was so entranced with them that I found I was using them almost too much.

Conditioning Place the woody stems in 2.5cm (1in) of boiling water for a few minutes and then allow a long drink.

Preserving By removing many of the leaves these pretty little calices will stay on the branches quite well for some weeks with no special treatment.

Acacia
Mimosa Wattle

Greenhouse shrubs, with delightful feathery grey foliage, which often makes these trees look as if they have been dusted with flour. Grown all along the Riviera though their home is Australia. Known throughout Australia as Wattle, a name given them by the early settlers, as they used the wood woven together to make the walls for some of their first houses. They were then covered in wet mud, hence a make-shift wattle and daub. They make quite tall trees in their natural surroundings, with cascades of tumbling yellow blossoms, which are a sight to behold, and a wandering perfume which prevails from the trees for a long way. Some kinds

Abelia grandiflora

can be grown out of doors in Britain against the shelter of a wall, but in very few places; the hardiest is *podalyrifolia* which grows well in Cornwall. Lovely arranged with daffodils or any early spring flowers. Remove a certain amount of the foliage to give accent to the colour. Unfortunately the fluffy balls of gold often turn hard and dark yellow within a few hours. Keep it excluded from the air as long as possible before arranging. It keeps extremely well in a polythene bag.

Conditioning After removing polythene, submerge the heads under cold water, then dip the stems into 2.5cm (1in) of boiling water for a few seconds and stand in a jug of warm water until the flower heads have dried off. This should give a little longer life to the fluffy heads. Several growers now pack the mimosa in polythene bags and attach a small packet of conditioning powder to add to the water in the vase, and I find this does help.

Acanthus
Bear's Breech

Hardy herbaceous perennial. A plant for every garden, growing well in full sun or semi-shade. (Personally I think they flower better in full sun.) The less they are disturbed, the better they grow. In ancient times the beautiful leaves were an inspiration to architects, who reproduced them on the tops of Corinthian pillars; now the plants grow wild in large clumps among the ruins of buildings in Greece and Turkey. The tall, spiky, purplish flowers last in water very much better than the leaves, though both are better cut after being left on the plant for some time. Preferably the flowers should be picked when all the buds right up the stem are nearly fully open. The leaves only last if picked in August or September and then treated as advised below. My favourite is *A. mollis latifolius*; also good, and much smaller, is *A. spinosus*. Acanthus is excellent mixed with large group-arrangements of summer flowers and its pointed shape has great structural value when used with rounded heads such as those of sunflowers or dahlias.

Conditioning The leaves should have the ends of the stems dipped in boiling water; then submerge the whole leaf in a solution of weak starch water for up to twelve hours. The flower stems are improved if dipped in boiling water, followed by several hours in deep cold water. Place the leaves in a polythene bag with a little water in it, tying the bag tightly to exclude the air, and leave for two days. The results are amazing; the leaves stay crisp and fresh for a long time and although I have not actually tried this with acanthus, it works miraculously with other leaves.

Preserving The flower heads dry very well if picked when they are all fully open all the way up the stem, then hung upside down to dry in a warm atmosphere.

Acer
Sycamore, Maple

Hardy shrubs. My favourite of all, for flower arrangement, is a variety of sycamore, *Acer*

Acer platanoides 'Drummondii'

pseudoplatanus brilliantissimum, which has apricot buds and later good apricot foliage in early spring. A beautiful tree in the garden and the foliage is a joy to use, particularly with such flowers as black tulips, to make a contrast of black and apricot. The pendulous flowers, resembling the common sycamore's, are tinged with peach and lime-green. In certain soils it quickly loses colour and I am fortunate in that mine remains interesting all the year round – possibly just the luck of planting it in a soil it likes. Generally speaking, sprays of acer are not ideal material for arranging, because they do not stand well in water. *Acer japonicum aureum* will however stand better than many. Like *A. pseudoplatanus brilliantissimum*, it is such an asset in early spring for its brilliant yellow-green leaves which keep their colour well into the summer and add, as do all these plants, a touch of sunlight to the garden even on the dreariest of days. I find it hard to bring myself to cut it as it is so very slow growing, but if you have the chance then it is an excellent background to a vase of yellows and is just the right shade for soft salmon pinks. *Acer negundo* 'Aureomarginatum' keeps its lovely variegation well through the summer, though the vivid lime-green and cream fade as the leaf matures. The Norway maple, *A. platanoides*, has the most wonderful lime-green flowers that open before the leaves break, so you get vivid green sprays on coal black branches which are superb, and add a touch of sheer delight to a vase of daffodils and tulips. Unlike other acers, the Norway maple lasts extremely well in water provided the branches are well hammered, or the bottom 5cm (2in) of bark peeled off before it has a long drink.

In addition to the ones I have mentioned, there are many varieties of acer renowned for their autumn tints, and this makes them a very valuable asset to any shrubbery or heath garden. Since my frequent visits to America, I have been enchanted with the brilliant colours of the sugar maples *Acer saccharinum*, but it obviously takes a lot of sunshine to produce these brilliant shades of red, like the red-hot ash of a wood fire. It is often possible to use a few sprays when in full autumn colour, although they do not last for very long, but I feel even a few hours' enjoyment is well worth while for some very special

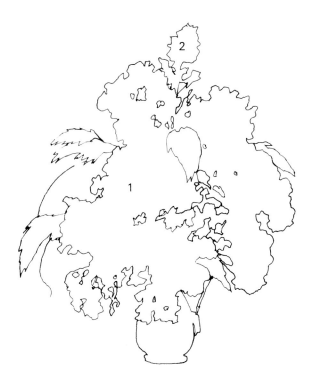

A water jug arranged with delicate and feathery plants ideally suited to a glass container.
1 *Alchemilla mollis* (Lady's mantle)
2 *Lasiagrostis splendens*

occasion, provided of course that the shape of the tree is not spoilt by picking branches at random; I cannot stress too often to pick with tremendous care. Leaves of autumn colour are fading naturally and there is nothing that I can recommend to make them last in water.

Conditioning Hammer the stems very well and place in deep warm water.

Preserving Individual leaves can be pressed and then mounted on wire stems by running a wire up the back of the leaf and covering with adhesive tape to make a false stem, often essential after pressing as the stems fall off easily.

Achillea 'Moonshine'

A silver and gold chalice that is cleverly designed with the Sydney Opera House illustrated at the base, it is shown here with a mixture of summer flowers.
1 Roses
2 *Viola* (Pansy)
3 *Digitalis ambigua* (Foxglove)
4 *Astrantia* (Masterwort)
5 *Lavandula* (Lavender)
6 Variegated strawberry leaf
7 *Codonopsis vinciflora* 'Tangshen'
8 *Clematis integrifolia*
9 Daisy

Achillea
Yarrow

Hardy herbaceous perennial. A flat-headed flower of deep yellow, useful for an arrangement in July and August as it has the great advantage of lasting well in water. There are no petals to fall and the flat heads give an excellent focal point in any vase. For a softer colour in pale yellow the variety I would recommend is 'Moonshine', which has a much smaller growth altogether and is good in clumps near the front of the border; the grey foliage is a considerable asset both indoors and out. There are of course many white varieties which are useful for small flower arrangements.

Preserving Dip the heads in powdered borax and either hang them upside down or stand them in a small jug with a small amount of water. I find this latter method preferable as it allows each flower head to retain a perfect shape. If hung in bunches, the stems tend to get imprinted on the flower head and leave a mark.

Acidanthera

Bulbous-rooted perennial. The one I like best is *Acidanthera bicolor* which has drooping flowers, white with a purple blotch in the centre, and a sweet scent. Used with a few *Begonia rex* leaves and a branch of berberis, and with a predominance of water, it can make an enchanting group in oriental style, in either a shallow lead container or a grey-green dish.

Aconite, Winter *see* ERANTHIS

Aconitum
Monkshood

Hardy herbaceous perennial. Monkshood is usually thought of as spikes of mauvish-blue hooded flowers on tall upright stems, rather like a delphinium. However, I strongly recommend *A. lycoctonum* which is more delicate in form in every way, having a more branching habit and spikes of delicious yellowy, lime-green flowers, excellent for arranging. The new pale blue form, *arendsii*, flowers from August to September just when a bit of blue for mixed arrangement is most useful. For a white group Alan Bloom highly recommends 'Ivorine', ivory spikes of well-clustered flowers growing on stiff stems.

Conditioning Cut and give it a good long drink up to its neck in warm water.

Preserving The seed heads dry well if hung upside down.

Acrolinium or Helipterum

An Australian wild flower growing in droves of pink and white in Western Australia, often carpeting the road verges with colour. Excellent for drying, having a daisy-like flower with dry papery petals, and very useful for small arrangements of dried flowers to give delicate colour in the winter months. It can be grown from seed, preferably started under glass and pricked out in May.

Actaea ranunculaceae
Baneberry

These very poisonous berried plants have come to my notice only recently and this was because they are happy in partial shade which makes them worthwhile plants for me at any time. The red berries mix well with any autumn colours and add a highlight to a brilliant red arrangement. I also like the white berries of *A. pachypoda*. It is important, however, to wait and enjoy the berried spray, rather than be tempted to pick the white, fluffy astilbe-like flowers. The red baneberry I have used in North America, and loved the glistening spikes of its red berries in its native land. It goes as far back as 1700, so it is a really old plant.

Conditioning This fluffy type of flower does not seem to last well, so I prefer to wait to pick the berried sprays. Remove any leaves and stand in a little really hot water for an hour or so.

Adam's Needle *see* YUCCA

Adiantum
Maidenhair Fern

Greenhouse plant. Sprays of heart-shaped tiny leaves on arched stems, so delicate and a delight to use for its light feathery effect in small vases. I have just been given two hardy varieties, one from America and one from Gloucestershire. I am very pleased about this as another range of plants I have come to love are hardy ferns. I find the maidenhair *A. venustum* particularly good for trailing out of a candle cup or similar type of

Adiantum cuneatum

vase, with a collection of 'mixed greens' or any delicate flower such as fritillaries.

Conditioning Submerge the whole stem under the hottest water in which you can hold your hand, wait until the water cools, and then tie into a plastic bag and leave in a cool place for one or two days.

Agapanthus
African Lily

Cool greenhouse evergreen. One of the oldest plants, used on roof gardens in Egypt and the Near East in the time of the Caesars. Its tall, round, ball-shaped flowers on slender stems are most commonly known in blue, though I have a white one growing well against a south wall. It is not very hardy and therefore more usually a pot plant. But in the last few years there has been a great development in the growing and hybridizing of hardy agapanthus. 'Headbourne Hybrids' range from deep to pale blue, varying in height and have a long flowering from July to October.

Agapanthus

Patens is another recommended hardy variety and well worth growing. It is lovely used in large groups in high summer and the rounded blue heads are particularly good to add to a blue and white arrangement in July or August. Excellent seed heads for drying.

Preserving Dry the seed heads by hanging them upside down.

Agastache animata

Sun-loving plants with a fragrant foliage rather like mint, and dense spikes of purple flowers. I have used it a lot in the United States to replace lavender and found it best to put a few stems together with some pink rosebuds or Japanese anemones.

Conditioning Place the stems in boiling water for a few minutes before giving them a long drink.

Agave

I am mentioning this exotic plant because so many people travel these days and are interested in what they see and from my very first trip to the south of France, I longed to leap out of the train and pick one of these wonderful brown seed head spikes. They really are so spectacular with their sword-like leaves and their handsome flower spikes. I have had the chance of using them many times since in America, Australia and on the Continent. The leaves have sharp spines and though lovely for a really big group, it is the side shoots of the flower head which I have enjoyed using, and the seed heads, so tall they are hard to pick even if one has the rare opportunity. They do grow in the warmer areas of the British Isles. I have grown some in Formentera, an island near Ibiza, and these lime-green heads against a blue Mediterranean sea are fantastic. The juice of the agave is used medicinally in ointment and has a soothing quality.

Conditioning Put the flower sprays into boiling water, fill up the container and allow a really long drink.

Preserving These seed heads dry off much better if allowed to dry naturally on the plant. You may as well pick and enjoy the seed heads as this plant will die after flowering, but happily they are always surrounded by lots of young ones coming up.

Ajuga reptans
Bugle

A compact spreading plant suitable for ground cover. 'Atropurpurea' has bronzy-purple leaves and there are two interesting varieties which I have started to grow – 'Variegata', cream blotch on pale green, and best of all for me, 'Multicolor' which is a real bicolour, creamy-green with a touch of maroon. These not only make good ground cover but a single floret will look superb in the centre of a green arrangement or in a moss garden of short-stemmed spring flowers.

Conditioning As the stems are so short the florets are quite difficult to arrange and, really, the ideal way I find is to soak them well in a shallow container and then put them in a plastic bag for twenty-four hours before arranging. This helps the stems to grow a little which makes them easier to arrange. I rarely use the flowers as the leaf florets are so much more attractive, but if you should use the flowers then place the ends of the stems in boiling water for a few seconds before giving them a long drink.

Alchemilla mollis
Lady's Mantle

Hardy herbaceous perennial. This feathery lime-green flower has a long period of bloom and is useful in high summer. Its lightness of form and delicate colour make it a most popular flower for arranging. The colour blends so well with so many others – yellows, reds, blues, almost any mixture of colours. But through these last few years I have arranged it on its own. I have a bronze vase which seems to suit it perfectly. Remove all the leaves as these tend to shrivel. It will dry off perfectly in water and keep a better colour this way all winter. It grows easily from seed; in fact it seeds itself freely, once established, and will flourish under most conditions although as it grows wild in the ditches in Scotland this shows that it must like moisture. The leaves are beautifully shaped and silky and their centres retain drops of rain which look like jewels. This plant can be increased by division or, as indicated above, by seed.

Alchemilla mollis

Preserving Remove foliage and hang flower heads upside down. It keeps quite a good green colour.

Alder *see* ALNUS

Allium

Hardy and greenhouse bulbous perennials. Members of the onion family. There are many decorative varieties. My favourite of all is *A. siculum*, which unlike many of the others has pendulous bells of greenish brown, flowering in May. *A. moly*, with its umbels of yellow flowers, blooms at a good time of year when yellow is quite hard to come by for flower arranging; *A. giganteum* with large well-rounded heads of purple flowers varying in size, has, as the name suggests, long stems; *A. karataviense*, one of the best of all, with short stumpy growth, well-rounded heads of white flowers growing from the centre of an umbel of blue-green, has ground-hugging leaves that are often variegated; *A. pulchellum* which has well-rounded heads I grow mainly for drying; and for its lovely seed head I grow *A. christophii* but I should add that it really does better in a greenhouse. There are many more. Their rounded heads add a good focal point in any flower group and the wide range of colour makes them a most worthwhile bulb to grow. Chives' flowers are also most decorative.

Conditioning Never put the stems in hot water as this increases the onion smell. A teaspoonful of chlorox or bleach in the vase removes any trace of smell and I can well recommend this.

Preserving Dry all seed heads by hanging them upside down. Hang large heads on individual strings to prevent them from losing their shape by pressing against one another.

Almond *see* PRUNUS AMYGDALUS

Alnus
Alder

Hardy deciduous tree. Extremely useful, especially in winter and spring. The catkins and the small cone-clusters on bare branches make lovely background shapes to set off a few flowers. *A. incana aurea* is one of the most attractive varieties, flowering very early with pink catkins. If these branches are picked in January, it is interesting to watch the catkins develop in water, and they can also be arranged with sprays of ivy or bergenia leaves in midwinter. Once it breaks into leaf, I feel it is valueless for the flower arranger.

Conditioning Hammer ends of stems well and put into warm water. The hotter the atmosphere, the quicker development.

Alstroemeria
Peruvian Lily

Hardy and half-hardy perennials. Known generally as a rampant lily-like orange herbaceous plant. The new ligtu hybrids are difficult to cultivate, but have a magnificent blend of colours from shell pink through to salmon. They need a warm well-drained position and hate disturbance. In fact it is very much better to sow the seeds where they are going to remain.

Constance Spry had great success in growing some at Winkfield in open trenches. Owing to their rather stiff form and multiple flower heads I find them a little difficult to arrange, but they can be very good in a mass arrangement (with a few dark coloured leaves), because of their lovely colouring and lasting qualities in water. If the flowers are allowed to remain on the plant they form a good seed head and it is advisable to pick these early and hang them upside down to dry. If the seed heads remain too long on the plant, the stems become so brittle that they are difficult to use. One variety that I have not mentioned before is *A. pulchella* from North Brazil, a fascinating colour combination of green and red. Well worth growing in a cool greenhouse as you can cut it over a long period. At Winkfield it grows profusely in the greenhouse but in South California I had the pleasure of cutting it in the garden.

Althaea
Hollyhock

Hardy perennial. As they may die out quickly, they are often grown as an annual or biennial. They also seed themselves very readily. Many colours from white through yellow, apricot, pink and red to nearly black, in tall rosettes of flowers all up the long stem. Very good to mix in a Dutch type of group in midsummer.

Conditioning Put ends of stems in boiling water for several minutes and then place in deep water, in the dark if possible, for at least forty-eight hours.

Preserving Once the seed head has formed, pick the stems and hang them upside down in a warm place until dry.

Amaranth Feathers *see* HUMEA

Amaranthus caudatus
Love-lies-bleeding

Half-hardy annuals. *A. caudatus viridis*, the green variety, is the one I would recommend here. The long tails of green are very good to

Amaranthus caudatus

Preserving Will retain only a fair colour after being hung upside down. However, their shape does help to vary the form in a dried arrangement.

Amaryllis
Belladonna Lily

Slightly tender bulbous plant with fragrant pink or white flowers in autumn. It needs the shelter of a wall for best results. For greenhouse culture, pot in August: one bulb to a pot (approximately 15cm, 6in). I love to use a few of these white lilies in a group of foliage in autumn; or to arrange them quite alone in a slender vase to show the delicate beauty of the pendulous heads. The flower stems are thick and need a suitable vase allowing plenty of room.

Amaryllis (greenhouse) *see* HIPPEASTRUM

Amelanchier canadensis

A deciduous shrub with bronzy foliage and white star-like flowers in May and with very good autumn colour. A plant that I have come to appreciate and enjoy. It is easy to grow, untemperamental, and very useful for arrangements in spring and autumn.

Conditioning Hammer the ends of the stems, place into boiling water for a few minutes and then give a deep drink in cold water.

Ampelopsis cordata

A vine with the most enchanting greeny-blue berries in small clusters. To my amazement I found it growing all over the fence on a piece of waste ground in the middle of a Washington DC suburb. The berries are seen to best advantage when the leaves are removed. I kept it in a plastic bag with no water and used it in many places on my trip. I tried it with mauve roses, purple grapes and grey begonia leaves and it really was a lovely mixture. Flower arrangers in North America should look out for it as it seems to grow in many areas there. Sadly I don't think there is enough sun for it in England.

give a change of form in any flower arrangement. There is of course the crimson variety, grown easily from seed. Feed the plants well for best results.

Conditioning Remove all the leaves as they wilt easily and spoil the effect very quickly.

Ananas comosus 'Variegatus'

Ananas
Pineapple

A. comosus is the commercial pineapple and is a native of Brazil and Colombia. It grows to about 1m (3ft) and has long, pointed and serrated leaves of grey-green. The fruit of *A. c.* 'Variegatus' is apricot-coloured and the tuft of leaves at the top a pale green edged with salmon to cream, its base leaves have creamy white margins and red spines. These fantastic fruits can be bought on good long stems so that one can use them in flower arrangements. Recently I have used them both at home and in the United States and, although very expensive, they lasted extremely well and were a marvellous talking point. Pineapples are such a thrill to use so keep a look-out for them, they are being grown as hot-house plants a lot now.

Conditioning Hammer the ends of the stems to allow them to take up as much water as possible. Cut a small piece off the stem when re-using as this keeps the pores open and allows the fruit to drink more freely.

Anaphalis margaritacea
Pearly Everlasting

A. margaritacea is a hardy perennial which spreads very easily, and this may make it a problem plant in the garden, but it has attractive grey foliage and clusters of everlasting-like flowers. It is useful in early summer in mixed vases.

Conditioning The foliage in the early stages needs to have the ends of the stems plunged into boiling water for a few minutes and then allowed a long deep drink. The flowers are better for this treatment too, though it is not so important.

Preserving Pick the flower heads in full bloom, remove all the leaves, tie the flowers in bunches and hang upside down to dry. The stems become very brittle and it is often necessary to make a false stem with a florist's wire. For dried flower pictures and small arrangements there is no more attractive flower. They look like small grey stars.

Anchusa

The hardy herbaceous perennial variety *Anchusa azurea*, or *A. italica*, growing 1–1.5m (3–5ft) is the one I like best. The annual *A. capensis* is also good. Anchusas are not really recommended for flower arrangement as, try as one may, it is hard to make them last well in water. However, because of the superb blue I feel I must mention them. I do occasionally put in a piece on a short stem to add blue to a mixed vase and find this the best way of using it.

Conditioning Shorten stems, dip the ends in boiling water for thirty seconds, and then allow a long drink in cold water for several hours.

Anemone
Windflower

Hardy herbaceous perennials, some tuberous-rooted. At the name, I always picture the brilliant colours of St Brigid and Caen in all the flower shops just after Christmas – what a delight! Arrange in a bright red dish or glass for maximum colour effect. Also I think of the wild anemones I picked as a child and the bitter disappointment that they were dead even before I reached home. For the garden, *Anemone blanda* gives a lovely patch of pink and mauve in early spring and lasts in a vase much better than expected. Beth Chatto's *A. magellanca* has given me a great deal of pleasure. *A. fulgens*, a brilliant scarlet variety with a very black centre, quite beautiful, is now marketed as a cut flower in great quantity. I cannot leave this section without a word about *Anemone japonica*, the autumn-flowering herbaceous anemone, lovely arranged with a few autumn leaves; it flowers in pink and white – I think I prefer more often to use the white, but I can never really decide.

Conditioning Dip the ends of the stems in boiling water for a few seconds and then allow a long cool drink. I find it better not to arrange them in Oasis as it tends to soften the ends in some way.

Angel's Tears *see* NARCISSUS TRIANDRUS ALBUS

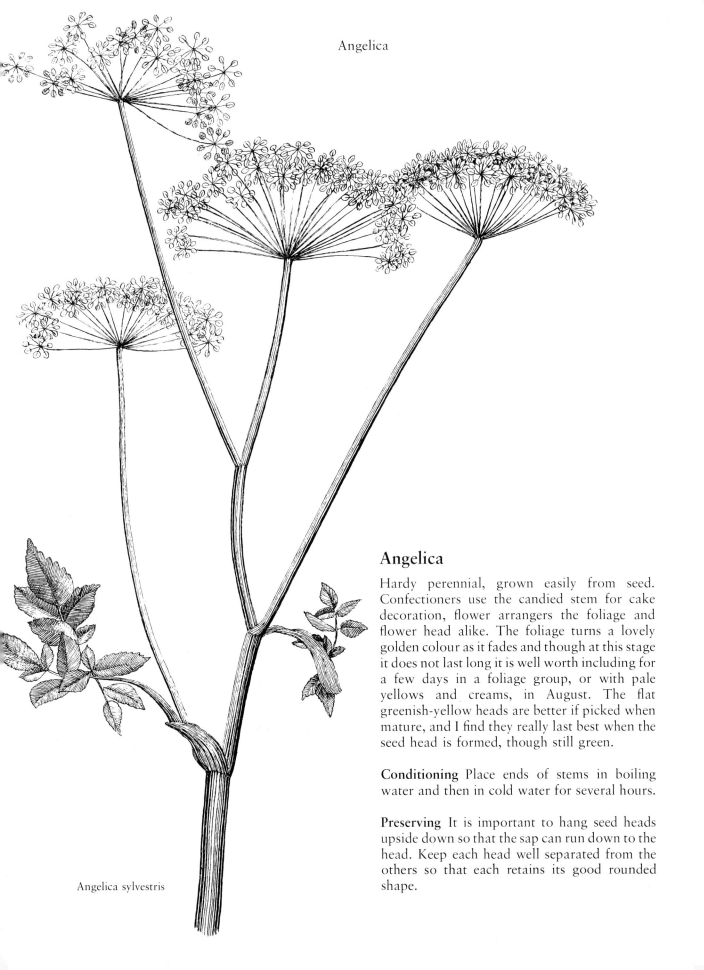

Angelica sylvestris

Angelica

Hardy perennial, grown easily from seed. Confectioners use the candied stem for cake decoration, flower arrangers the foliage and flower head alike. The foliage turns a lovely golden colour as it fades and though at this stage it does not last long it is well worth including for a few days in a foliage group, or with pale yellows and creams, in August. The flat greenish-yellow heads are better if picked when mature, and I find they really last best when the seed head is formed, though still green.

Conditioning Place ends of stems in boiling water and then in cold water for several hours.

Preserving It is important to hang seed heads upside down so that the sap can run down to the head. Keep each head well separated from the others so that each retains its good rounded shape.

Anthemis

Hardy perennial. *A. cupaniana* is a good grey foliage plant useful in a grey border as it is dwarf and spreading, and for pieces of foliage for a small group in greys and pinks or shades of lilac. No special treatment required.

Anthurium

Greenhouse. Spade-shaped flowers with a shiny texture rather like American cloth. These last well and look beautiful arranged with their own striking foliage or with various hard green foliages. Colours now range from reds to every shade of pink and apricot. From Honolulu the flowers are sent all over the world.

Packing If a small water-filled balloon is attached to the end of each stem by tying tightly with elastic bands, the flowers (packed in stiff boxes) can travel for thousands of miles.

Antirrhinum
Snapdragon

Grown from seed and treated as an annual. The new double varieties are well worth growing, especially the Penstemon-flowered 'Bright Butterflies' Mixture, as they are hard to find as plants. They last well and flower profusely until the first frost. They have a good range of colours and last better as a cut flower than most people imagine. Attractive arranged in a basket with mixed annuals or alone. Often forced through the early spring and then widely sold as a cut flower; the stems tend to be brittle as they have grown to great lengths under glass and need careful handling.

Conditioning If cut straight from the garden, a good drink for an hour or so, up to their necks in water, is all that is necessary. If forced, dip ends into boiling water before giving a long drink.

Aquilegia
Columbine

Hardy perennial. One of the earliest plants, often seen in old paintings. The original flower is double-petalled. The long-spurred hybrid varieties are more delicate, and in a much wider range of colours; they look delightful arranged alone in silver or glass, or picking up a colour combination in a mixed vase. Columbines also have beautifully-coloured foliage in late summer.

Conditioning Place in warm water for an hour before arranging. They will last very well if faded blooms are removed to allow new buds to open.

Preserving Let seed heads form, cut and hang in bunches upside down.

Aralia

Hardy shrub. *Aralia elata* (or *A. chinensis*) can be planted out of doors in a sheltered place, and grows to 6m (20ft) in Cornwall, with heads of ivy-type flowers 0.6m (2ft) across, and handsome large spreading leaves. *A. elata aureomarginata* is the one I love; the green and yellow leaves are superb for a large group, and I like to use them whenever I have the chance.

Conditioning Dip the ends of the stems into boiling water, and then allow a long drink in deep water for several hours.

Arbutus unedo
Strawberry Tree

Half-hardy evergreen tree with white flowers and strawberry-like fruits which keep the tree colourful most of the winter. These fruits are highly decorative and mix well with red flowers or with arrangements of fruit and flowers.

Conditioning Hammer stems well and keep for several hours in deep water.

Arctotis grandis

Half-hardy South African annual. The daisy-like flowers with glistening petals are white and backed with pale blue. *A. acaulis* is often wrongly named and many seed catalogues advertise them as 'large-flowered' arctotis. If you have a sheltered spot you will enjoy these many-coloured, daisy-like flowers. They have a wonderfully wide range of colours through pinks and purples and all shades of orange and brown.

Conditioning Dip ends of stems in boiling water after cutting. If possible cut in full sun, as the flowers tend to close up very quickly especially in the evening and will not reopen easily.

Arisaema

A very interesting plant of the arum family, *A. candidissimum*. Their hooded, striped flowers of pink and green which blossom before the leaves appear stand out in the border in June. They add a touch of novelty and have very effective leaves. They do not last long but are of great interest for the specialist flower arranger.

Conditioning Dip the ends of the flower stems in boiling water for a few seconds before giving a long drink.

Artemisia

Hardy perennials. Very pretty silvery foliage and good in all kinds of groups, especially with mixtures of greys or with pink and white. Quite one of the most useful of all the grey foliages as the artemisias last very well in water. *A. ludoviciana* is perhaps my favourite as the stiff grey spikes last such a long time. You will get some nice curving lines if you allow it to keep its natural growth, so I try not to tie it up too tightly. 'Lambrook Silver' is much softer in form and feathery in appearance. I use them both through July and August and often get some new growth in the autumn. *Artemisia lactiflora* has white plumes on tall stems, excellent for large groups for church decoration during July and August.

Conditioning Hammer the woody stems or place the ends in 2.5cm (1in) of boiling water and then allow a long deep drink.

Artemisia gnaphalodes

Arum italicum marmoratum

Preserving *Artemisia ludoviciana*: once the flower is over, the grey seed plumes if hung upside down dry extremely well.

Artichoke, Globe
Cynara scolymus

One of the best of all plants for the flower arranger, as the leaves are very useful all the year round and the flowers in every stage, from bud to full flower to seed head. It is grown easily from seed and is edible, of course, and delicious. I am always torn between eating and decoration!

Conditioning The leaves last much better if they have been on the plant for several weeks before

being cut. Hold ends of stems in boiling water for thirty seconds and then submerge completely in a bath of cold water for one hour. The flower heads last very well.

Preserving Hang heads upside down in a warm atmosphere, at any stage from green through purple to brown.

Arum

A. maculatum, Cuckoo pint or Lords-and-ladies, is more often used for its foliage. The greenish almost transparent flowers with purple stamens are beautiful, but die off very quickly. For better value, allow the berries to form and you will have a beautiful head of orange berries that mix well with flowers or foliage. The leaves last very well; their shape is so good I find I use them continually in early spring. *Arum italicum pictum* is an improved form and produces white-veined leaves in January or even earlier – this in itself is a joy – and I find it useful right through to May. It grows best in damp and partial shade, though it can be grown in open ground. A well-recommended plant.

I have used the leaves in several of the arrangements illustrated in this book.

Conditioning Submerge wild arum leaves in starch water for a few hours, before arranging. The flower heads last a little better if the ends of the stems are dipped in boiling water for thirty seconds.

Arum Lily *see* ZANTEDESCHIA AETHIOPICA

Aruncus sylvester
Goat's Beard

Hardy perennial, growing to about 1.5m (5ft) with large plumes of creamy-white flowers in June. Formerly known as Spiraea, as so I still think of it. It very quickly loses its fluff and so can be disappointing when cut, but I do use it occasionally as the leaves are very decorative.

Conditioning Boil the ends of the stems and then put into deep water.

Preserving When the flowers fade, hang the creamy-brown heads upside down.

Arundinaria
Bamboo

A hardy Japanese shrubby plant with slender stems furnished with grassy foliage. Generally considered difficult when cut as the leaves tend to curl; however, see the method below which is used in America to help solve this problem.

Conditioning Place the ends of the stems in boiling vinegar for two minutes and then allow a long drink in deep warm water.

Arundo donax variegata
Reed

A good striped reed in cream and green or white and green. Not very satisfactory or long-lasting when cut, as it tends to curl, but I do use it in early spring for a graceful effect in a group of foliage, and replace when necessary.

Conditioning Dip ends of stems in boiling water and afterwards give a long cold drink.

Asparagus

A. sprengeri or *A. plumosus* was once almost obligatory – as the so-called fern used for all types of floristry in the early part of this century, often overwhelming the flowers themselves in, for instance, a hand-bouquet. Largely owing to Constance Spry's influence this conventional use has almost disappeared. However, I often use the autumnal sprays of foliage and berries from the asparagus bed; these delicate plumes add a transparent effect to large groups which include colouring beech leaves or other autumn tints.

Aspidistra lurida
Parlour Palm

Certainly a plant that changed ideas on flower decoration have brought back into favour. Only a few years ago it could hardly be given away and now they are fetching fantastic prices and the demand is still rising. The variegated kind is the most popular. Used stylishly in a shallow container, it takes on excellent shapes. It preserves very well – an added delight – and needs the minimum of attention. Percy Thrower considers it stands neglect better than any other plant, and I think the leaves last longer than any other plant. I brought some leaves back from Bermuda in November and three months later they were still fresh in the vase.

Preserving Put the stems of the leaves in a solution of one part of glycerine to two of water and leave undisturbed. This means waiting in patience as the leaves take anything from six to nine months to dry. However, they will reward you by turning a lovely creamy-biscuit colour and with careful handling will last for years.

Aster
Michaelmas Daisy

True asters are hardy perennials and best grown and arranged grouped alone. There is nothing more effective than a mass of their purples and pinks in the autumn sunshine, or indoors in large bowls or copper pans, rather than when mixed with other flowers. The annual china aster *Callistephus chinensis*, grown from seed, has a wide range of excellent colours, from white and pinks to all shades of mauve, and lasts in water extremely well.

Conditioning Michaelmas daisies last better if the ends of the stems are well hammered and placed in boiling water, then allowed twelve hours in deep water. Pick off the faded blooms as often as possible as they can make the stem look dead long before it actually is.

Astilbe
Spiraea

Hardy herbaceous perennials. The hybrid varieties have a wide range of colour in delicate pointed plumes of pink to deep red. Often disappointing when used as a cut flower, but delightful as a rich brown seed head.

Preserving Cut when the flowers have lost their colour and are a pale green or brown. Hang them upside down or stand in shallow water to dry off.
For other herbaceous 'spiraeas', see Aruncus and Filipendula.

Astrantia major
Masterwort

Hardy perennial. *A. major* loves shade and seeds easily. It has good foliage and pleasing star-shaped flowers with an odd crisp look. Some varieties: *A. m. involucrata* which has extra long shaggy segments and a pale green colour is really an outstanding variety. Sadly it does not seed freely. *A. m. helleborifolia* has a collar of broad

Aspidistra lurida

segments in a lovely rose-pink, and it is worth feeding it well to get the very best results. *A. major Sunningdale* variegated, hybridized in 1966, has, as the name implies, the most attractive variegated leaves, well divided and blotched with yellow and cream. The flower is naturally nothing very special.

Conditioning The variegated leaves need careful treatment. If you submerge the leaves under water for an hour or so, then tie in a polythene bag with a little water in it for twenty-four hours, they will last. The flowers need no special treatment.

Preserving These flowers look as if they would dry easily but in fact they are rather difficult. The only way I find I can keep them is to place the flower stems in a solution of glycerine and water. They take on a creamy-brown look and last for a very long time. It is well worth doing.

Athyrium filix-femina
Lady Fern

Possibly the fern I find most useful of all, for its graceful outline.

I have become fond of so many varieties of fern that I have started a little fernery under a north-facing wall and near a water tap – not particularly elegant but I think it gives them the conditions they will be happy in. (See also Polystichum.)

Conditioning Submerge young growths in warm water for a few hours.

Preserving Place stems between sheets of newspaper and press under a heavy weight.

Athyrium goeringianum
'Pictum' (Japanese Painted Fern)

One of the most delightful ferns in existence, with delicate fronds of pink, mauve and grey. It seems very hardy which amazes me as it looks as if the first frost would bowl it over. I have used it in a flower arrangement and it made enormous impact, but you have to take a chance that it may let you down. If you leave the fern until it is really mature then it is more likely to live in water. Arranged with 'Doris' (pale salmon) pinks, lavender and some love-in-a-mist, it really is enchanting.

Atriplex hortensis rubra

Hardy annual with red foliage and spikes of red seed in late summer that make it a very useful plant for flower arranging. The red seed heads mix well in a vase of dahlias, and with a few bronze leaves make a good background for any brightly-coloured flowers. There is also a yellow-leaved atriplex, *A. hortensis aurea*. The spikes dry naturally in water but gradually lose their colour, so I prefer to remove them and store them away for winter use, when they add colour to a vase of dried flowers.

Conditioning When the plant first comes into leaf it needs special care. The ends of the stems must be put into boiling water, and then allowed

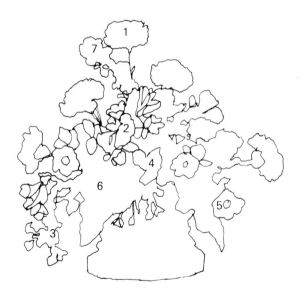

To make this arrangement a little more interesting I bought the carnations and freesias to add to the pieces that were available to cut from the garden in early spring.
1 *Dianthus caryophyllus* (Carnations)
2 *Freesias*
3 *Helleborus foetidus* (Stinking hellebore)
4 *Helleborus corsicus*
5 *Helleborus orientalis* (Lenten rose)
6 *Arum italicum pictum*
7 *Euphorbia robbiae*

a long drink in the usual way. As the seed head forms and the plant matures, a long drink is all that is required, and it is at this stage that I find it most useful.

Preserving Remove leaves and the seed spikes can be dried off in water, or tied in bunches and hung upside down to dry in the warm.

Aucuba japonica
Spotted Laurel

Hardy evergreen. A shrub I never thought much of until I decided to plant one; since then I have used it often. It lightens a group of mixed evergreens in any month of the year, though I use it most in early spring. The female bushes have clusters of brilliant red berries.

Auricula
Primula

My grandmother called these delightful primrose-like flowers 'dusty millers' which well describes their dusty white leaves. They have a delicious smell and last much better in water than the polyanthus. A range of beautiful colours – even down to a green-and-black, though this one is not really hardy, but a plant for the cool greenhouse.

Conditioning Place in deep warm water for several hours.

Drying The little seed heads are charming if left till well formed on the plant, and then stood in the barest amount of water until they have really dried off.

Australian Gum *see* EUCALYPTUS

Autumn Crocus *see* COLCHICUM

Avens *see* GEUM

Azalea

Used as house plants at Christmas, *A. indicum* (*Rhododendron simsii*) or small varieties

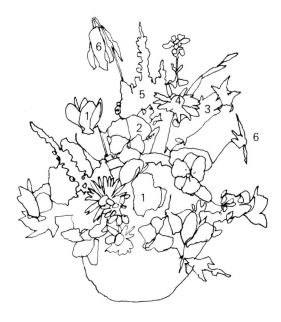

A small Spanish basket filled with a collection of summer treasures.
1 *Cyclamen neapolitanum*
2 *Viola* (Pansy)
3 *Gentiana asclepiadea* (Willow gentian)
4 Daisy
5 Heathers
6 *Clematis integrifolia*

in shades of white and pale to deep pinks are generally very popular. Bury the pot in soil and keep in the shade of a tree from May to September, repot and bring in again, and your plant can last many years. Always water with rain water as tap water may contain lime which azaleas dislike. Visiting Seattle and California over the years I have been fascinated and enchanted by the azalea plantings there. Often these are the evergreen varieties. A sight I will never forget was a wall covered in white wisteria which had an underplanting of white azaleas. It had to be seen to be believed, a touch of magic. Although a group of white, or green-and-white flowers is what I probably love most for the house, it had never occurred to me to try this colour pattern outside. The outdoor varieties including Mollis (tall), Kurume (dwarf), Ghent, and others are some of the loveliest of all shrubs. For sprays of flowers or autumn-tinted foliage they are superbly decorative. Their delicate branching habit makes them a wonderful flower to arrange – especially if you can lay your hands on enough to have a vase full of them. However, they are somewhat slow-growing and if the plants are new and small, then you must pick with care and just use a few sprays to add background to a vase in shades of apricot or flame.

Conditioning As they have woody stems either remove a layer of the outer skin by paring off or hammer well, before allowing a long drink.

Ballota pseudo-dictamnus

Hardy perennial. The contorted, curved and almost arching sprays make it most useful for arranging, giving a lovely natural outline in any vase. The flowers are insignificant, borne as tiny grey-green funnels that ring the main stem, but they become visible as the leaves are removed.

Conditioning Put the ends of the stems into boiling water and then stand in deep water, but

Ballota pseudo-dictamnus

do not submerge, for, as with so many grey-green plants, the tiny hairs on the stems are flattened by the water and lose all their silvery-grey colouring.

Bamboo *see* ARUNDINARIA

Baptisia
False Indigo

Hardy perennial. A pea-shaped dark-blue flower rather like a small lupin. Useful in a small mixed summer vase as blue is such an asset to a mixed group.

Barbados Lily *see* HIPPEASTRUM

Barbeton Daisy *see* GERBERA

Bay Grape
Sea Grape

The Bay Grape trees grow on the seashore in Florida, Bermuda and the Virgin Islands and I expect in many other areas in that latitude.

Stumpy trees with rounded tough leaves that turn the most lovely colours as they are maturing, they last for weeks and weeks. It is the one leaf that I love to bring back from any of these places but I have to warn you that though they last well they do need a false stem which can be made from a florist's wire bound with crepe paper. They are beautiful in their dried stage or, best of all, as they are just turning colour – mixed with fruits they make a wonderfully rich picture.

Bay Tree *see* LAURUS NOBILIS

Beetroot
Beta

Leaves and seed heads are good in a flower group. Some of the ornamental beets are most handsome with well-shaped, reddish-green leaves; *Beta vulgaris cicla* or silver beet has large green leaves with prominent midribs in green and scarlet. Even the edible beets provide some excellent leaves to use as a foil for red roses or dahlias.

Conditioning The leaves flag easily. Their stalks should be dipped in boiling water and then they should be completely submerged in a bath of cold water overnight. Or experiment with the starch method, by immersing the leaves overnight in a weak starch solution.

Preserving Allow seed to form, cut and hang stems upside down to dry.

Begonia

B. rex is really a greenhouse plant, but I always have it on my kitchen window-sill, and cut off leaves all the year round for use in all kinds of ways: with fruits, with tulips in spring, and with summer flowers to add a touch of the exotic. The flowering begonias are of little value for cutting – the heads drop off their stems so quickly; but odd blooms may be used for floating in bowls as they have a wonderful colour range.

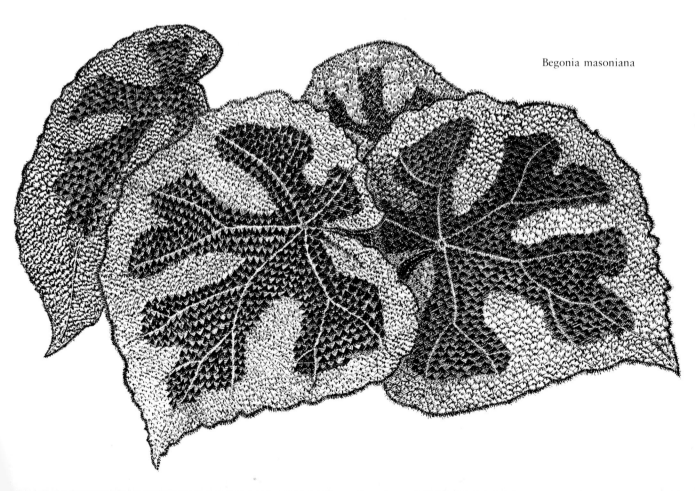

Begonia masoniana

Semperflorens varieties, generally planted out as bedding plants either as an edging or *en masse*, are small plants that I have a new respect for. Not only do they last well in the garden but I have often used small pieces as cut flowers and they have been most useful. The bronzy foliage often outlives the flower and looks well with apricot-coloured rosebuds or small dahlias. Unwin's 'Organdy' mixed makes a marvellous carpet of colour in the garden for weeks on end.

Conditioning *Begonia rex* leaves should have the ends of the stems dipped in boiling water for thirty seconds. Then submerge in cold water, dry off and arrange keeping the stems as much below the water as possible.

Belladonna Lily *see* AMARYLLIS

Beloperone guttata
Shrimp Plant

This has salmon-red bracts in drooping spikes surrounding small white flowers. A plant for the greenhouse and well worth while for small sprays picked to put in a vase, where they will add a spontaneous cascading effect. In Australia I noticed they grew in small hedges dividing gardens, with also a lime-green and yellow variety that I had never seen before.

Conditioning Boiling water treatment is essential.

Berberis
Barberry

Hardy evergreen and deciduous shrubs with ornamental leaves and colourful berries – red, purple, or blue-black. My favourite evergreen kinds are *B. darwinii* and *B. stenophylla*, each with yellow-orange flowers in spring, and *B. wilsoniae* and *B. rubrostilla*, each with arching sprays of iridescent coral berries in autumn. *Berberis thunbergii* turns a beautiful autumn colour, and *B. thunbergii atropurpurea* has excellent purple foliage all summer.

Conditioning Hammer ends of stems or peel off some bark to make absorption of water easier.

Bergenia
Megasea

Hardy perennials. The large-leaved fleshy megaseas are now better known as the bergenias; there are many varieties and some dispute arises in the horticultural world as to the naming of them. *Bergenia crassifolia* has spoon-shaped leaves and very early-flowering paler pink flowers. *B. cordifolia* is one that I use all the year round; the large heart-shaped leaves are superb. Mr Foss, formerly of Constance Spry, often says that if you grow only one plant in your garden, then it must be this. A plant misused in Victorian days and dumped on the flint rockery, often in the shade, because of being so good-natured, seeming to thrive in any conditions. Some of the

Bergenia 'Abendglut'

leaves may turn a lovely colour in late summer and look beautiful with a few Peace roses. The green leaves I use in the winter with a vase of 'mixed greens'. The flowers are also effective, and are nice to cut in May, though to me they are of secondary importance. 'Ballawley Hybrid', with large handsome leaves that turn mahogany colour in the winter, is one that I am thrilled to have and I would like to mention two more that I have grown recently. (I see that Graham Thomas in his superb book, *The Modern Florilegium*, mentions eighteen varieties.) The only one that I would want to cultivate for its flowers – beautiful and white – is B. 'Silberlicht'. The flowers are usually rather clumsy, and strangely enough do not last very well. I do use the pale pink blooms of *B. crassifolia* especially in early spring when they add a real splash of colour to a moss garden, and can be tucked in on their very short stems. Generally speaking, it is for their foliage that I grow and love these plants and I have found *B. abendglut* or 'Evening Glow' to be the one which has the best bronze leaves in winter.

Conditioning Soak the leaves completely in a bath of cold water for a few hours, dry off and arrange.

Beta *see* BEETROOT

Betula pendula
Silver Birch

Silver birch is one of the most graceful of all trees, and I love to use sprays from the bare branches in winter, or later the young green foliage and small catkins to provide a delicate background for daffodils.

Conditioning Hammer ends of stems well and stand in deep water for several hours.

Billbergia nutans

Greenhouse evergreen. Its unusual pendulous flower has the strange but attractive contrast of lime-green petals and bright-pink bracts. A greenhouse plant much recommended.

Bird of Paradise Flower *see* STRELITZIA

Blandfordia
Christmas Bells

The Christmas plant in Australia, low-growing in fiery red, and sold as the British sell holly for Christmas decoration. A fleshy-rooted greenhouse plant in Britain.

Bleeding Heart *see* DICENTRA SPECTABILIS

Blessed Thistle *see* CNICUS BENEDICTUS

Blue Cedar *see* CEDRUS ATLANTICA GLAUCA

Bluebell
Scilla

Wild bluebells are often thought poor flowers for bringing indoors. But this is only when they are picked on too long a stem. Cut not more than 10cm (4in) long and massed tightly in a basket or tin, they will last very well and their scent is delicious. They can last as long as ten days while gradually their bright blue fades almost to white before they die off completely. When picking, never pull but cut; the white end, which must be removed in any case before arranging, provides the substance the bulb needs for flowering next year. Wrap in polythene or paper as soon as cut, as they droop very quickly if exposed to the air, and take a long time to recover.

Conditioning Cut stems fairly short and place in deep warm water for several hours.

Bocconia *see* MACLEAYA CORDATA

Boronia megastigma

Beautiful scented plume of magenta-maroon and yellow, growing wild in Australia where it is sold in small bunches by flower sellers in September. I used it a lot in decorations in Australia, but unfortunately never have enough to cut in England. Constance Spry loved its fragrance and often had a pot of it in her room.

From left to right: Lagurus ovatus, Milium effusum
aureum, Phalaris arundinacea 'Picta', Zea mays, Holcus
mollis 'Variegata', Festuca ovina, Briza maxima

Bougainvillea

Famed for its curving sprays of rich colour on walls and arches in warm climates. A hothouse plant in Britain and magnificent to use.

Conditioning I found it lasts fairly well if first the stems are dipped in boiling water and then the whole spray is completely submerged in cold water for six hours. Store in a plastic bag away from the air.

Preserving I bought in Kenya some excellent individual sprays of florets of bougainvillea on firm grass false stems which had kept their colour quite well and had a waxed look. I am not quite sure how they preserved them but I think the flowers must have been dried very carefully by hanging upside down and then been waxed.

Bouvardia

An enchanting star-like small flower growing in trusses – white, pink and scarlet. A greenhouse plant, but sold quite frequently and used chiefly for florists' sprays or bouquets. No perfume, although I always expect one.

Box Tree *see* BUXUS SEMPERVIRENS

Bracken *see* PTERIDIUM

Briza media
Quaking Grass

Hardy ornamental flowering grass. Graceful to use with cut flowers and, when dried, to arrange with the more solid seed heads of poppies, cardoon, and others, to add a light touch to a winter vase.

Preserving Leave on the plant until the flowers are really open; then cut and bunch, and hang upside down to dry.

Brunnera macrophylla

Hardy herbaceous plant with pale blue forget-me-not flowers. I like to use these to add the ever

Brunnera macrophylla

important touch of blue to any little mixed vase in June, but my main reason for growing brunnera is to have the variegated leaves of *B. macrophylla variegata*. It is a fascinating plant as the leaves increase all summer. I do find that to keep the variegation it is necessary to split up the plant quite frequently. I have mine in full sun though they enjoy partial shade.

Conditioning The flower heads last best if you put the ends of the stems into a little boiling water and then give them a long deep drink. I only use the leaves of the variegated plant and I find it best to pick in advance and put the leaves with just a little water into a polythene bag, seal it and leave for twenty-four hours.

Brussels Sprouts
Brassica gemmifera

The red variety, besides being edible, is interesting for decoration. The purplish-red rounded leaves are most attractive. Try them in winter as a foil for a few expensive red roses.

Conditioning Never use hot water for any brassica. Soak well in cold water for a few hours.

Buddleia davidii hybrid

Buddleia davidii

An excellent summer-flowering shrub, attractive to butterflies and often known as the 'Butterfly Bush'. Adds colour to the shrub border at rather a dull time of year. Sprays combine well in vases of mixed summer flowers; the white variety can be added to green and white groups, the mauve and the purple to pinks and blues. Does not last well despite all treatment, but can be replaced without much trouble after two days if necessary.

Conditioning Dip ends of stems in boiling water and then give a long deep drink.

Preserving Before picking, allow flower heads to lose colour and become a brownish spike, then store till required.

Bugle *see* AJUGA REPTANS

Bulbs

Bulbs for indoor culture should be planted in late September or early October, in fibre or small shingles. Narcissi, crocus and daffodils are all very attractive planted in large bowls and covered in layers of shingle with just the tops of the bulbs peeping out; add water and no soil at all. Keep in the dark until the small shoots appear. These start pale green but will soon become a brilliant green once they are in the light. As they get bigger they need more water, so that they end up literally standing in water. If you decide to plant bulbs in fibre, then soak it very well and squeeze out any surplus water. Put a layer in the bottom of the bowl, place the bulbs on it, giving them enough space to develop, and then fill up with fibre leaving just the tips sticking out. Keep in the dark for several weeks, then the tips will have become pale green; then take them out and stand in a warm room. The warmer the room the quicker they develop and it is quite a good idea to keep some of them in different rooms so that you don't have them all coming out at once. Be sure to buy specially prepared hyacinths if you want them to bloom by Christmas, and remember that they take fifteen weeks from planting to blooming.

Bulrush *see* TYPHA

Bupleurum rotundifolia

The first time I ever saw this dear little plant it was growing at the edge of a cornfield where the seed must have got mixed in with the grain, and I fell in love with it. Grassy blue-green leaves and terminal umbels of greeny-yellow flowers. Not spectacular but enchanting for small arrangements and particularly good with one or two saxifrage leaves or tellima. Well worth growing from seed.

Burning Bush *see* DICTAMNUS

Buttercup *see* RANUNCULUS

Button Snake Root *see* LIATRIS

Buxus sempervirens
Box

Evergreen shrub, excellently dense and slow-growing for topiary, but useful for arrangement in arching sprays, if unclipped. The variegated box, *B. sempervirens aureo-maculata* and *B. sempervirens argentea*, are especially useful and I use them a great deal in winter.

Preserving With a great deal of patience you can achieve creamy sprays of box. First of all hammer the ends of the stems and then put them into glycerine and water and forget all about them. They take weeks to suck up the mixture but in the end they are well worth waiting for.

Caladium

Deciduous perennial house plant. A plant with beautifully ornamental foliage: large leaves of greenish white veined in darker green, or pale-pink leaves veined with crimson. When cut from the plant in England, the leaves do not last very well; the best effect is gained by washing the roots and inserting the whole plant into a vase – this can add charm and lightness to a vase of foliage in greens and white. In the United States these plants are used to great effect as bedding plants or round terraces and pools, being brought in during the winter and repotted for next spring. On many of my autumn visits to the United States I have had a lot of fun being allowed to pick the last leaves and, much to my surprise, they lasted extremely well.

Conditioning If cut leaves are to be used, dip the stalk in boiling water, before submerging the whole leaf in cold water for several hours.

Calathea zebrina
Zebra Plant

A good ornamental house plant which I find useful in miniature indoor gardens, in winter and early spring.

Calceolaria
Slipper Flower

Half-hardy or greenhouse plants. A wide range of orange-red slipper-like flowers. Generally used for bedding-out schemes and used little in flower arrangement, but a piece in a coppery or more subtle shade can look attractive in the centre of a small summer vase.

Calendula
Pot Marigold

Hardy annual. A mass of marigolds in a wooden bowl or a basket brightens any dark corner and gives a glorious feeling of sunlight. These flowers are long-lasting in water. I am fond of the ball varieties, especially a pale lemon yellow which looks cool and fresh in high summer, arranged with grasses and green love-lies-bleeding. Unwins have a nice mixture of colours in their C. 'Pacific Beauty' which are much better for blending than the vivid orange, and they last very well indeed.

Conditioning Give a large drink, up to their necks, in deep water.

Californian Tree Poppy *see* ROMNEYA

Callistemon
Bottle-brush Tree

A native of Australia. The flowers are excellent for a modern style of arrangement and last extremely well. I use them as often as I can get them, liking them best when dried.

Preserving Hang them upside down and they dry very well.

Callistephus *see* ASTER

Calluna *see under* ERICA

Camassia quamash
Bear Grass, Wild Hyacinth

A hardy bulbous plant with spikes of blue flowers in July. C. *leichtlinii* a good pointed outline for a mixed group of summer flowers and excellent for a vase of blues, July being the only month for a good vase of tall blue flowers. The rather shy C. *l.* 'Plena' has rosettes of creamy-yellow flowers all up the stem.

Camellia japonica
Tea Plant

Hardy evergreen shrub. Now more widely grown than ever before. Though tender, they do well outside in a sheltered north or west aspect – this prevents the early morning sun from reaching the blooms while they are still in the grip of frost, when they would become scorched and unsightly. They like the dappled shade of a small deciduous tree, and acid soil. Although expens-

Camassia quamash

ive initially, they will well reward you with an abundance of white, pink or red blooms in early spring, to say nothing of magnificent dark glossy foliage. This I enjoy in winter more than I can ever express: by itself in a white slender jug or mixed with evergreens of any kind. If you prefer not to pick the flower sprays, then use the heads alone and have them floating in a bowl.

Conditioning Hammer the hard woody stems of the foliage and give a long drink.

Campanula
Canterbury Bell, Bellflower

Hardy annuals, biennial and perennials. In July, when many summer flowers droop readily and shed petals, these are one of the best-lasting subjects for cutting. They look cool and pretty and have become very popular over the years. Of the hardy perennial varieties, *C. latifolia*, *C. persicifolia*, *C. latiloba* and *C. pyramidalis* are some of my favourites. *C. lactiflora* 'Loddon Anna' is a delightful soft pink. Though I have never grown *C. burghaltii*, I was given it for my lecture at the RHS in 1977 – and what a charmer,

Campanula lactiflora 'Loddon Anna'

with its large, pendulous grey-lilac bells. Used with some grey foliage and soft pink Chaucer roses, it really is a delight. It does not last quite as well, sadly, as some of the *persicifolia* types which are outstanding. These seeded themselves freely in my Grandmother's garden in Scotland and it was from her that I got my love of the campanula family. The biennial Canterbury bells I recommend both for the border and to cut. For the rock garden, there is a wide range of alpine campanula well worth growing.

Conditioning Place in deep water for several hours. Remove all faded flowers, and each bud should open out.

Canary Creeper *see* TROPAEOLUM

Candytuft *see* IBERIS

Canna indica
Indian Shot Plant

Greenhouse perennial. Used for bedding and cutting, but it will not stand British winters. Handsome foliage in red and green, and yellow and flame-coloured flowers on strong, thick stems. It is marketed in Britain occasionally and looks well with mixed foliages.

Conditioning For the leaves, dip the stalks in boiling water and then submerge in cold water for several hours. The flower stems need boiling and then should stand in cold water.

Cantaloup Melon
Cucumis melo cantalupensis

This may seem odd to include, but its grooved shape is so decorative and gives an air of festivity, as when placed in a vase of mixed fruit and flowers for a buffet table.

Canterbury Bell *see* CAMPANULA

Cape Gooseberry *see* PHYSALIS

Cape Jasmine *see* GARDENIA

Cape Lily *see* CRINUM

Capsicum

Greenhouse. Grown in Britain now much more widely than ever before and last year I even saw them growing outside in a very sheltered corner. The fruits are better known as sweet peppers or chillies. I use both the red and the green fruits in vases of foliages, or with fruit and flowers. Their shiny skins have a lovely texture and give highlights to any arrangement.

Cardoon
Cynara cardunculus

Hardy herbaceous perennial. Of the artichoke family, a little hardier than the globe artichoke and therefore used for decorative purposes more widely. Good leaves and excellent seed heads. A plant I would never be without. See also Artichoke (*Cynara scolymus*).

Carnation *see* DIANTHUS

Carpenteria californica

A shrub that, as the name implies, comes from California, and will need a sheltered place in the garden. It produces a wealth of single white flowers with a mass of golden stamens, resembling a single white rose. Having seen it in full flower in June at Winkfield Place I cannot wait to grow it. I used it in a green and white arrangement and these clear, single flowers made a marvellous focal point.

Carpentaria californica

Conditioning Place the ends of the stems into boiling water for a few minutes and then give a long drink. Keep the flower heads well above the water-line, as they are very delicate and bruise easily.

Carpinus betulus
Hornbeam

A large tree bearing sprays of green catkins in early spring before the leaves appear; extremely pretty as background material in a vase. In the summer, they form showers of tiny keys, which turn from green to brown, delightful at all stages.

Conditioning Hammer the woody stems and give a long drink.

Preserving Place stems of the green keys in glycerine, remove before they turn brown, and occasionally they stay green or golden; or the keys can simply be hung upside down and when dried they are very effective.

Carrot
Daucus carota

I use carrots occasionally with fruit, flowers and vegetables, but I also like to use the lacy flower (it is rather like cow parsley) after it has gone to seed, both fresh and dried. In addition carrots have good coloured foliage.

Preserving Allow the seed head to form, then hang it upside down.

Castanea sativa
Sweet Chestnut

This is lovely to use in its flower stage, removing the foliage until you are left with the fluffy yellow spikes of the flowers, which are especially good when arranged with lilies.

Preserving Put the stems in glycerine and use as a change from beech leaves. I have also used the prickly cases which hold the nuts. Dried off and mounted on wires they make an interesting spray for a dried group.

Catananche caerulea alba

Catananche caerulea

Strangely enough it was not until this year that I became conscious of this plant. It has star-like purple flowers, so useful for a mixed summer vase. It is a 'cut and come again' plant and flowers more or less continuously for four months, liking a dry soil and lots of sun. It's wise to take seed, or root cuttings after three years as this continuous flowering takes its toll, and this way you will always have something to cut.

Catmint *see* NEPETA

Cattleya
Orchid

Stove plant. The opulent varieties with purple colourings are usually worn as a spray or carried in a bouquet. Not really recommended for use in a group; as well as being expensive, they are difficult to arrange as the stems are short and the petals so delicate. As the years have passed I have had much more chance to use these orchids, from private greenhouses in America and out of doors in Hawaii and Australia. I find quite the best way to use them is to place the stems in a flower pick or cigar holder – both equally good – as they keep the short stem in water and at the same time provide an elongated stem which is easier to work with. In Australia I had an opportunity to use the white cattleyas with cascades of white jasmine, and white open roses, an arrangement that I don't suppose I will ever have the luck to do again!

Ceanothus

Hardy and half-hardy shrubs, both evergreens and deciduous. 'Gloire de Versailles' is one of my favourite deciduous varieties. I love a tuft of this fluffy blue flower in a vase, but I have never found any way of making it last in water, and so it does mean replacing the stem each day.

Cedrus atlantica glauca
Blue Cedar

This magnificent tree has beautiful spraying branches and lovely cones. Its deep blue-grey goes so well with a mixture of greys and for winter decoration it can be put with eucalyptus foliage and a few pink chrysanthemums.

Drying A really good branch is well worth saving after use in a vase. Hang it upside down to allow the needles to fall, and it is excellent then as a background or gummed and glittered for Christmas.

Celmisia

These beautiful New Zealand daisies have large white daisy flowers with clear yellow centres and handsome pointed sword-like leaves with a grey look. I use both flowers and leaves. I love them and grow them with great difficulty in my Hertfordshire garden but in Scotland they flourish.

Celosia
Feathered Cockscomb

This brilliantly coloured plume in red, yellow and orange looks a little like amaranthus upside down. It is a plant I have never been very taken with but I know on my autumnal trips to the United States that I frequently find it to be most useful. It is best of all dried because it keeps its colour remarkably well and it does add character as well as colour to any dried arrangement.

Conditioning Put the ends of the stems into boiling water for a few seconds and then allow a

Celmisia spectabilis

long drink. If picked in a very young stage, it does not last at all well.

Preserving I think one gets the best results by immersing the flower heads in silica gel. The colour then keeps perfectly. The heads will dry off quite well if you put the stems in shallow water and leave in a hot, dry place.

Centaurea
Cornflower, Sweet Sultan

Hardy annuals. Grown from seed, cornflowers (C. *cyanus*) make a good splash of colour and look their best, I think, arranged in baskets with grasses. Sweet sultan (C. *moschata*) in white and a soft pink-lilac is a better lasting flower for the house; it stands well and makes a good focal point in any vase.

Ceratostigma *see* PLUMBAGO

Cercis siliquastrum
Judas Tree

This has showers of purple racemes and is so beautiful that I wish it were not so rarely available. A tree that is not often grown, sad to say, chiefly because it is not very hardy and is slow to flower.

Chamaecyparis
Cypress

Hardy evergreen coniferous trees. These evergreens are used mainly for winter decoration, and especially for Christmas. I like to gum and glitter short pieces to arrange with fir cones and perhaps fruit and candles for a Christmas table. In the garden they have great architectural value as single trees or to contribute height and shape to a shrub border. Many different varieties in a wide range of greens and yellows.

Cheiranthus
Wallflower

Hardy annual. Wallflowers as we know them come in a lovely range of warm colours –

browny-golds and rich reds, through to cream and pale yellow. Because of their hard woody stems they do not last very well in water unless they are picked fairly short. They seem to arrange best in a mass, either in a wooden box or basket or a copper bowl; in this way even if the petals do fall, they fall on each other, and the flowers do not look so sad when they gradually begin to die. 'Ruby Glow' is the most beautiful colour, almost purple, and this I think is quite one of the most unusual to grow. They are one of the few flowers that seem to last very much better if they are arranged on their own and not mixed with other flowers.

Conditioning Cut with stems not longer than 10cm (4in) and give them a long drink in warm water before arranging.

Cherry Pie *see* HELIOTROPIUM

Chimonanthus
Winter Sweet

Hardy deciduous shrub. C. *praecox* (C. *fragrans*) has pale golden flowers deepening to red at the centre and of all winter shrubs is quite the most delightful for scent. It has, however, a rather straggly form.

Chincherinchee *see* ORNITHOGALUM

Chionodoxa
Glory of the Snow

A little bulb which produces star-shaped flowers of excellent blue colour, with white throats. Increases every year to give a cloud of blue in early spring, and is lovely when used for a touch of colour at this time in a 'moss garden', with crocus or other suitable companions.

Chlorophytum comosum variegatum

Greenhouse and house plant. Long pointed leaves, with a cream stripe up the centre, arching over like the spray of a fountain. Useful with ornamental foliage. It has the added attraction of long wands of stems that produce young plants. Often known as baby-bearing plants, like *Saxifraga sarmentosa* 'Tricolor', and *Tolmiea menziesii* or 'piggyback' plant.

Choisya ternata
Mexican Orange

Hardy evergreen shrub. Useful both for its good green hard foliage and for its clusters of lovely sweet-scented white flowers which appear in late spring.

Conditioning Hammer the stems well, before giving a long drink.

Christmas Rose *see* HELLEBORUS

Chrysanthemum
Chrysanthemum, Ox-eye Daisy, Marguerite

Greenhouse half-hardy and hardy perennials. The name covers a wide range of plants from the ox-eye daisy to the ones we think of as chrysanthemums proper, the greatest stand-by for winter flower arrangement. There are many varieties in each class, such as incurved, anemone centred and American spray, in all colours and grown all the year round. Koreans are one of my favourites, partly because they are single; all singles are so easy to arrange and most effective for the focal point in a vase. My favourite colourings are the pale yellow and apricot but I would hate to live without 'Wedding Day', the single white which starts with a green centre. It flowers very late and is superb. Annual chrysanthemums with daisy-like faces are especially useful to place centrally in a mixed group. *C. maximum* 'Esther Read' a double white perennial must have a mention, as with little trouble you will get a long flowering period of this variety which lasts extremely well even in hot weather. It is sad to see them dyed in all colours and sold in practically every country in the world – dreadful.

Conditioning Place the ends of the stems in boiling water, then leave in deep water up to their necks.

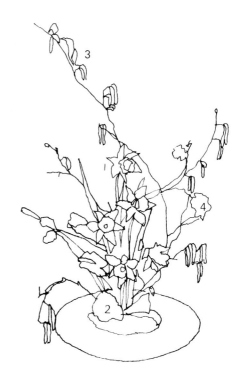

A very simple arrangement with a branch of catkins, a few daffodils and some hamamelis, all in a base of galax leaves.
1 *Daffodils*
2 *Galax* leaves
3 *Corylus* (Hazel catkins)
4 *Hamamelis* (Witch hazel)

Cimicifuga

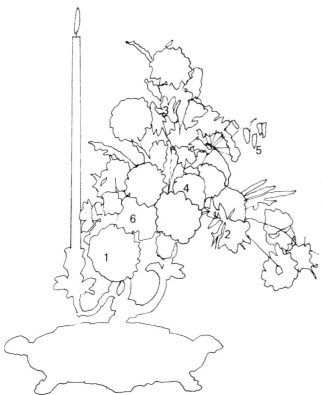

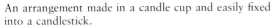

An arrangement made in a candle cup and easily fixed
into a candlestick.
1 *Dahlias*
2 *Lonicera* (Honeysuckle)
3 *Alstroemeria ligtu* hybrids (Peruvian lily)
4 *Sedum*
5 *Briza maxima* (Pearl grass)
6 *Tellima grandiflora*

Cimicifuga cordifolia
Bugbane

Hardy herbaceous perennial. A plant that has
become increasingly popular. Plumes of creamy
flowers on coal-black stems. *C. racemosa* is
taller and particularly attractive for growing in
woodland.

Conditioning Scald the stems in boiling water
and let them stand in deep water for several
hours.

Cineraria *see* SENECIO

Clarkia

Hardy annual. Flowers in July and comes in a wide range of colours – purples, through pinks of all shades, to white. A very good annual to grow for flower vases as it lasts in water so well. Remember to pick when it is almost in full flower right up to the top of the stem, otherwise the budded tip of the stem tends to droop easily. It is attractive either arranged in bowls by itself or added to mixed groups of blending colour.

Conditioning Dip the stem in boiling water for a few seconds and then allow a long drink.

Preserving Remove any foliage and arrange in full flower in shallow water. It dries off very well and the less it is disturbed the better as this prevents the petals from falling.

Clary *see* SALVIA

Clematis
Virgin's Bower

Hardy climbers and herbaceous perennials. The climbing varieties, both evergreen and deciduous, are very rewarding, giving a wealth of bloom if they really like their position; they like their heads in the sun and feet in the shade and prefer lime soil. As a rule they do not stand well as a cut flower, though they are ideal for the centre of a vase and I use them as often as I can. The little herbaceous one *C. integrifolia* is one my grandmother loved, and the plant I took from her garden some years ago gives me a great deal of pleasure; unlike the climbing varieties these last very well in a flower arrangement without any special conditioning. I must also mention *C. heracleifolia* whose attractive soft Wedgwood blue flowers are sweetly scented and are borne on stiff stems on a sprawling plant, flowering for many weeks in late summer. Again it not only adds great interest to a flower vase, but gives the much wanted touch of mauvy-blue. The seed heads of *C. davidiana* are fluffy and very effective, as are the long sprays of old man's beard, *C. vitalba*, the wild clematis, which I use continually in all its seed head stages.

Conditioning The large-flowered and climbing varieties should have the ends of their stems placed in boiling water for a few seconds and then be given a long drink for two to three hours. The stems are sometimes short, so be sure to place in a shallow bowl and prevent the petals from getting wet, as they quickly become transparent. Although I have never tried this, the Japanese often use their alcohol treatment for clematis, placing the stems in a small bottle of pure alcohol for several minutes, before standing them in water for a long drink.

Preserving The stems of old man's beard may be hung upside down to dry the seed head, though I find that if you pick before the seed is too fluffy they last extremely well in a solution of glycerine and water; I can thoroughly recommend this.

Cleome spinosa
Spider Flower

Half-hardy annual. I have used them a great deal in Australia but rarely in Britain, though in the last few years I have seen them in quite a few gardens and, grown as an annual, they are most effective. Interesting for the flower arranger who is on the lookout for something different. If you can find them they are certainly attractive with their rounded spined heads of pink or white florets.

Clerodendron bungei

A hardy deciduous shrub reaching a height of about 2.5m (8ft). It has fragrant rose-purple flowers during late summer. The flower sprays are very decorative when the heart-shaped leaves have been removed.

Clianthus puniceus
Parrot's Bill

Greenhouse climbing shrub. Parrot's bill describes it very well and there is little to add. I seldom have the opportunity of using it as a cut flower, but it is most unusual and has pleasing feathery foliage which is suitable for a mixed group.

Clivia
Kaffir Lily

Greenhouse perennial. A handsome head of upright trumpet-like flowers in shades of orange, very useful pointed leaves and lasts in water extremely well. Being spring-flowering it is an asset for a large group for a church or some special occasion – at a time when most flowers are so delicate and therefore have little substance for the centre of a vase. For a good colour combination mix it with forsythia and daffodils.

Clivia miniata

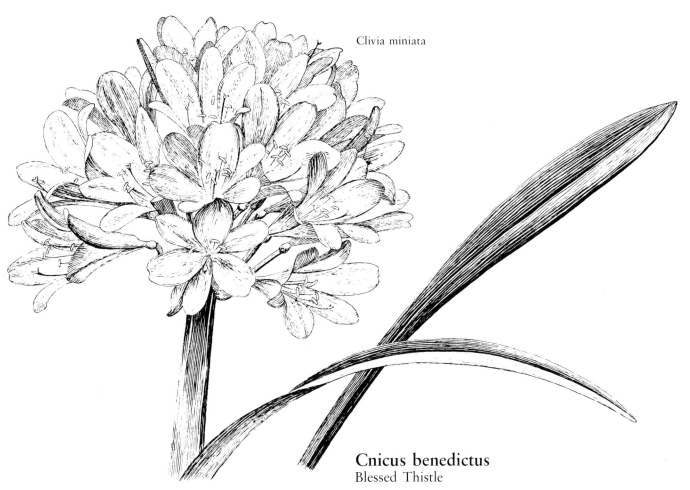

Cnicus benedictus
Blessed Thistle

Annual. Extremely decorative green leaves with white blotches, but very prickly and difficult to handle. The flower is of little interest.

Conditioning Stems should have the ends well boiled; then give a soaking in cold water.

Cobaea scandens

72

Cobaea scandens
Cups and Saucers

A half-hardy perennial, usually grown as an annual, *C. scandens* has trumpet or bell-shaped flowers of delicate lilac or pale green. A really enchanting climbing plant, quick growing and well worth while as an annual. Sometimes it can be persuaded to survive a winter if given a sheltered position and if the weather is not too severe. The seed heads are pretty: not very good for drying, but they last well in water.

Codiaeum
Croton

Tender evergreen shrubs with beautiful ornamental foliage, sold in bunches of individual leaves and extremely useful, especially in winter. I have had the fun of picking long stems and using them in large foliage groups in Bermuda. I have found them most decorative arranged with fruit and flowers.

Conditioning The leaves last very well if the ends of the long stems are plunged into boiling water, and the whole leaf is then completely submerged in water for several hours.

Codonopsis vinciflora 'Tangshen'

A new plant for me and in my opinion worthy of a place in any garden though I have never had the fun of arranging it. Enchanting pale china-blue bells which give you a wonderful surprise as you lift their heads, to find brilliant orange and maroon markings. 'Tangshen' twines up a shrub enjoying partial shade, and has exquisite greenish bells with purple markings. See the photograph on page 32.

Colchicum
Autumn Crocus, Meadow Saffron

A delightful autumn bulb, very rewarding though it does need careful planting. The lovely mauve and white 'crocuses' appear straight out of the ground with no foliage at all, making a wonderful splash of colour just as it seems everything else is dying off. In spring, however, when they might well be forgotten, the plants throw up a multitude of green leaves, which are not very attractive; because of this it is advisable to plant round trees. One of the best ways of growing them I ever saw was as underplanting in a bed of azaleas; the turning foliage of the azaleas and the mass of purple colchicum made a beautiful display in autumn and the leaves were not too conspicuous in the spring. When cut the flowers last well; one or two stems of the very large white varieties arranged on a pin-holder in a shallow silver bowl are hard to surpass.

Coleus
Flame Nettle

Greenhouse perennial. Beautiful ornamental foliage in a wide range of colour – flames and reds, but my favourite is the lime-green. It is coming into wider use as a cut plant, though usually thought of as a greenhouse or bedding-out plant for parks or gardens.

Conditioning The stems must be dipped in boiling water, then given a long cold drink, but do not submerge in case of transparency.

Columbine *see* AQUILEGIA

Conditioning and maintaining

If you are going to go to all the trouble of picking flowers and then arranging them it is well worthwhile to try and make them last in water just as long as possible. The initial treatment of flowers after picking is of considerable importance. There are different theories about the best time of day to pick. Gardeners, by and large, feel the morning is best as the flowers have regained overnight the moisture that they lose during the day. While agreeing with this theory, I do not necessarily keep to it: partly because I find that blooms removed from the plant with the dew still on them are inclined to wilt more quickly; and also because flowers last much better if they have several hours in deep water. I prefer to pick at night and then leave them in deep water till next day.

Avoid picking in full sun (except for flowers like arctotis and gentian which close up easily) and get all stems into water as quickly as possible; once a stem flags, it takes a long time to stiffen up again. I take a jug of water round the garden with me in hot weather to prevent this from happening. As you pick the flowers, remove all the bottom leaves, especially any that go under the water-line. This prevents the water from becoming stagnant quickly. It also saves a confusion at the top of the vase, you can see where you are placing the next stems and ensure that they really are under water. Even if you do not use any of the special treatments I give later it is most important to cut all soft stems and hammer hard any woody ones. Then place the flowers in deep water for up to twelve hours. I find that the use of plastic has altered our lives considerably, inasmuch as you can pick into a plastic bag, and this retains the moisture and saves carrying round a bucket. I like to carry a plastic bag in the car all the time as I am often tempted to pick by the wayside and if the stems are put into plastic and away from the air then they really last twice as long. It is contact with the air and dehydration which makes them wilt so quickly.

If you are buying flowers, it is of course much more difficult to know how fresh they really are, but flowers more often die from being fresh and not having had a really good drink than because of being too old. As soon as you get them home, put them quickly into water, first snipping the dry ends as this enables them to take up water more quickly. Try to get them wrapped so that the heads are out of the air; equally important in both summer and winter.

A glance at the stems will indicate how long they have been in water. If they look dark in colour and at all slimy, do not buy. With such flowers as lilies and daffodils it is quite easy to see how fresh they are by the amount of pollen on the stamens. When a lily bud first opens, the pollen is hardly noticeable. Often the stamens are removed altogether before the pollen can stain the flowers, but if by gently tapping a bunch of daffodils you shake off any pollen then it is better not to buy! Nearly all fresh flowers such as daffodils and chrysanthemums have a definite sheen on a newly-opened flower. With roses and tulips, one glance will show you a closed bud or a fully-blown flower. As one gets far more effect from a really open flower, I usually like to buy two or more bunches in various stages – some in tight bud and some in full bloom. I have been interested for a long while in the conditioning of cut flowers so as to make them last better and you may like to experiment yourself with some of the methods I shall suggest. We are learning more all the time about the movement of sap, and cell structure, and an outcome of this is the boiling water treatment – one of the discoveries that has enabled me to use many different kinds of foliages that previously seemed to wilt as soon as removed from the plant.

Here are some of my methods of conditioning:

Hammering and peeling With really woody stems of shrubs such as lilac and laburnum, either hammer the bottom 5cm (2in) of the stem, or scrape off the outside bark, leaving the white under-stem showing for at least 5–7cm (2–3in). Be very careful that the whole of the white part goes well under the water-line or the stem will not last. Then remove any foliage that will go below water, to prevent discolouration of water, clogging the cells in the stems so that they cannot drink freely, and bad odour. Also remove heavy or unwanted leaves that may obscure flower heads or berries. This will reduce the transpiration as well.

Boiling water treatment This is another way of treating the stems of woody plants. I find it particularly good for roses and the leaves of many hothouse plants, such as *Begonia rex* and caladium. Place the stem ends in a jug with 2.5cm (1in) of really boiling water for about a minute, then fill up the jug with cold water and leave the stems in it for several hours. To prevent the flower heads from getting scorched by the steam, put a towel round the top of the jug, or, as in the case of very delicate flowers such as clematis, cover the flower head itself in tissue paper.

Searing Hold the stem ends in a gas flame or burn with a match. This has the same effect as the boiling water, but is very much easier when you are taking odd leaves from a stem of, say, spurge or poinsettia, which will result in the bleeding of the white rubbery substance known as latex. Searing stops this bleeding at once. It is also suitable for poppies and hollyhocks, though generally I find it quicker and easier to place the ends in boiling water. However, it can be useful if you are re-cutting ends that have already been boiled. After shortening the stem a little, just hold the stem in the flame of a lighted match for a few seconds.

Floating Leaves such as arum, and all kinds of ferns, should be floated or submerged for twelve hours if possible. Fill a bath or sink with tepid or cold water, but avoid hot water as it will scald and completely ruin any delicate leaf. But never submerge completely any grey foliage as this spoils the silvery-grey effect. I think this is because the silver effect is usually created by a coating of very fine hairs on the leaves, and once really wet the leaves look quite green and take a long time to dry. Heads of hydrangea, which wilt quickly, recover overnight if submerged in warm water. Because leaves are soaking wet after this treatment always leave them on a piece of newspaper to dry. I have found the following piece of advice given to me by a friend in Nottingham to be most effective and particularly good for young and tender hosta leaves which, when picked in early May, are difficult to condition. Cut the leaves from the plant and place the ends of the stems into boiling water until you count twenty. Then put about 5cm (2in) of water into a plastic bag, lay the leaves in it, seal the bag and leave overnight. When I was in Hawaii I found it worked well with bougainvillea and tender leaves of tropical exotics, begonias and castor oil plant.

A plastic bag placed over a completed vase and left in a cool place means that you can make the arrangement the day before and it will remain very fresh – useful tip for party and table flowers.

Starching One solution suitable for most purposes can be made by dissolving a teaspoonful of instant starch in a little under 1l (1½pt) of water. Submerged in it overnight, arum leaves and ferns stiffen slightly and this makes them last much longer. It is also good for bracken before pressing and using for winter decoration.

Boiling vinegar A tip I heard in the United States, where it is used for such subjects as bamboo. Put 2.5cm (1in) of boiling vinegar into a jug and insert the stems for five minutes, then allow them to have a long drink of water.

Cutting the stems under water This is a method used by the Dutch growers, and the exhibits on their stand at the Chelsea Flower Show seem to stay fresh almost better than any others. The idea is to stop any air entering the stem and forming an air bubble which would prevent the assimilation of water. Wire netting in the vase may make this difficult to accomplish. It is best to cut the stems in this way in a bucket of water and leave them in it to have a drink; afterwards take care to keep your finger over the end of the stem until you get it into the vase.

Spraying This is particularly helpful where there is central heating. It increases the moisture content in the air, reduces transpiration from the leaves, and prolongs their life. It is excellent for hydrangeas, which seem to drink through their heads, and also woody-stemmed flowers such as rhododendrons, which absorb moisture more slowly. Both flowers will last longer if given a long drink and an overhead spray immediately after picking.

Filling the hollow stems with water Hold the hollow stems of such flowers as lupins and delphiniums upside down, fill with water and plug them with cotton wool or Oasis. This takes quite a time, but is well worth while if they are needed for some special occasion.

Breaking stems There is divided opinion about this. However, I constantly break, both for speed and lasting; I find it has much the same effect as hammering and the flowers last extremely well.

Retaining the roots Occasionally when I have a very large group of flowers to arrange, I find it most helpful to use a whole pot plant – many of

which, such as *Begonia rex*, when cut, do not stand well in water without special treatment. If you remove the plant from the pot and wash the soil from the roots, it can be put straight into the vase; or if extra height is needed, insert the roots in a polythene bag and tie on to a cane at the height required.

Warm water By warm, I mean the temperature at which you can comfortably insert your hand. All cut flowers revive well in warm water, and I usually fill up my vases with warm water if this is available. If flowers arrive limp, cut the stems and then place them in warm water and they will revive almost immediately.

Aspirin and other aids Many people use aspirin to help flowers to last, and it is especially good for tulips. On very good authority I have been told that sugar feeds the flowers and that a teaspoonful of sugar and one aspirin is the ideal combination. The aspirin keeps the water clear, as sugar – although flowers like it – does tend to clog the cells and gradually defeats its aim, by not letting the stems take up water. Charcoal is excellent for keeping the water clear, and in Australia they often use alum. The Dutch product, *Chrysal*, has very good lasting properties, and I can thoroughly recommend it. Read the instructions carefully, for you should put the flowers into it for a drink and then tip the Chrysal water into the vase. However, I have used it just in the flower vase, the flowers having had their preparatory drink in cold water only, and it is worth using like this for a special occasion. A little bleach is good in a vase which has either onion or cabbage, and prevents any odour. I find a teaspoonful of Phostrogen is excellent. Anything that may help to give the flowers longer life is worth trying.

Alcohol To use this for flowers may seem odd but it has been used in Japan for many years, for preserving special subjects. Many of the Japanese studios keep a small bottle of pure alcohol for putting stems of flowers such as wisteria, clematis and water lilies into for several minutes; I cannot say that I have had any experience with this, but I did come home and try my hellebores in gin! Though they appeared at first to hang over the vase, I must admit that after a long drink they really lasted extremely well. I am told the Japanese inject alcohol into the stems of water lilies and they stay open even at night, although the only method that I find really satisfactory with water lilies is inserting melted wax between the petals which stops them closing.

Cotton wool Putting cotton wool into a bowl and then filling it with water, is the ideal way of keeping small, almost stemless flowers: stephanotis, orchids, and gardenias.

Protecting petals – tissue and polythene film Stretch a piece of tissue paper over a bowl of water and fix with an elastic band. Puncture holes in the paper and slip the stem ends into the water. In this way the flowers can drink but the petals remain unaffected. The very thin polythene film used in the kitchen for covering pots, etc., will do equally well.

Pricking the stems With a needle prick right through the stem just under the head for tulips, hellebores and polyanthus (primula in North America). This prevents an air bubble forming and the flower will drink more freely. An alternative method is to take a needle and make a fine cut from the head to the base of the stem down the length of the stalk. This is particularly good for hellebores.

Filling the vases The filling of vases, once they have been arranged, is most important. I start with the vase three-quarters full before I begin an arrangement; the water gives the vase stability and it is not so likely to fall over. After the arrangement is completed you should fill the vase up to the top. If this causes problems I suggest you put one finger over the edge of the vase so you can feel the water rising inside.

After care When I'm renewing a vase I find it best to cut stems rather than to risk upsetting the whole arrangement by pulling them out. A few moments spent daily removing heads and leaves will refresh the arrangement – I rarely rearrange a vase as there never seems to be anything worth using again. Keep the vase filled with water at all times and make certain that none is spilled underneath as it can stain furniture badly. A small glass mat under the vase can help prevent this happening. Should you have water marks on furniture I can recommend two methods of removing them. One is by mixing together a little olive oil with some coarse salt and rubbing it gently over the mark. The other, which needs more care, it to put a drop of methylated spirit on to a soft cloth, dip it into a little linseed oil and rub over the stain. This will take out most difficult stains. After a flower arrangement is finished, remove the wire and thoroughly wash the vase. Then, as I mentioned earlier in the book, scald the netting to clean it thoroughly, and replace in the vase. It is important to clean vases each time you empty them otherwise water marks will become impossible to remove.

Convallaria majalis
Lily of the Valley

Hardy herbaceous perennial. Sweetly-scented sprays of little bells, in pink as well as white, about 15cm (6in) high. Lovers of shade, they grow well in any surroundings, doing well in small town gardens which makes them a general favourite. They are easy to force, so are in great demand for bouquets at all times of year. Almost the nicest way to arrange them is to make a posy of the flowers in your hand and surround them with a frill of their leaves, tie with string to keep them in place, and put them in a small bowl or vase. The ornamental foliage of the variegated *C. lineata* which I saw only recently in Frances Perry Hay's garden in Enfield makes a most unusual planting. Though I have never heard of it I am told it has been around since 1835! Well worth looking for and most useful for a mixed foliage arrangement.

Conditioning If they are picked straight from the garden, little care is needed; just cut the ends of the stems and place in deep water for an hour or so. The forced blooms are rather fragile and are better if the bunch is wrapped in tissue paper and stood in a little warm water; then fill the jar right to the top and let them stay overnight in deep water.

Convallaria majalis

Coreopsis

Convolvulus *see* IPOMOEA

Coreopsis

Hardy annuals and perennials. Brownish-yellow daisy-like flowers with a good 'face' which makes them a useful central point in a vase. The annuals, being on rather slender stems, are more difficult to arrange than the firmer perennial varieties. Late summer plants, well recommended.

Cornus
Dogwood

The red and yellow shoots of dogwood, indigenous to North America, are beautiful in winter, giving welcome colour to a shrub border. I recommend several species: *C. alba sibirica* 'Westonbirt' has leaves with excellent autumn colour and when these fall you are left with brilliant scarlet stems all winter. *C. stolonifera flaviramea* has bright yellow-green bark and both of these give a graceful outline shape for a winter arrangement, with perhaps a bunch of single chrysanthemums or early daffodils.

Cornus mas is a delightful species, flowering very early in the spring; it has clusters of tiny yellow flowers which show up well on the bare brown branches before the leaves appear. It is also excellent arranged with a few daffodils. One of my favourites is *C. kousa* with open large white bracts appearing in May or June, strawberry-like fruits in the autumn and gorgeous autumn-tinted foliage. This is a lovely flower for arrangement, for it has an oriental delicacy and one or two sprays make a decoration in themselves, arranged alone in a shallow dish or bowl. *C. florida* is the State flower of Virginia and to see these beautiful small trees together with the Red Buds (*Cercis canadensis*) is a sight I will never forget. *C. nuttallii*, the famous dogwood so often seen in western North America, preserves most beautifully, though alas not so well in England, probably because of the damp climate.

Conditioning Strip off about 5cm (2in) of bark from the end of the stem and give a long drink in warm water.

Preserving The branches of fully open American dogwood can be preserved excellently by putting the branches into silica gel. The process takes a great deal of powder and continual warmth but the effect is fantastic once it is done.

Cortaderia
Pampas Grass

Hardy herbaceous perennial grass with handsome white plumes growing out of tall clumps of fine grassy foliage. It was used a great deal by the Victorians as an ornamental plant in shrubberies or planted on sweeping lawns to give a feeling of height and grandeur. We use it for background for large groups in midsummer, and it has proved invaluable for flowers arranged in the Albert Hall, in London, and really large buildings. Because of its size it is of little use in the average house or for small vases, and there seems no way in which it can be cut down to look in proportion; though I think I have seen small pieces taken from the sides and used in some Australian examples. I have seen a pink one, but it is rather unusual.

Preserving When the grass is dry, about the end of September, pick and bunch the heads and hang them upside down to dry completely, for use in winter groups.

Corylopsis

Hardy deciduous flowering shrubs. *C. spicata*, which needs a sheltered position, flowers as early as February, with pale-yellow drooping spikes adorning bare branches. *C. veitchiana* flowers in April, and the lovely variety *C. willmottiae* flowers in March and April. I grow the first and last mentioned and although they don't really flourish in my cold garden, they always give me a few precious sprays of flowers at a very sparse time of year. The flowers of some varieties are sweetly-scented and the leaves often turn a good colour in autumn.

Conditioning Hammer stems well and peel off up to 5cm (2in) of bark from the end of the stem, before placing in warm water.

Corylus
Hazel

Hazel catkins are amongst the first spring flowers; to get the maximum enjoyment from them be sure to bring them into the house in their early stage just after Christmas. Hammer the stems well and keep them in a warm room in deep water and you'll be surprised how quickly they come out. *Corylus avellana contorta*, with its spiral twisting and arching stems, is almost a 'must' for any flower arranger. One stem of a lovely shape is an exciting background for a few well chosen flowers at any time of year. For decoration indoors and out I love the deep purple foliage of *C. maxima atropurpurea* (the purple-leaf filbert). In vases it makes a good background for merging with red flowers or for contrasting with browns and yellows.

Conditioning Hammer ends of stems well and peel off bark up to 4–7cm (2–3in). Place in warm water for several hours.

Corylus avellana

Cotoneaster ·

Hardy evergreen and deciduous shrubs, bearing scarlet or black berries in autumn and winter, when berries of all kinds add a brilliance of colour and form to any group of flowers. Pick with care always, so as not to deform the tree. Possibly one of the best known varieties is C. *frigida*, though C. 'St Monica' and C. *watereri* are considered better, almost evergreen and the berries a better red. C. *wardii* is excellent, with orange-red berries and slender arching sprays with silver-backed leaves. Coming mostly from Central China they stand most conditions very well. I always feel tempted to pick the sprays of white blossom in spring, but try to wait for the berries as they are of much greater value.

Conditioning Sprays when flowering are better after being dipped in boiling water for one or two minutes and then given a long drink in cold water. For berries, hammer the woody stems well, before giving a long drink.

Preserving The berries can be placed in a solution of glycerine, though I have never been very successful with this method. Lately I have tried spraying the branches with hair-lacquer and found this more satisfactory (they kept their colour and it seemed to prevent them from shrinking too badly) but I still hope for the perfect answer.

Crambe cordifolia

This plant was given to me many years ago without a name but with a good reputation! I planted it in the wrong place, not realizing it would grow so big, moved it and lost it. It has large deeply-lobed leaves and in July it bears a spectacular mass of tiny white gypsophila-like flowers. The leaves do not last well in water but small pieces of the flower heads look well in a late summer green and white arrangement.

Crataegus monogyna
Hawthorn

Hardy tree with a wealth of pink or white blossom in May (it is often known just as 'May'),

making the lanes look and smell delightful. It holds for many people a superstition that it might have been from this tree that they made Our Lord's crown of thorns. From this comes the notion that it is unlucky to bring it into the house. However, having used it often in its berrying stage, I have become used to the idea of bringing it in, and love to pick its arching sprays when in flower. I remove all the leaves and use it in an oriental type of arrangement in a Chinese vase or ginger jar. A variety worthy of a mention, which I have used in Long Island, is C. *maracantha* having excellent autumn colour and large, rounded red berries. They also have vicious long thorns but these are easily removed before arranging.

Conditioning Hammer ends of stems and put in warm water.

Preserving The sprays of berries remain quite a good colour for keeping to use in the winter, and if you can paint them over with a coat of clear varnish this preserves them extremely well.

Crinum longifolium
Cape Lily

Hardy deciduous bulb. C. *longifolium* flowers well in late summer. It has trumpets of pink or white (C. *l. album*) massed at the top of thick succulent stems, and looks lovely when used with branches of lime flowers from which all the leaves have been removed. Excellent for large groups for weddings or other special occasions. C. *powellii* and its white variety is a lovely hybrid, but rather less hardy.

Crocosmia crocosmiiflora
Montbretia

Still often listed as *Tritonia crocosmiiflora*, this is a hardy perennial with sword-like leaves and orange flowers that have a delicate habit of growing on arching sprays. Flowering late into the autumn, it is extremely useful and makes a good foil for the more solid flowers of dahlias. The leaves also are useful, and press well as they change colour and are nice to use in the winter. Varieties with larger flowers and very hand-

Crinum powellii

some, too, are *C. aurea* and *Carmin brillant* best described as having rich tomato-red buds. They last extremely well in water.

Preserving Cut the leaves as they turn and press them between sheets of blotting paper to keep their colour.

Crocus

Hardy bulb. One of the greatest delights in early spring is to see a carpet of crocus growing in the grass under the trees. They cut better than is generally expected and can be used in clumps to give a splash of colour in an indoor moss garden. The species varieties, blooming so early and a joy to behold, are for me the best of all.

Crown Imperial *see* FRITILLARIA

Cryptomeria japonica
Japanese Cedar

Hardy evergreen. An ornamental conifer with bright green foliage in early spring, turning to shades of bronze and crimson in winter. I use it at all times of the year, but mostly in autumn, as it is such a good foil for all the varying shades of chrysanthemums.

Conditioning Hammer the ends of the stems and place in warm water.

Cuckoo Pint *see* ARUM

Cucurbita
Gourd

Half-hardy annuals. Decorative small marrows for which seed is now easily obtainable from any reliable merchant. The gourds have all kinds of variations and combinations of colour, such as green and orange or yellow, or striped green and white. Some have smooth skins and others are very lumpy. When picked, they are very ornamental placed in a bowl or dish with a few fresh or preserved leaves, or mounted on wires and used to hang among fresh or dried material in a vase.

Preserving Never pick your gourds until they are really ripe. They are best left until the first frost. Then give a coat of clear varnish; this excludes the air and prevents them from going soft and mouldy. In this way they keep for months.

Currant *see* RIBES

Cut flowers *see* CONDITIONING AND MAINTAINING

Cut-leaved Elder *see* SAMBUCUS

Cycas
Sago Palm

Stove plant. Handsome dark-green leaves with well-shaped, feathery fronds, which I rarely have the opportunity of using while they are fresh. However, they are preserved commercially and used then by many florists in wreath work. I sometimes use them at Christmas-time either glittered, or painted white or gold and then glittered. If mounted on long canes as false stems to give extra height, they are most useful in big group-arrangements for special occasions.

Cyclamen
Sowbread

Hardy and greenhouse plants. The greenhouse cyclamen, *C. persicum*, sold in pots in autumn and winter are decorative just as they are, or when taken out of their pots and used in a planted garden with a collection of other plants; they last surprisingly well like this. Less well known, but still more attractive are the alpine varieties for

Cyclamen persicum album

the rock garden or wall. These delicate little flowers look charming in a china hand or similar small vase. It is often possible to buy them in bunches from a florist's in both spring and autumn. *C. coum* flowers in the spring; it has the most lovely cerise colouring and is delightful arranged in a bed of moss with a collection of little bulbs and spring bits and pieces.

Care of plants The potted plants are killed more often by over-watering than by anything else. Even neglect is far better for their chance of survival. Water only when really necessary; it is often preferable to wait until the leaves start to wilt. One old lady I know, who has a superb plant, uses cold tea every few days and it certainly looks wonderful on this diet!

Cydonia oblonga
Quince

Hardy deciduous tree. Quinces are used more often for jelly than for flower arrangement, but a few sprays of the fruit in a vase of mixed flowers or in a combination of fruit and flowers look delicious. I only wish they were less hard to come by. I once did a vase of clusters of quince and green grapes with a collection of mixed yellow flowers and hope to try this out again one day.

Cymbidium
Orchid

Orchids have a strong fascination for many people, and are now more widely grown than ever before; even the small-greenhouse owner is launching forth. One of their greatest merits to me is that they outlive almost any other flower in a vase. Cymbidiums are one of the most beautiful of all. After being able to use them in Sydney almost whenever I liked, I felt I would never enjoy doing another fruit and flower group without putting in a spray of this orchid, which has beautiful arching sprays blooming right down the stems and a delightful colour range: soft pinks to rose red and green to cream. The bought flowers are an excellent investment in early spring; expensive as they are, they will outlive a bunch of daffodils four times over. Arrange them with a bare branch of exquisite shape, preferably in a vase of oriental design.

Conditioning Cut the ends of the stems on the slant and stand in deep water. Every few days remove from the vase and cut a small piece off the stem. This ensures that the plant can drink properly.

Cynara cardunculus *see* CARDOON

Cynara scolymus *see* ARTICHOKE

Cynoglossum amabile

Hardy perennial. Easily grown from seed, this plant makes a lovely patch of blue in any flower border. It is better to treat it as a biennial and raise fresh stock each year. A small piece of the brilliant blue is an asset to any vase of mixed flowers. It resembles a large forget-me-not, and deserves to be better known.

Conditioning Cut the stems and place in warm water until this cools; then arrange.

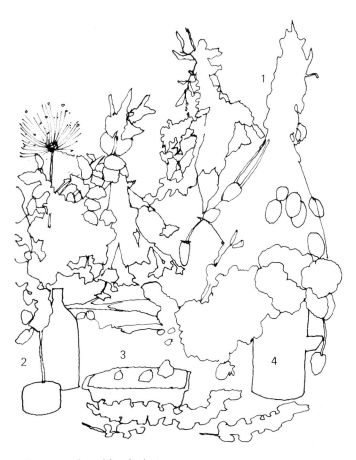

Leaves and seed heads drying.
1 Air drying by hanging bunches upside-down.
2 Preserving in glycerine and water.
3 Drying in hot sand or silica gel.
4 Drying by placing the stems in water.

Cypripedium
Lady's Slipper Orchid

Greenhouse. A type of orchid that may be a little less expensive than most others. They are generally greeny-brown and yellowish in colour, though they come in a range of unusual colours in the hybrid varieties. Some time ago their prime use was to be worn as a spray or 'corsage', but they are good in vases for home decoration. They last extremely well as a cut flower. I have used them with mimosa with all the foliage removed, and placed the whole group on a convex mirror to add a reflection.

Conditioning Cut the stems on the slant and cut off a small length every few days.

Cytisus
Broom

Hardy deciduous and evergreen shrubs. Well known for their sprays of cascading bloom in spring, in all shades of yellows and reds to browns. *Cytisus praecox* is one of my favourites and one of the best varieties for flower arrangement. None last really well in water, alas, once in bloom, but the sprays add a beautiful curve to any vase or bowl. The foliage, however, is in constant demand among those who like the rather stylized effect it can produce.

Conditioning Flowering broom lasts better if given a few minutes with the ends of the stems in boiling water, and then a long drink.

Preserving Once you have coaxed the branches into the shape you want, they will stay like that for a long time. How to do it: you can shape the sprays by tying them into position, or sometimes it is easier to put the branch into a nylon stocking when you can twist and contort it to any shape you like. Then submerge it under water for at least twenty-four hours. Dry it off well and you have a shaped green branch that you can use all winter.

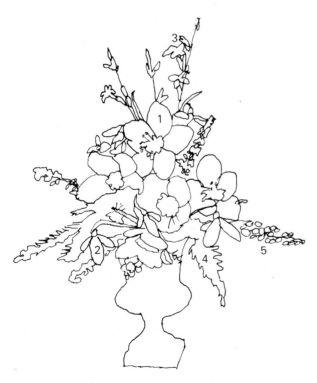

An attractive late January arrangement.
1 *Helleborus niger* (Christmas rose)
2 *Galanthus nivalis* (Snowdrop)
3 *Jasminum nudiflorum* (Winter jasmine)
4 *Ericas*
5 *Mahonia bealei*

Daffodil *see* NARCISSUS

Dahlia

Half-hardy tuberous-rooted perennial in many varieties: cactus, quilled, large, fancy, pompon, peony-flowered, semi-double, decorative, and so on. One of the most useful flowers of all for arrangement, having such a good 'face' for giving a central point of interest in any vase, and such a clear rounded outline for showing up from a distance; also a wide and helpful range of colour. It is hard to choose which to grow but I would like to recommend a few that I would hate to be without. First, a selection of apricot colours as I find they give the central point to any autumnal vase with pieces of turning autumn foliage: 'Waverley Pearl', apricot waterlily; 'Katisha', deep apricot; pompon 'Graham McKenzie', lovely creamy apricot. For a red that mixes with pinks and looks stunning in a mixed red arrangement, 'Cherry Wine'; for soft pink, 'Delicious' and good lilac, 'Chorus Girl'. 'Jescot Jim' is a good clear yellow, and I love white – 'Polar Beauty' and 'Baseball' give two sizes. As I grow mine for cutting I try to have a wide variety in different shades. For the last few years I have covered the tubers with straw and polythene and so far I have not lost any. This does save much work in lifting and storing. I do recommend that you take a few minutes and go and see the plants in flower if you can. We are so lucky in Hertfordshire having the Aylott nurseries near as we can see and buy the best in England.

Conditioning I think a little boiling water for a few minutes for the ends of the stems, and then a long drink, is as good a method as any. A teaspoonful of sugar and an aspirin added to their water and they really should last very well.

Preserving I have seen some extraordinarily well preserved dahlias; these were dried in a shallow box by the hot sand method.

Danae racemosa

Hardy evergreen berry-bearing shrub. Has good arching stems of bright shiny green elliptical leaves which last for a long time in water and are very rewarding. I find it is rather tender.

Conditioning Hammer the stems and give a long drink. Nothing more is necessary.

Preserving Place the stems in a solution of glycerine and water and allow a long wait. Then you are rewarded by lovely wands of cream sprays lasting for weeks.

Daphne

Greenhouse and hardy deciduous and evergreen shrubs. Daphnes of all kinds are very useful for vases and bowls and the many sweet-scented ones will fill a warm room with their fragrance

Daphne

in early spring. *D. mezereum*, the most common, with purple or white flowers followed by shiny red berries, often flowers in January if grown in a sheltered spot. Spurge laurel, *Daphne laureola*, the evergreen variety growing wild in woodlands, lasts for weeks in water, which adds greatly to its popularity. For its heavenly perfume *D. odora variegata* (or *D. odora aureomarginata*) is one of my favourites – fresh and lovely with tufts of verbena-scented pinkish-white flowers and evergreen foliage – but it does need some protection. *D. pontica* is a hardy evergreen shrub that will succeed even in heavy soil or under overhanging trees, and produces its fragrant yellowish-green flowers amid bright green foliage in April.

Conditioning Hammer stems well or place the ends in boiling water for a few minutes, and allow a few hours in cold water.

Datura
Trumpet Flower

Half-hardy and greenhouse annuals. Many species I do not know at all, but the thorn apple or *Datura stramonium* is extremely useful. It has rather insignificant flowers, but lovely thorny-looking seed heads on angular branches, that dry well and are very pretty indeed, sprayed and glittered for Christmas decoration. A much-debated plant because it is poisonous to cattle; as with all such plants, great discretion should be used as to where and how it is grown. *Datura cornigera*, the greenhouse species in Britain (growing in magnificent trees in the tropics) has superb trumpet flowers; the long heads on slender stems make them difficult to arrange and they are best cut short, almost to their necks, and massed together in a shallow bowl. In this way they will last quite well. They are rare in any case and not generally used.

Preserving Pick *Datura stramonium* when the seed heads form and start turning from green to creamy brown; remove all the leaves and hang the branches upside down.

Day Lily *see* HEMEROCALLIS

Dead Nettle *see* LAMIUM

Delphinium
Larkspur

Hardy annual. The name larkspur is usually restricted to the annual delphiniums. A most useful annual with tall spikes of mauve, pink and white flowers, which give good outline to a group of summer flowers – lilies or roses and so on.

Conditioning Remove all the green foliage that goes below the water-line, as it will very quickly turn the water green; then hammer the stems and put them in warm water.

Preserving The flowers dry well if left standing undisturbed in shallow water.

Delphinium

Hardy herbaceous perennials. Showy plants for the border and one of the most popular and best of the blue plants. Their tall spikes are most suitable for large vases of any kind. Beautiful for church decoration, but especially if you add some of the white species as blue is a difficult colour for artificial light – so often looking black and not blue at all. The white varieties and the pink have begun to appeal to me more and more. The American Pacific hybrids are well worth growing from seed. You get a chance to use some of the most lovely offbeat colours. 'Butterballs' is one everyone should try and get, with clusters like clotted cream. The Belladonna hybrids I can thoroughly recommend as they bloom continuously. They are a much smaller plant and do not require the same amount of staking as the taller varieties. They have a good range of blues, and a white form. So much easier to arrange than the giant stems of the larger plants.

Conditioning If you are using the spikes for a special occasion, I think it is well worth while to fill the hollow stems with water and plug the ends with cotton wool. For general use, give a good long drink in deep water before you begin arranging.

Deutzia gracilis

Preserving The seed heads can be used for winter decoration if the stems are cut when the heads are well formed, and hung upside down to dry. To preserve the spikes for colour, hang each stem upside down when in really full bloom and dry off in a warm room. The individual florets can be dried by the hot sand method for pot-pourri, or in miniature dried groups.

Deutzia gracilis
Japanese Snow Flower

Hardy deciduous shrub. A lovely shrub with delicate pink or white clusters of flowers on dark stems, and flowering before the foliage – which adds to its charm. Much appreciated for cutting as it comes a little later than the spring azaleas and lilacs, and so is very useful indeed. It makes a good background for any mixed flower vase.

Conditioning Hammer ends of stems well and soak well in cold water.

Dianella

A new treasure I have just been given, a small iris-like plant which after flowering has the most wonderful bright blue berries. I can't wait for a chance to arrange it.

Dianthus caryophyllus
Carnation

There are two distinct kinds of carnation. The border carnations grown out of doors and flowering in the garden in June and July, are smaller than the carnations that are grown so widely under glass. I love the sweet-smelling small carnations that one can grow easily from seed and propagate by layering. They have a wide range of colours – reds to deep purple, soft pinks and white. They grow on fairly long stems about 30–45cm (12–18in), and for the best blooms really require staking and the flower buds reduced to one per stem. Still, I am quite happy to have them on their clustered stems and never mind if the stems have a curve or twist due to being allowed to grow freely without staking; it is often so much easier to arrange flowers that have curving rather than upright stems. These flowers scent the summer night air, and are lovely cut short and used with lavender for a guest's bedroom, or on a small table in the living-room. The larger and not so hardy carnation grown under glass is, I suppose, sold more frequently than almost any other flower, and is used a great deal in flower arrangement both in mixed groups and arranged alone. It is the one flower that really does last better if it is put into a vase and arranged alone, with no other flowers or unrelated foliage. I find them rather dull like this and much prefer, if I can, to mix them with other flowers in a combination of colours to suit the tones and hues of the vase concerned. They look particularly good with grey foliage, artemisia or eucalyptus.

Preserving Use the hot sand treatment to keep their colour. For details of this treatment see page 99.

Dianthus
Pink, Sweet William

Of the many hardy varieties of dianthus the best are the garden pinks – sweet-smelling, delicate and attractive arranged in bowls either alone or with little pieces of grey foliage, or mixed with summer flowers. Grow from seed or cuttings. A delightful variety of single annual pink, ranging in colour from pure white to crimson, is the 'Brilliant Fringed Mixed'.

Sweet williams always seem oddly named *Dianthus barbatus*, but here is where they should come. They are not only good for cutting, as they last so well in water, but they are most effective in the border, making a splash of colour for several weeks. I love to see a bowl of sweet william just on their own, or they can be arranged in a basket. They mix well with many summer flowers, and their wide range of reds makes them extremely useful to put into a vase of 'clashing reds'. The smaller and dwarf varieties are effective in the front of the border. I

have taken a new liking for these flowers, partly because this year I had a few gaps in the border and just before I opened the garden to the public, I wanted a bit of instant colour. Up at the Royal Show a little while before I had bought some potgrown *Dianthus* 'Magic Charm' and they really lived up to their name and flowered for weeks. At the seed trial grounds at Histon I was very taken with two comparatively new varieties: 'Orchid Lace' with a frilly edge, and 'Snow Fire' compact single flowers, white with a red centre. Personally I like the self-coloured best but these others are worth a mention.

Conditioning Cut the ends of the stems and give a long drink.

Dicentra spectabilis
Bleeding Heart

Hardy perennial. This very old-fashioned little flower has acquired a new popularity, thanks to the 'flower movement' of modern times. I have

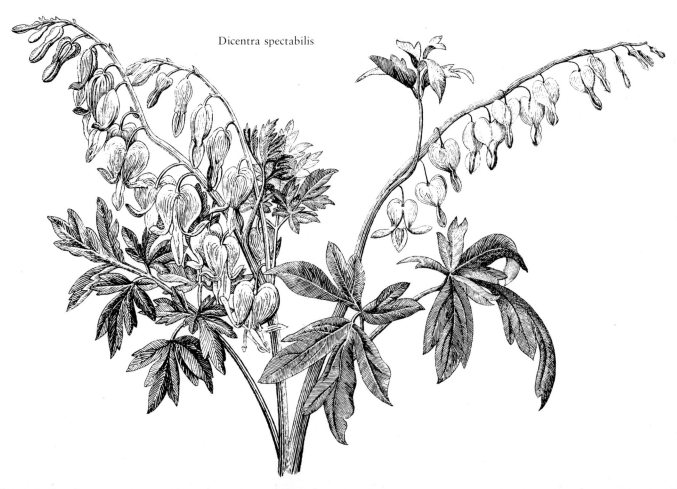

Dicentra spectabilis

Diervilla florida variegata

become extremely fond of it. There is a choice of old-fashioned names for it: Dutchman's Breeches, Lady in the Bath and many more. It has arching sprays of small flowers, rather like little lockets, hanging from delicate stems, and its strong pink with a touch of white makes it a good mixer though I really prefer to arrange it by itself, so as not to detract from the lovely form which I feel is its greatest charm. A plant that forces well and is sometimes to be found as a pot plant.

Dictamnus albus purpureus
Burning Bush

Another old-fashioned plant that has come back into favour. I use it whenever I can. Flower-spikes in pink and white – rather like a lupin at first glance. When the flower fades, it leaves a nice-looking green seed head.

Conditioning Place stems in warm water.

Preserving Hang the seed heads upside down.

Dieffenbachia picta
Dumb Cane

Greenhouse plant, with lovely green and white spotted leaves. They are most decorative, and for some very special occasion it is worth while to buy a whole pot and use the leaves individually as you need them. They are such good lasters in water, that this is not as extravagant as it may sound. A few of these handsome leaves placed low in a vase just make a big group stand out. I find that when possible I like to put the whole pot in a bowl of mixed greens in winter. In this way the plant lasts much better and makes a marvellous focal point.

Conditioning Having cut the stem from the plant, place the ends in boiling water for a few seconds, then allow a long drink.

Diervilla florida
Weigela

Weigela is the name I have always used for this shrub. I consider it a great asset to the shrub border, as it flowers in May to July. If you remove the leaves before arranging it, you will have delightful sprays of pink or reddish flowers that look very attractive as a background in a mixed summer vase. The variegated variety (*D. florida variegata*) with green and white foliage on dark stems is worth growing.

Conditioning Strip off 5cm (2in) of bark from the bottom of the stem, before placing in water.

Digitalis
Foxglove

Hardy biennial. Suttons have the seeds of the lovely hybrids 'Excelsior' which have very nice spotted bells hanging all round the stems. (Suttons also listed a primrose-coloured one but sadly it is no longer available.) You can still buy the seed of 'Apricot' and I would hate to be without it, but it rarely comes true from self-sown seeds so you must re-sow. They are in such delicate colours and arrange so well in a vase of mixed pastel flowers that I feel every garden should have some; liking shade, they fit into any odd corner. Quite one of the best flowers for cutting as they don't drop their petals as so many summer flowers do. There are of course some perennial varieties that are well worth growing. *Digitalis mertonensis* is crushed-strawberry pink; *D. grandiflora* (*D. lutea*) and *D. ambigua* are yellow.

Conditioning Place the ends of the stems in warm water and allow them time to have a long drink.

Preserving Gather the seed heads when formed, remove leaves and hang upside down to dry.

Dimorphotheca
Star of the Veldt

Hardy annual. This enchanting little daisy-like flower comes from South Africa where it grows wild in drifts on the mountain sides. It stands about 30cm (1ft) in height and comes in shades of orange, apricot, buff and salmon. Grown in Britain as an annual, it is charming for a patch of colour in the front of a border. Unfortunately, as it closes its petals at night, it can be a bit disappointing as a cut flower and there is little I can suggest to prevent this. I use them either alone or mixed with other small summer flowers.

Dipsacus fullonum
Teasel

How I have come to enjoy the common teasel, growing as a wild or native plant on both sides of the Atlantic. I have picked it in Virginia, Indiana, California and in Sussex and my native Hertfordshire. One wonders where it came from originally. The seed heads are what I find the most useful in their green stage or turning brown. Cutting the head in half, though I am often loath to do it, gives a very effective star-shaped flower with a shiny, creamy centre and a frill of spikes round the outside. These can be used for many dried arrangements and produce a flower with a face that modern flower arrangers desire.

Conditioning No special treatment, though in its early stages before the flower head is mature it is important to put the stems into a little boiling water and then allow a long drink.

Preserving Pick the teasels as they turn colour from green to brown, remove the foliage and hang them upside down to dry. The stems can be placed in a solution of glycerine and water but this is not essential. It does, however, give them a silky look and feel, and of course, they last indefinitely.

Dog's Tooth Violet see ERYTHRONIUM

Dogwood see CORNUS

Dondia epipactis see HACQUETIA EPIPACTIS

Doronicum
Leopard's Bane

Hardy herbaceous perennials. This yellow daisy flower is, I think, well worth growing – not because it is at all spectacular, but because it comes so wonderfully early that it is more than welcome, giving a bright spot of colour which is so cheerful on a cold day. It will grow in shade, which makes it more welcome still. It mixes well with forsythia and daffodils.

Conditioning Place in warm water.

Dracaena

A hothouse plant with superb foliage. D. fragrans victoriae is my favourite, having broad cream leaves with a prominent green stripe down the middle. The purple-leaved varieties are most useful too, to make a good contrast in a foliage group or to give a hard outline to a more confused group of flowers.

Preserving If you put the leaves in glycerine and water they turn a lovely colour, but it requires great patience as they can take anything from two to three months to absorb the mixture.

Dracunculus vulgaris
Dragon Arum

Hardy tuberous-rooted arum type of exotic plant in mauvish-black with mottled leaves. It would be quite superb for flower arrangement, but gives off a vile smell – in spite of which I have used it! I have now learned that the smell is to attract the bluebottles for pollination, and once pollinated the smell disappears. I was lucky enough to be able to use two for my RHS lecture and with aubergine, black grapes and grey leaves the arrangement really was rather spectacular. But they only last a few days.

Dragon's Head see PHYSOSTEGIA

Drying and preserving

In the past drying and preserving was done so that one had material for the winter months when flowers were scarce and expensive, but now dried or preserved flowers and leaves are used in many months of the year. Since the oil crisis the cost of general maintenance and

Dracaena fragrans victoriae

heating of glasshouses has increased so much that the price of flowers has risen enormously. Now we need to use preserved leaves not only in winter but in almost any month of the year. And after using dried arrangements in the winter I start putting fresh flowers and leaves into them, usually at the end of January. Hellebore, a favourite of mine, brings a promise of spring and makes the arrangement look quite different.

Searching for dried materials is a most interesting and educative process – even the common grasses have a use. Drying should be done all through the year because if you dry at different stages of development, you get a change of colouring. If you pick a few stems of wheat or barley when green, then when turning yellow, and when fully ripe and deep gold, drying at these various times gives much more interesting colour values. So with putting beech leaves into glycerine at different times; the leaves will vary in size – small ones in the early sprays and larger ones as they develop – and will also vary in colour. For pressing the same applies. Bracken can be pressed when green, then a few fronds as they turn pale cream, and some later still when a deep rich brown. It is quite possible in the autumn to gather seed heads and some foliages that have dried off naturally by themselves. The only difficulty is to pick them at just the right stage as they 'weather' quickly and become very brittle. Seed heads that have been hung upside down – hence allowing the sap to run into the head – seem to handle much more easily and are not nearly so fragile. Also, I would strongly advise you to remove a vase of dried flowers as soon as you feel these have served their purpose, and store them carefully away, so that the best can be used again another year.

Having collected what you can, even if it may not appear very exciting, then look in the shops. It is often so worth while to buy a few of the interesting drieds that are imported: wood roses from Honolulu, banksia from Australia, lotus seed pods from the Orient will all add an exotic charm to your own dried materials.

Drying by hanging or air drying The drying of seed heads and some flower spikes is not as difficult as some people imagine. The most commonly used way and quite the easiest is to air dry them. What is essential, however, is to find a suitable place for doing this. Garden sheds or garages may be quite satisfactory in a hot, dry summer but in some years they may be too damp. It is vital that the material dries as quickly as possible and for this you need a really dry, airy room. Remove all the leaves from your stems as soon as you pick them. This is most important for two reasons. Firstly, it is necessary to assist dehydration as much as you can – and leaves kept on the stems retain the moisture in the stem, and so prolong the drying period. Secondly, the leaves quickly shrivel and die, and then have to be removed, and this is much easier to do when the stems are stiff and fresh; once they are dry they become brittle and are more likely to crack and break. Hang the seed heads in bunches, tying them with string, plastic-covered wire, elastic bands, or pipe cleaners. Make the bunches small to avoid overcrowding; in fact, I often prefer to tie each stem individually, as this can give you a more perfect specimen in the end. If they are bunched too closely together, one head can get caught in another, and as you pull these apart when they are dry, they often get damaged. Heads of yellow achillea damage very easily and if all the heads are tied together the stems press into the heads, leaving a hole in the finished specimen. Leeks which have run to seed develop marvellously attractive heads – they too, like achillea, should be dried separately so that their shape and structure is protected. I usually stand these plants in a flower vase, so that the heads remain perfect while they are drying. This takes up a lot of space, however, and the hanging method is the more useful.

If drying in a shed, place the nails so that there is a gap between each bundle, allowing plenty of air to circulate round them. Light material, such as grasses, takes about a week to dry and heavier material up to three weeks, depending greatly on the warmth of the air. The quicker the subjects dry, the better colour they keep. Watch them every now and again: stems, as they dehydrate, tend to shrivel and to slip out of their string. Either re-tie, or remove them if they are ready, and store in cardboard boxes, being careful to put the lids on and keep them away from the light. I dry all my seed heads by this method:

hollyhocks, verbascum, cardoons, and also some flower heads such as delphiniums, but these need to be tied individually or as soon as you pull them apart they will shed their petals. Helichrysums – or straw flowers as they are sometimes called – must be dried head hanging down so that the sap runs into the head. I find it best to insert a florist's wire right down the middle of the head, through the calyx, otherwise the flower head flops over. Remove all the leaves and hang the stems carefully so that each bloom has room to open as it dries. Having the wire already in the stem, you can add other wires to it later to lengthen the stem. Statice, and any other similar flower, is best treated in this way. I hang the smaller and more precious things, a few branches at a time, over the warmth of the boiler. When picking for drying, be sure to leave the flower heads on the plant until they are really fully open up to the tops of the stem in the case of acanthus, or larkspur and delphiniums; otherwise, the tips with the unopened buds will hang over.

Drying in water This is the best way to dry the heads of hydrangeas and other difficult flower heads, oddly enough. Cut hydrangeas when the flowers are well out – when they have been in bloom for several weeks and the heads are changing colour from pink to red and blue to green. Remove all the leaves and stand the stems in a vase with a small amount of water. Keep them over the boiler or in the linen cupboard, in as much warmth as possible. The quicker they dry, the better colour they keep. Molucella or Bells of Ireland, with delightful stems of bell-shaped flowers, dry either green or a lovely shade of creamy-parchment. Stand the stems on a pin-holder in shallow water, so that they take on charming natural curves; and then place them in a jam jar, still with a small amount of water, until they dry off completely. The seed heads of hostas I also dry in this way, picking the heads when they are green and watching them open out until all the seeds are showing.

Glycerine This is perhaps the most progressive way of doing it and where we have really had a lot of fun. Preservation by this method is long-lasting, the stems keeping their natural shape and form, and deepening in colour as they absorb the glycerine. Particularly good for leaves and branches. Mix the solution with one part glycerine and two parts hot water and place this in a narrow vase or jar so that when the subject is put into it the solution goes as far up the stem as possible. Hammer woody stems well, 5–7cm (2–3in) up the stem, and allow them a deep drink of water for several hours, especially if they have been picked for some time and may have flagged. Then put them into the glycerine and leave for about ten days, or until the stems have changed colour. Green leaves gradually turn brown as the solution creeps up the stems. Coat the leaves with a little of the mixture dipped in cotton wool; this prevents them from curling, and can be repeated as often as needed. Cut off poor branches and those with imperfect leaves so as to save the glycerine. (This is one reason why I like to preserve my beech leaves early before the leaves get damaged by insects.) Take out the branches before the mixture drips off the ends of the leaves, and store in a box.

Leaves of the berberis *Mahonia bealei* or of the variety 'Charity' are wonderful subjects for this method of preservation. Take each leaf and stand it in the glycerine solution – it can take up to three weeks to show results but these leaves go a wonderful goldy-brown colour and once they have reached this stage, they never change, so you have a leaf to use for months and months. Beech leaves are generally the most popular and turn a splendid copper colour. Sprays of lime flowers picked just before they are fully open, and with all the leaves removed, provide lovely sprays of delicate flowers that make a nice light background for other dried flowers. Sprays of hips and cotoneaster berries also take up glycerine very well. So does old man's beard – the sprays acquire a pink glow, and although after some weeks in a hot room the flower heads do go more fluffy, they stay on the stems very well and do not shed. The leaves turn a delightful bronze and although they curl after a time, they can be cut off later. Try experimenting with ivy berries; these need to be completely submerged for a while and though rather limp they help to give another form to a dried arrangement. Contrast and colour and shape are, after all, what one is looking for.

Laurel (*Prunus lauracerasus*) and *Magnolia grandiflora* are of course both evergreen and so it may seem a waste of time to preserve them. If you do so, however, you will have an upright stem of bronzy, leathery leaves with a wonderful texture – such a help to use either as individual leaves or in a spray, to mix with the lighter and more delicate seed heads. The bold leaves of *Bergenia cordifolia* and *B. crassifolia*, and the keys of hornbeam, also add interest and different form to a dried group. Separate leaves of ivy and whitebeam can be preserved by submerging them in the solution. For flowers in glycerine, three that come to mind are *Astrantia major* and Bells of Ireland and *Erigeron giganteum*. Seed heads of *Sisyrinchium strictum* take up glycerine very well and go a marvellous black. You may wonder whether it is worth the effort but one big advantage is that they do not shed and have a slightly shiny effect which is very pleasing. This goes too for clematis seed heads, and is a real advantage as they do shed easily.

Flowers and seed heads are useful but most important are the leaves. Though they change colour from green to shades of brown the leaves retain their natural curves and three-dimensional effect. Try for yourself using *Choisya ternata*, *Cotoneaster salicifolia*, *Elaeagnus macrophylla*, *Danea racemosa*, the common boxwood *Buxus sempervirens*, all excellent subjects.

Skeletonizing This is a difficult process requiring endless patience, but most rewarding. Large leaves of *Magnolia grandiflora* and some of the hybrid rhododendrons can be skeletonized by soaking the leaves in a strong solution of soda and water and allowing them to decay. This happens more rapidly if they are kept in a place where the heat is constant; on the side of a solid-fuel boiler is ideal. When the green matter has decayed, remove it very carefully, so that you are left with the skeleton. Take care not to break the mid-rib – this is the most difficult part of the operation. You may find skeletonized rotting leaves on the ground under the trees of the hybrid rhododendrons, and magnolias and hollies; these are small, but delightful painted with gum and glittered for Christmas. It is possible to buy skeletonized leaves, processed in eastern

Europe, and we have used them in bridesmaids' bouquets and mounted on bare branches of beech or oak. With each leaf fixed to the branch with a piece of silver wire, they make ethereal sprays that are a marvellous background for a winter group.

Pressing This is for flat sprays of beech branches, ferns of all kinds, bracken, and all sorts of autumn-tinted single leaves. Sprays of leaves can only be pressed if their natural habit of growth is flat. It is best to lay out the material on a thick layer of newspaper, cover with another layer and put them under heavy books or some weight – though I find under the carpet best of all. It is important that leaves do not overlap, and take care to see that they are not curled or folded as once they are dry they cannot be straightened, and this may spoil the shape of frond or leaf. The advantage of pressing sprays of beech is that they retain their lovely colours, whereas when they are preserved in glycerine they become much darker and, generally, a copper colour. Bracken presses extremely well and by using it in all its shades you can have a wide range of colours, from green to cream and brown. The green hedgerow ferns also press well, and the royal fern *Osmunda regalis* gives tall delicate fronds of autumn colours which are most useful for tall vases. It is sometimes necessary to put a florist's wire up the back of a leaf, once it is pressed, to give it support. A thick wire caught in several places will keep it upright and firm. Smaller leaves need to have a false stem added: put a wire up the back and attach it with adhesive tape, then use an additional wire to provide a stem. Stems of anything that is pressed always break off so easily. Single leaves of sweet chestnut or acer give a lovely bit of colour when placed at the base of a dried group. I was given the tip of submerging bracken and ferns in weak starch water for several hours before pressing, which makes the sprays remain much firmer – a great help if the ferns are to be treated or perhaps painted for using at Christmas-time. Crocosmia leaves press well and keep a good autumn colour. It is always helpful to have spiky leaves to give different form. All pressed material takes on a very flat look, but it mixes well with spiky and rounded seed and flower heads.

Preserving in silica gel and hot sand Silica gel uses the same principle as the hot sand methods and though delicate blooms and leaves are achieved which look lovely and retain their colour and natural charm, it is hard for flower arrangers in Britain to make them last. In the controlled temperatures of apartments and houses in the United States it is quite a different matter. The atmosphere is dry and warm, ideal conditions for these dried flowers. I have seen lovely sprays of dogwood that were so realistic that I could not believe that they were not real, or should I say, fresh. But it would be almost impossible to do this in Britain. Using them under glass, as I do every now and then, I find that they keep their colour and add greatly to a picture made of flowers and shells, which is how I enjoy them most.

Preserving in sand is an American method that I know little about from experience, but I have seen some remarkable results. In this way, it is possible to dry to keep the true colour of the flowers very well indeed. For the best results you need to select straight-petalled and light-coloured blooms, but I have seen good results with roses, sprays of ivy, sunflowers, dahlias, marigolds, zinnias and bells of Ireland – mostly in not too dark colours. Get a box for the sand – one that will allow you to cover the whole flower completely. Shake in a layer of dry, fine, warm sand and place in the flower head. Stems of roses should be removed and replaced by a wire, and the rose then laid in so that the sand can be sifted over it. Placing the rose-flower head up, take a handful of sand and carefully let it sift round the outer petals, circling the sand stream round each layer of petals until the whole head is completely covered. Leave the flower for about four days and then scrape away a little of the sand and test the petals to see if they are crisp and dry; they can then be removed and stored in boxes in a warm place for the winter. Zinnias are better dried face downwards, and the sand sifted over in the same way as for roses; the stems stick straight up and will dry off quite well in the air; if they seem brittle when removed, an additional wire stem must be made. For the drying of larkspur and delphiniums slightly longer boxes are needed so that the whole stem can be laid on the bed of sand, and, again, sift it over so that you submerge the entire spike. It is always better to take the smaller stems and side shoots of delphiniums, as these dry very much more quickly; naturally anything that is very fleshy takes a considerable time to dehydrate. Small flowers such as pansies and love-in-a-mist all dry well, and are most attractive if used to line a glass bowl to hold pot-pourri.

Finally I feel I must draw attention to the way I most enjoy having my own dried flowers and this is with a mixture of fresh and dried, as seen in the picture on page 215. This is a semi-permanent arrangement. The fresh material is changed every now and then, but the background of dried remains the same, a great time-saver for the busy housewife.

Dusty Miller *see* AURICULA

Eccremocarpus scaber
Chilean Glory Flower

Half-hardy. Except in mild climates, this is usually grown as climber rather than a herbaceous plant as it tends to need the shelter of a wall. It flowers in midsummer – small bells of orange and yellow – and its vivid colouring mixes well with all the 'autumnal' shades.

Conditioning Place the ends of the stems in boiling water for two seconds before giving a long drink.

Echinops ritro
Globe Thistle

A hardy perennial, thistle-like, as the name implies, this has nice rounded blue heads for giving a central point to a vase. They stand well in water and look as if they should dry well, but I find this is more difficult than one expects, as they so often shed their spikes or petals.

Conditioning Hammer their woody stems and allow a good drink.

Preserving Strip off all foliage and hang upside down to dry.

Echium
Viper's Bugloss

Hardy annuals, biennials and perennials. The large thick spikes of mauvey-blue flowers are one of the few good blue flowers (and it is strange that there are so few) that stand well in water. I have found *E. vulgare* growing wild in Norfolk, and it has been well worth a detour to go and look for some. They seem quite easily grown, though I am always surprised that they are not grown more often, when, because of their colour, they combine with other flowers so attractively. Not only are they pretty in the flower stage but superb in the first green seed head stage. After picking it wild in Norfolk I was amazed to find the same echium growing in southern California.

Conditioning Place ends of stems in boiling water for a minute, before giving a long drink.

Edelweiss *see* LEONTOPODIUM

Elaeagnus

Hardy evergreen shrubs that I have come to love more and more. All the varieties are a positive delight especially in the winter. The one I use most of all is *E. pungens aureo-variegata* (*E. maculata*), which has green and brilliant-gold foliage; and one can cut it the whole winter through. I like to use it with any mixture of winter flowers or foliage. In the garden it looks just like a ray of sunshine. It will do well in full sun or partial shade and can be grown from a cutting or grafted. If you have a mild climate you can grow *E. angustifolia* (Oleaster). It is a delightful shrub looking as if it is covered with a layer of white cotton wool.

Conditioning Hammer the stems well, before putting in water.

Preserving Place stems in a solution of glycerine and leave for several weeks.

Elder *see* SAMBUCUS

Embothrium coccineum

One of the most breathtaking shrubs I have ever seen, but as it is very tender it is rarely seen growing in Britain – and so I have scarcely ever had the fun of using it at home as a cut subject, to add brilliance to a group of mixed reds, as I did in Australia. Some of the best I have seen are growing at Bodnant in North Wales. It needs acid soil.

Conditioning The stems must be placed in boiling water, before being given a long drink.

Enkianthus campanulatus

Beautiful shrub with tiny bell-shaped flowers hanging in pinky-orange clusters from the branches. They are at their best in May and in autumn. Liking peaty soil, they cannot be grown everywhere; but if conditions suit them then I can thoroughly recommend them. They are at

Enkianthus campanulatus

Epilobium angustifolium album

their best arranged with apricot and flame colours, and particularly with azaleas and tulips.

Conditioning Hammer ends of stems well.

Epilobium angustifolium
Rosebay Willow Herb, Fire Weed

A hardy perennial weed that gets the name of Fire Weed because it springs up everywhere after fire. This is very noticeable in the country and it was quite remarkable in London after the Blitz in the city; seeds seemed to appear from nowhere and the following year bomb sites were a blaze of red. Its red is a vivid carmine, and is breathtaking growing in sheets of colour in midsummer. It has tall spikes of flower and lovely pink seed heads, but these want careful watching as they suddenly burst open in a warm room and shed their fluff over everything. However, although it is a vicious weed in the garden, it is very effective picked and arranged in a mass – for either a party or some special occasion, as try as one may it is difficult to make it last with certainty even with all the known treatments. The seed heads are light and pretty mixed with more solid dried flowers all through the winter.

Conditioning Pick and put it into water at the earliest minute, as it quickly wilts and is very difficult to revive once it has gone down. Put the ends into boiling water, and then allow a long drink.

Preserving As soon as the flowers have fallen, pick the seed heads and dry by hanging the heads upside down.

Epimedium

Hardy herbaceous perennials. An attractive plant and shade-loving, which makes it the more rewarding. I like to use it in flower and for its foliage. The flowers are pink or cream according to the variety, the leaves almost heart-shaped, turning a lovely bronzy colour in autumn: it is advisable to use them only when they are mature. It is only fair to mention that the flowers do not stand very well in water; in fact, try as I may I find they last only a day or so.

Conditioning The stems of both flowers and leaves are improved if you place the ends in boiling water, before giving a long drink.

Eranthis
Winter Aconite

Hardy tuberous-rooted perennial. This delightful yellow flower has the shape of a buttercup with a frill of green round the petals. A real herald of spring that flowers before any of the other bulbs; useful in a 'spring garden' in a carpet of moss with a few snowdrops or early primroses. One of the best varieties with longer stems and more coppery-coloured foliage is *E. tubergenii*.

Eremurus
Foxtail Lily

Hardy herbaceous perennial. *Eremurus robustus* is an extremely handsome plant with very tall spikes of pink flowers, slightly resembling a lupin. I have never had any luck getting it to flower a second year, but I know many people who have had great success. There is a lovely orange species, *E. bungei*, which is very much

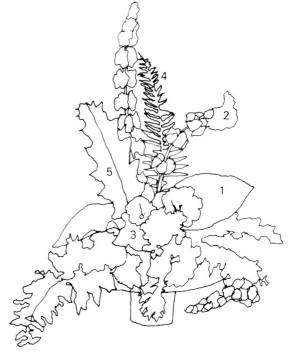

A mixed green arrangement with feathery ferns and bold leaves.
1 Variegated *hosta*
2 *Molucella laevis* (Bells of Ireland)
3 *Pelargonium*
4 *Polystichum setiferum* (Soft shield fern)
5 *Onopordum arabicum* (Grey thistle)

smaller in height and therefore more generally useful as the flowers can be used in much smaller vases. However, *E. robustus* has been a joy to us in really big groups in Westminster Abbey on many occasions.

Conditioning No special treatment required.

Erica
Heather, Heath and
Calluna
Ling

Better known as heather to all of us. I use small pieces in little vases in February with winter jasmine, the odd Christmas rose and the first of the spring bulbs. I also like to have sprays when they have died off and are a nice brown colour, going in well with an arrangement of dahlias or chrysanthemums. They are being grown more and more, and wisely so, as they make for trouble-free gardening; once established, they spread rapidly and give colour all the year round. There is a variety for every month of the year. One of the most interesting in my opinion is called *Calluna vulgaris* 'H. E. Beale' it has a crop of double flowers all the way up the stems, and lasts for weeks in a little water.

Preserving The flowers of the tall Mediterranean varieties dry naturally on the plant; they have a tendency to drop, but I feel it is well worth using a few sprays for their delightful browny colour. The 'H. E. Beale' heather, on the other hand, is better dried off standing in a little water, and retains its delightful pink colour for months.

Erigeron
Fleabane

Hardy herbaceous perennial. Daisy-like flowers which prefer full sun and make a splash of colour for the front of the border; good to cut and useful for putting in mixed summer flower groups. The hybrids now generally grown come in a range of pinks and mauves.

Conditioning Place the stems in boiling water for a few minutes, before giving a long drink.

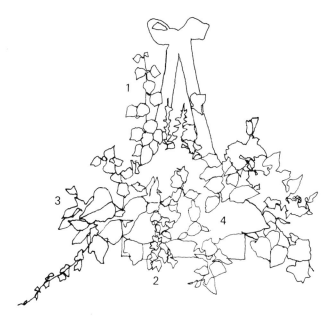

A very useful arrangement for winter with an interesting mixture of ivies.
1 *Hedera helix* 'Goldheart'
2 *Hedera helix* 'Glacier'
3 *Hedera helix* 'Marginata'
4 *Hedera colchica dentata* 'Variegata'

Eryngium giganteum

Eryngium

E. giganteum, sometimes called Miss Wilmott's Ghost, is a hardy biennial with green and white ornamental foliage and grey-blue flowers in summer, surrounded by spiny bracts; these dry well and can be used all winter. As they are biennial you are without them for a year until you get them established, and this is hard. The best variety is 'Slieve Donard'. The wild sea holly (*E. maritinum*) is also effective in a flower arrangement and excellent for drying. The perennial *E. planum* is rather more slender, and there are many richly-coloured forms of it. The *E. alpinum* 'Donard' form is graceful, shaggy and blue, one of the best. I see George Smith recommends *E. proteiflorum*, well named, as it does have a look of Protea about it, but you may also find it named as 'Delaroux'. It is not possible to describe all the varieties, and I suggest it is best to go and see them in flower.

Preserving The best way I find to deal with the eryngiums, which were always disappointing, is to place the flower stems in a solution of glycerine and water. That way they stay open and retain a good silvery buff colour.

Erythronium
Dog's Tooth Violet

Hardy bulbous perennial. These enchanting little bulbs have delicate drooping flowers with turned-back petals in pale pinks and creams, with many variations in their hybrid forms. They flourish in the protection of grass and increase rapidly. I enjoy using them in small vases and try to show the beauty of their unusual form. I think without any doubt the 'Pagoda' variety is a 'must', and it lasts surprisingly well in water.

Conditioning Give them a drink, and as they are very fragile great care must be taken not to bruise the petals.

Erythronium

Escallonia montevidensis

good subjects for flower arranging. They come in July and August at a very welcome time of year when not many other shrubs are in flower. 'Apple Blossom', with pink and white flowers, and 'Pride of Donard', with vivid red flowers, are just two of the many excellent varieties.

Conditioning Hammer the ends of the stems or put them in boiling water.

Eschscholtzia
Californian Poppy

Hardy annuals. Poppy-like open flowers, in many bright hues, that thrive on poor sunbaked soil. They have finely-cut and glaucous foliage. My very first memory of them is of my delight as a child at being able to pull off their little green hats as they were bursting into bloom, and so hasten the process! Nowadays, I like to arrange them in a basket and enjoy their blaze of colour.

Escallonia

Hardy or half-hardy evergreen or deciduous flowering shrubs, growing well in sheltered gardens or by the sea. The arching sprays of blossom, rose-tinted or white, make them very

Eschscholtzia aurora

Conditioning Dip ends of stems in boiling water for a few minutes, before giving a long drink.

Eucalyptus
Australian Gum

Tall trees with attractive ornamental grey foliage and flowers varying from fluffy pink to shades of scarlet and cream. These trees give Australia its beautiful hazy grey look. Britain is lucky in being able to import 'pads' of *E. populifolius* (a lovely round-leaved variety) and *E. globulus* (with pointed leaves) in large quantities in the winter; these leaf sprays last well and are excellent and economical to buy. There are several hardy varieties well worth growing in Britain. *E. gunnii* can grow to 4.5m (15ft) with great speed and if protected for the first winter should get well established; it is ideal for cutting.

Preserving If the ends of the stems are placed in glycerine and water, it takes on a lovely reddish look and lasts for months. *E. populifolius* is particularly good.

Eucharis grandiflora
Amazon Lily

Greenhouse bulbous evergreen plant. I have always called this bulb the 'Easter lily'. It grows on stems about 60cm (2ft) in height with open drooping white flowers; when I lift its head I always think I am looking at the loveliest and purest flower of all. Because so much of its beauty is lost if the head hangs, it is better arranged on short stems and is more generally used for sprays and bouquets.

Eucomis
Pineapple Flower

Although some species are hardy in mild climates, these plants are generally grown in a greenhouse. In early July they produce stout stems carrying spikes of greenish-white flowers, and ending in a dense tuft of green leaves – hence the name. If you can grow them, they are most rewarding. I like to use them mixed in with a green and white group.

Eucryphia

Slightly tender shrub, with open single rose-like flowers; so like philadelphus that for a long time I mistook it for a late variety. *E. glutinosa* is perhaps the hardiest eucryphia, though I think that the hybrid *E.* × *nymansensis* is still more beautiful in flower. It lasts much better if you remove most of the foliage as soon as you pick it.

Conditioning Having stripped off the leaves, put the ends of the stems in boiling water, before giving a long drink.

Euonymus

E. europaeus is best known as the Spindle Tree bearing lovely pink berries in the autumn. It grows wild on many of the chalky hills in Britain, in Wiltshire particularly. *E. europaeus fructu-albo* has white berries instead of pink. As with all berried trees and shrubs, the spindle tree can be arranged with a wide variety of materials; because of its awkward angular habit it is better as a background. The evergreen species of euonymus are invaluable, particularly the variegated *E. radicans* or *E. fortunei* 'Gracilis', which will cling to a wall rather like ivy, and the small *E. radicans variegata*, with green leaves margined with white, often acquiring a tinge of pink in winter. These are both helpful to put in winter vases, and like all variegated plants immediately add a light touch to a vase of evergreens. *Euonymus fortunei* has lovely lime-green new growth edged with cream, and though I am tempted to pick this, it is very much better to leave it to mature on the plant. Like so much young growth it does not stand too well. 'Silver Queen' is small leaved and will climb but it needs support. The nicest thing about it is the pink tinge that the leaves take on in winter which makes it excellent for arranging with a few Christmas roses and yellow jasmine. *E. japonicus argenteo variegatus*, the most brilliantly variegated, has rounded leaves looking as though they were splashed with cream paint. I often use a spray of this to cheer up a dried group.

Conditioning Hammer the stems well, before putting in water.

Euphorbia

Euphorbia
Spurge, Poinsettia

Tender and hardy plants of many varieties, nearly all of them useful in flower arrangement. *Euphorbia fulgens*, a greenhouse species that is on sale in January, has orange flowers all along the stems, in arched sprays; an expensive luxury, but such a glorious flower to enjoy at a sparse time of year. The poinsettia, *E. pulcherrima*, is another lovely exotic plant, which we have come to look forward to seeing in the shops at Christmas-time; generally thought of as a flower with brilliant red bracts, though thanks to Thomas Rochford we can now also avail ourselves of all the beautiful white species that he has brought from America and propagated in Britain. I have used these white poinsettias for weddings in December and consider them a godsend as they give character to any vase of mixed foliage. A point I must make clear is that they last much better if you wash the roots and

do not cut the stems. All euphorbias bleed when cut and great care must be taken to condition them first. So much for the hothouse varieties. The hardy herbaceous plants are a 'must' for the flower arranger's garden. *Euphorbia polychroma* has brilliant yellow bracts in early spring, giving a touch of sunlight to the border, and is good to cut. *E. robbiae* has lovely evergreen foliage and large yellow-green flowers. It makes a useful ground cover. *E. lathyrus*, or caper spurge as I call it, has no striking colour, only green spikes and funny green seed heads, but is good to cut in winter, and has the added advantage that it is reputed to be a mole deterrent – I think this is quite true. *E. wulfenii*, with delightful tall spikes of yellowy flowers in May is something I can never get enough of; it has the most lovely shape and colour, will mix with any other flowers and lasts for weeks in water. *E. wulfenii* 'Lambrook Yellow' is one of the best varieties.

Varieties do differ, partly due to the soil conditions and sun. The euphorbias that cling to the side of a rock in the south of France or in Formentera are the most wonderful lime-green colour so it looks as if they prefer being starved. The orange heads of *E. griffithii* are also very worthwhile, lasting for a long time in the border as well as in the house. *E. sikkimensis*, about 1m (3ft), has crimson stems and red-veined leaves with yellow bracts in July. The annual *Euphorbia marginata*, perhaps better known as 'Snow-on-the-Mountain', has leaf bracts that look like flowers, in green and white and is excellent for mixing in a green and white vase in midsummer. It stands very well in water once the stems have been burnt and given a long drink. *E. myrsinites*, at its best hanging over a wall, is another example of how starvation results in a mass of rounded lime-green heads on long trails of glaucous leaves. *E. wallichii* is a variety I have not got but am most anxious to see, after Graham Thomas's glowing write-up of it. These are my favourites but there are many more varieties.

Conditioning It is most important to treat all spurges carefully. They bleed a white liquid from their stems, so never leave them out of water for any length of time. Scald the ends of the stems in boiling water before giving them a long drink.

Evening Primrose *see* OENOTHERA

Everlasting Flower *see* HELICHRYSUM

Everlasting Pea *see* LATHYRUS

Fagus sylvatica
Beech

Deciduous tree. Beech in all its varieties – copper (*F. sylvatica purpurea*), cut-leaved (*F. sylvatica laciniata*) and others – is used a great deal for flower arrangement. It is excellent as a background in almost any vase. It is often preserved both at home and commercially and so can be used nearly all the year round; not only the foliage, but the nuts as well in all stages of devlopment. I have had great success putting them in glycerine.

Conditioning Hammer ends of stems well before putting them in water.

Preserving Beech leaves absorb glycerine almost better than any others, turning a lovely shade of copper in a matter of days. Hammer ends of stems well, allow a long drink, then place in the solution of glycerine, in July or August. If the branches are first put in a salt and water solution, this will result in variation of leaf tones in the final result.

Fatsia japonica
Fig Leaf Plant

Hardy, or nearly hardy, evergreen shrub, with rounded deeply-cut leaves that are extremely useful in a vase of mixed foliage. As the summer goes on the lower leaves start to die off and these change to a lovely creamy yellow which adds a bold touch to an autumn group of yellow and reds. It will grow quite well in any really sheltered garden. I am always surprised to see it growing in London gardens, but these are usually well protected by buildings. The green and variegated varieties make good house plants.

Preserving The leaves may be put in glycerine and water and removed when they have turned pale brown.

Felicia bergeriana
Kingfisher Daisy

Annual. A slightly tender little plant, but well worth growing for its long blooming period of brilliant blue daisy-like flowers. I like to use it in very small vases, remembering that because of its delicate form it can easily be overshadowed by other flowers.

Fern *see* ATHYRIUM, NEPHROLEPSIS, OSMUNDA, PTERIDIUM

Ficus elastica
India-Rubber Plant

A greenhouse or house plant that is a handsome decoration in itself, but odd leaves are effective and helpful for a touch of the exotic in a mixed green group.

Filipendula

F. hexapetala flore-pleno, the double form of dropwort, is a hardy herbaceous perennial with creamy-white plumey flowers in June. It is most effective for giving a light touch to a vase of delicate summer flowers. My grandmother always grew it, and used it often with cream sweet peas for the centre of her table. It lasts surprisingly well with no special treatment. The flowers of many varieties of *Filipendula* in a wide range of reds and pinks, to white, with fluffy flat heads, are attractive in groups of mixed summer flowers, though I often feel they are better value if you leave them until their green seed head stage; they look most attractive then in a foliage arrangement, often drying off to

Filipendula ulmaria

a desirable brown shade, when they can be used all through the winter. *Filipendula ulmaria* is one of my favourites for the golden patch of sunlight that these plants give any border, with their bright lime-green to golden feathery foliage.

Conditioning Hammer ends of stems well and put into warm water.

Preserving When in its seed head form, cut and remove the foliage, stand the stems in 2.5cm (1in) of water and allow them to dry off slowly in a warm atmosphere.

Flame Flower *see* TROPAEOLUM

Flax *see* LINUM

Flowering pot plants *see* HOUSE PLANTS

Foeniculum
Fennel

Really a herb, but used in flower arrangement for its feathery light foliage and attractive yellow flower. Easily grown from seed, it is a good flower for anyone making a new garden and wanting quick results for picking. Giant fennel has a big seed head much used for dried arrangements.

Conditioning Place the ends of the stems in boiling water for two seconds, before giving a long drink.

Preserving When the seed has set, hang the stems upside down to dry.

Foliage colour guide

Lime-greens and yellows This list of plants is given as a guide so you can see what is likely to be available. I find lime-greens and yellows enormously useful in flower arrangements, and the lime-greens particularly valuable as a foil to the red section of the spectrum.

Acer japonicum aureum, yellow leaves, turning deep crimson in autumn.
Acer negundo aureo-marginatum.
Achillea 'Moonshine', herbaceous, pale-yellow flowers.
Amaranthus caudatus viridis, long green-white tassels, grown as annual.
Angelica, perennial, leaves fade to good lime-green.
Atriplex hortensis aurea, yellow-leafed annual.
Aucuba japonica, green spotted lime-coloured leaves, evergreen.
Cornus alba (Dogwood), striped green and white tapering leaves.
Cornus stolonifera 'Flaviramea', yellow-barked dogwood.
Corylopsis spicata, shrub with bright yellow flowers in early spring.
Cupressus macrocarpa lutea, pyramidal yellow-green evergreen.

Cytisus praecox, early-flowering cream broom, low growing.

Daphne pontica, early-flowering daphne, yellow-green flowers in April.

Decorative Kale and Cabbage, green and white, red grown as annual.

Elaeagnus pungens aureo-variegata, lime, green and yellow foliage in winter.

Euonymus europaeus fructu-albo, yellowish-white, form of spindleberry.

Euphorbia (spurge) all varieties, particularly *E. wulfenii* (or *E. veneta*), *E. epithymoides* (or *E. polychroma*).

Fennel, bi-annual, good golden flowers.

Filipendula ulmaria variegata, yellow foliage.

Forsythia intermedia 'Beatrix Farrand', large yellow bells in spring.

Hosta fortunei albo-picta, lime-green centre, dark-green edge.

Hosta fortunei albo-picta aurea, golden small leaf.

Hosta fortunei 'Yellow Edge', a rare form with brilliant gold edge surrounding grey-green centre.

Hydrangea paniculata, pointed creamy-green heads.

Hydrangea quercifolia, white fading to green, foliage a lovely autumn colour.

Ligustrum ovalifolium aureum (Golden Privet), golden-foliaged shrub, one of the most useful.

Mahonia japonica, racemes of lime-coloured sweetly-scented flowers in winter and early spring, good foliage.

Malus 'Golden Hornet', attractive yellow berries in autumn.

Mentha gentilis aurea, lovely golden ground cover (needs to be well-conditioned).

Nicotiana alata 'Limelight', lime-green annual.

Parrotia persica, shrub, with yellow and red autumn colour.

Philadelphus coronarius aureus, golden-foliaged shrub.

Pieris formosa, shrub, with greenish-white lily of the valley-like flowers.

Scrophularia nodosa variegata, lovely green and white blotched leaves.

Sedum rosea (*rhodiola*), lime-green flowers in spring.

Skimmia japonica, shrub, if grown in full sun, leaves are lime-green.

Spiraea opulifolia lutea, golden-foliaged plant.

Stachyurus praecox, deciduous shrub growing to 3m (10ft), yellow flowers in February.

Syringa vulgaris 'Primrose', primrose-yellow lilac.

Ulmus glabra aurea, the Golden Elm.

Zea mays japonica, annual maize, with green and white striped foliage.

Grey foliages After greens and yellows, grey foliage plants, which seem to be mostly herbaceous, are a tremendous asset for the flower arranger. You will notice in the Drying references in Part Two that many of them preserve extremely well, which is always rather surprising.

Artemisia, all varieties.

Cardoon (or Artichoke).

Chrysanthemum haradjanii.

Cineraria maritima (*Senecio cineraria maritima*).

Eryngium planum, grey-blue.

Eucalyptus gunnii.

Eucalyptus perriniana.

Helichrysum petiolatum.

Onopordon acanthium, perennial. The Scots or Cotton Thistle.

Ruta graveolens 'Jackman's Blue'. Rue, vivid blue-grey mass of tiny leaves.

Santolina neapolitana.

Senecio laxifolius. A shrub, similar to *S. greyi*.

Stachys lanata, 'Lamb's Ears'.

Thalictrum speciosissimum glaucum.

Verbascum 'Broussa', good grey leaves and seed heads.

Forsythia
Golden Bells

Hardy deciduous shrub. With clever pruning *Forsythia intermedia spectabilis* makes a lovely shrub, a mass of golden flowers in early spring clustered on dark stems before the leaves appear; it is a good foil for daffodils. Varieties differ in shades of yellow; one of the best is 'Beatrix Farrand' triploid, the result of an experiment carried out by John Taylor of New Zealand. He injected this plant with colchicine and has produced the most amazing sprays of huge, pale yellow blossoms which are really superb. I have been given some cuttings and am looking forward to seeing the results. Forsythia is quite one of the best things to force, but it does take about five weeks to come into full bloom. I find it best to pick some sprays in January, and then to hammer the ends of the stems well and put them in warm water in a warm room after twenty-four hours in the cold. This gives sprays of bloom in the house several weeks before they flower in the garden.

Conditioning Hammer ends of stems well, before putting in warm water for several hours.

Fortunella margarita
Kumquat

A delicate citrus, bearing small almost oblong oranges. I have seen them growing in California and Australia, and have used small sprays in a vase of mixed apricot colours. I have bought the fruit in England and mounted some on wires and used them in the winter quite often – but this is not quite the same.

Foxglove *see* DIGITALIS

Francoa ramosa
Maiden's Wreath, Bridal Wreath

Slightly tender perennial plant with ornamental foliage and spikes of white flowers in late summer. The sprays are delicate and pretty in vases of all kinds of flowers, particularly good mixed with whites and ideal for wedding groups.

Conditioning Hammer the stems well, or put them in boiling water.

Freesia

A tender cormous plant with the sweetest smelling flowers of all. The hybrids of *F. refracta*, so improved in recent years, now come in every shade of yellow, and white, mauves, pinks and reds. Hybridization is largely due to the Dalrymple brothers who lived in the New Forest and spent the greater part of their lives working to get the results that we see today. It is now hard

to visualize the spindly little yellow flowers they once were. I like to see them arranged in a mass on their own, or in a silver sauce-boat. However, they do mix well with other flowers and can be put in a vase of, say, mixed pinks or reds to pick up a particular colour. The really large white freesias make a lovely bride's bouquet, as do the new and exciting double blooms.

Fringed Pink *see* DIANTHUS

Fritillaria
Crown Imperial, Fritillary

Bulbous. The crown imperial has an elegant flower with hanging bell-shaped blossoms in

Fritillaria meleagris

orange or yellow colouring, and a tuft of leaves at the top of the spire, rather like the top of a pineapple. The bulbs need good drainage and as they are loved by slugs it is very necessary to have plenty of anti-slug mixture available. Excellent subjects for arranging in really large groups (they look their best in copper or wooden containers) and one of the first of the really long-stemmed flowers to come into flower, so that they are welcomed by all who have to cope with big vases each week.

The best known of the smaller species is *F. meleagris*, or Snake's Head Fritillary, standing not more than 30cm (1ft) high, with delicate nodding heads chequered in pale and deep purple. They flourish in turf, growing naturally in water meadows, and seemingly enjoying the moisture and protection that grass can give them. I really feel when arranging them that one must keep the fragile effect of their delicate stems and drooping heads; so as not to detract from this, they are best silhouetted against a plain background.

Conditioning They stand extremely well in water and so require no special treatment, apart from the usual long drink.

Fuchsia

Tender and hardy deciduous flowering shrubs, often growing as hedges in southern Ireland and many other places with a mild climate. They have made a big comeback in recent years, after a spell of neglect following their popularity in Victorian days. Dazzling mixtures of pinks and petunias, scarlets and purples – that sometimes seem wildly improbable. I love to use their clusters of bell-shaped flowers as a cut flower, but there are few opportunities as the hothouse varieties are seldom cut; also I think few people realize that they last so well in water. However, a chance to use them is always rewarding for the cascading bells which hang over the edge of vase or container. Numerous varieties are hardy in the south of England. 'Alaba' has bright green leaves and pale pink flowers and another you will enjoy growing is 'Versicolor' whose foliage is strikingly variegated with grey-green and white and yellow with rose-pink tinting. Its

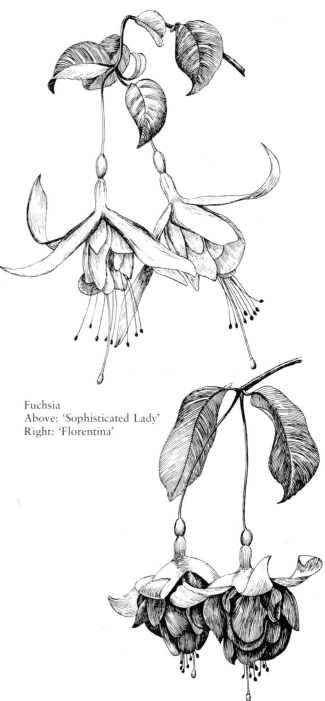

Fuchsia
Above: 'Sophisticated Lady'
Right: 'Florentina'

flowers are similar to those of *gracilis* but I like to grow it for its lovely foliage.

Conditioning Put the ends of the stems in boiling water for a few minutes, before standing in water for a long drink.

Funkia *see* HOSTA

Gaillardia
Blanket Flower

Hardy annuals and perennials. Has good showy daisy-like flowers in summer, often in contrasting shades of red and yellow. They give a good centre to any vase, and mixed with any turning foliage look extremely well. The hybrid varieties last very well in water.

Galanthus
Snowdrop

Hardy bulb, blooming in winter and spring, and not everyone realizes that there is such a large number of varieties. In fact they bloom in one species or another for about four months, the earliest coming like a breath of spring in December. *Galanthus caucasicus* is one of the earliest to flower and *G. elwesii* is one of the finest, with broad glaucous leaves. They all have drooping white bell-like heads, with a variety of markings in the form of different bands of green from the tip of the petals to the edge of the calyx. Lovely to pick for the house and to put in tiny vases or to use in a bowl in a bed of moss. Beverley Nichols suggested uprooting a few clumps and replanting them in bowls in the house – they do look very attractive; when these are finished, the bulbs should be separated for planting again in the garden. This splitting up is a very good thing in any case from time to time and should be done immediately after flowering while still green.

Galanthus byzantinus

Galax aphylla
Fairy's Wand

One of my great delights in lecturing in America is to find that nearly every florist from San Francisco to Chicago can produce bunches of these enchanting little leaves, rounded, leathery, about 10cm (4in) across, on tough wiry stems. They are green in summer but turn a lovely burnished bronze. They last so well that I often bring some home to England. One of the highlights of my trip last fall was to go walking in the Appalachians where they carpet the ground along with a creeping staghorn type of moss, surrounded by wild azalea – a flower arranger's paradise. These galax leaves seem to fit into any arrangement, tucking into the base of any small vase and adding greatly to the design. Their pet name comes from the fairy-like, delicate little flowers though I have never actually seen the plant in bloom. I do hope that some of you with acid soil conditions will try to grow it. I cannot think why it is not more widely grown in England.

Galtonia candicans
Giant Summer Hyacinth

Hardy bulbous plant. The white bells of G. candicans flower in August. Its nice long stems make it a most useful cut flower to mix with shorter subjects for a late-summer wedding. There is a green variety G. princeps that is beautiful but very rare.

Gardenia
Cape Jasmine

A tender evergreen shrub with sweetly-scented white flowers; the double-flowered form Gardenia jasminoides is generally grown. It is used chiefly as a spray to be worn or for a bride's bouquet. However, I love to have gardenias in the house, if I can, in a small bowl or done as a pyramid.

Conditioning Every care is required to prevent the flowers from being bruised as they get discoloured at the least touch. For special care overnight, stretch a piece of tissue paper over a bowl of water, secure with an elastic band, make small holes in the paper and push the stems through. This keeps the petals out of the water.

Garrya elliptica

Hardy evergreen shrub that grows well on a north wall, though it makes a beautiful tree of good shape if allowed to grow in the open. The male plant bears grey-green catkins in winter and is one of my favourite shrubs. I think it looks particularly effective with orchids.

Conditioning If you want to force it, it is important to hammer the ends of the stems, before putting in warm water.

Preserving Takes up glycerine beautifully.

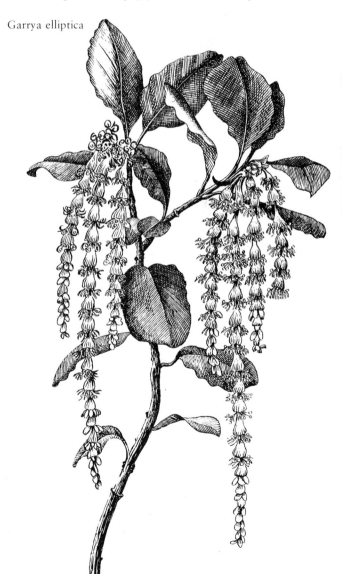

Garrya elliptica

Gaultheria

I think it is the berries I like in this evergreen flowering shrub. I have had the opportunity of using *procumbens* or partridge-berry, which after producing a rather nondescript flower has brilliant red berries. Good plants for ground cover.

Genista
Broom

Hardy deciduous flowering shrubs of the pea family. The Plantagenets took their badge from *G. anglica*. The spreading *G. lydia* is a delightful low arching shrub covered in spikes of clear yellow flowers in June. Small pieces used in the house add the much needed touch of yellow to a mixed summer group. All genistas need plenty of sun, so they make good subjects for the heath garden.

Conditioning I find that, like gorse, the stems last best in water if they are first well scraped with a sharp knife a little way up from the base. Be extremely careful that the exposed white part of the stem is well under the water in your arrangement.

Gentiana

Hardy perennials. There are many varieties of this adorable little trumpet-shaped blue flower: *G. acaulis*, a lime-lover and spring-flowering; *G. verna*, small but brilliantly blue, also in spring; *G. septemfida*, with flowers right down the stem in summer; *G. sino-ornata*, the one I find I can grow most easily and I use continually in the autumn. A few of these little bright blue flowers make a charming table decoration – just on their own in a small shell or bowl. The willow gentian, *G. asclepiadea*, is little grown but well worthwhile and wonderful to pick in July and August, again giving this useful touch of blue to any mixed flower arrangement.

Conditioning Always pick when fully open. Remove quite a number of the leaves and put the stems in warm water and allow to cool before using.

Geranium
Cranesbill

The bedding plants generally referred to as 'geraniums' are really pelargoniums. Cranesbill are hardy perennials, ranging from dwarf kinds grown on the rockery to those for the herbaceous border. The best kinds to grow are *G. pratense* and *G. grandiflorum*, both bluish purple. *G. sanguineum*, a brilliant magenta, is one I am particularly fond of; it grows a little taller and flowers for a long period, at least three months, which is a great advantage. *G. pratense* has the added attraction of lovely coloured leaves in the autumn, although once cut these do not last very long.

Conditioning Always place the ends of the stems in boiling water for a few seconds, before giving a long drink.

Gerbera jamesonii
Barberton Daisy, Transvaal Daisy

In a very warm part of the country *G. jamesonii* and the hybrids derived from it can be grown out of doors, but elsewhere they are really only suitable as greenhouse plants. Native to South Africa, they naturally thrive in sunshine, but are being grown in Britain, under glass, more and more, selling in great quantities as cut flowers and used for bouquets and sprays. I find they last well and I like them in vases; as they are grown nearly all the year round under glass, they are particularly useful when other flowers are scarce. I use them with dried material as all their golden and apricot shades go so well with it.

Conditioning Place ends of stems in boiling water, before giving a long drink.

Preserving Although I have not tried this, I feel that they are the kind of subject that should react well to the American hot sand treatment.

Geum
Avens

Hardy perennial. A showy red, yellow, or orange flower only suitable for small containers as a cut flower, because it will only hold up its head if cut on short stems. I use the red ones most of all as they have such a brilliant colour.

Conditioning Cut with short stems and dip in boiling water for a few seconds, before giving a long drink.

Ginkgo biloba
Maidenhair Tree

Deciduous tree with attractive foliage rather like enlarged sprays of maidenhair fern, hence its common name. I pick the leaves in autumn, when they turn to gold.

Conditioning Hammer ends of stems well, before giving a long drink.

Gladiolus
Sword Lily

Half-hardy corm. Vigorous spikes of flowers in a wide variety of colours. The corms are rewarding to grow as they produce good blooms easily, though better results are obtained with additional feeding and plenty of moisture. The smaller blooms, such as the dainty *G. primulinus* and 'Butterfly', are more useful for the flower arranger; they are much easier to arrange and have a lovely range of soft colours. On the other hand, the really large stems can be a joy for a big group and give so much scope for a wide choice of reds, pinks and petunia to mix together in a big 'clashing red' vase. By planting in batches each week, one has a long picking period. Lift and store the corms every autumn.

Conditioning Cut the ends of the stems under water and remove a small piece every four or five days. Always remove the dead flowers; with the stems in water, all the buds will open eventually. If by chance you have too many gladioli coming into flower at the same time, it is better to pick them when the buds are just showing colour and leave them out of water, preferably on a cold stone floor or in a cardboard box with the lid on; cut the ends of the stems and put them in warm water when you want them. They can be left like that for a week or more.

Gladiolus primulinus 'Sulphur Queen'

Preserving If you ever let the flowers go to seed, they are very nice in a dried group after being hung head down to dry off.

Gloriosa
Glory Lily

Greenhouse tuberous-rooted climbers. Tender red and yellow gaily-marked lily with turned-back petals. Rare, as they are natives of tropical Africa. I have had fun using them with mixed reds or fruit and flower groups, to which they add a delightful exotic effect.

Glory of the Snow *see* CHIONODOXA

Gloxinia

Tender tuberous-rooted plants with trumpet-like flowers, their texture more like velvet than anything else, in the richest red and purple colours. As they are greenhouse plants, they are not generally considered a cut flower. It often must seem such a waste to cut them, but for some special occasion I cannot begin to tell you how lovely they can look, their rich colouring enhancing a vase of cut flowers quite superbly. If you are tempted to cut a stem or two, I can assure you that they will last extremely well.

Godetia

A good hardy annual in long-stemmed and dwarf varieties, with an excellent colour-range. I like the shell-pink, salmon and mauve, as they blend so well with various colours, and there are many good crimsons and reds, which go well in vases of 'clashing reds', a lovely white one and a startling shade of orange. If you don't grow them yourself, bunches are often on sale in the summer-time. They are a good stand-by as they last so well, and can be put in a mass or used as odd stems as part of a colour scheme.

Conditioning The stems are tough, so it is as well to hammer them before giving them a long drink.

Golden Bells *see* FORSYTHIA

Golden Chain *see* LABURNUM

Golden Privet *see* LIGUSTRUM

Grevillea

Greenhouse and tender shrubs. *G. rosmarinifolia*, though half-hardy, can be grown in a shrub border in the southern counties of England, but requires the shelter of a wall. The greenhouse shrub *G. robusta* (Silk Bark Oak) has delicate fern-like leaves, standing well when cut, which gives it an advantage over many other fern-like subjects. It is also a good subject for preserving in glycerine.

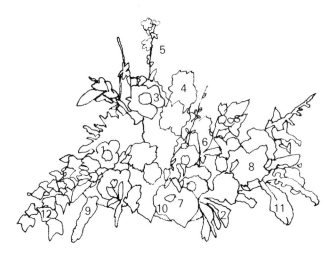

A mass of small spring flowers in a bed of moss.
 1 *Helleborus niger* (Christmas rose)
 2 *Helleborus foetidus* (Stinking hellebore)
 3 *Helleborus orientalis* (Lenten rose)
 4 *Ornithogalum thyrsoides* (Chincherinchee)
 5 *Jasminum nudiflorum* (Winter jasmine)
 6 *Iris histrioides*
 7 *Galanthus nivalis* (Snowdrop)
 8 *Petasites japonicus giganteus* (Butterbur)
 9 *Mahonia bealei* × 'Charity'
10 *Tellima grandiflora*
11 *Arum italicum pictum*
12 *Hedera* (Ivy)

Conditioning Put ends of stems in boiling water for a few seconds, before it has a long drink.

Guelder Rose *see* VIBURNUM

Guernsey Lily *see* NERINE

Gunnera manicata
Hardy herbaceous perennial. A very handsome water-loving plant with the most enormous leaves, rather like a rhubarb. Best used in early spring before the leaves have fully grown. The flowers and seed heads of *G. manicata* are superb, but so large that they are of little value except for really huge groups.

Conditioning The leaves should have their stalks dipped in boiling water and then be completely submerged in a bath of cold water overnight.

Gypsophila
Chalk Plant

Hardy annuals and perennials. This flower used to be looked on as a foil for carnations and sweet peas; however, I feel those days have gone, and we now prefer these other flowers unobscured and unfussed. By the same token we like the charming cloudy hazy feeling achieved by having gypsophila quite alone, arranged in a glass goblet or urn to make the most of its ethereal lightness. There are many kinds, both double and single, in pinks and white.

Preserving Carefully hang upside down to dry.

The indoor tray garden.
1 *Begonia rex*
2 *Solanum capsicastrum* (Winter cherry)
3 *Calathea makoyana* (Peacock plant)
4 *Primula obconica*
5 *Helxine soleirolii* (Mind your own business, Baby's tears)
6 *Zebrina purpusii*
7 *Hedera helix* 'Glacier' (Ivy)
8 *Iresine herbstii* (Bloodleaf)

Hacquetia epipactis
Dondia

A delightful spring-flowering plant that is worth its weight in gold. The small daisy-like flowers have green petals and a yellow centre. It has short little stems and is only useful for very small vases. However, it gives a good centre to any

Hacquetia epipactis

really small vase in February, or can be added to a 'moss garden' of early primroses and early little bulbs. It grows well in the rock garden and flowers freely in partial shade, but is better if left undisturbed and if you want to split up the plant this must be done after flowering. It lasts surprisingly well in water and needs no special attention.

Haemanthus
Blood Flower, Red Cap Lily

A bulbous plant for the greenhouse. *H. multiflorus* is the one I know and like best: it has erect lily-like scarlet flowers on stems about 30cm (1ft) high. The cut flowers can be bought in the autumn.

Conditioning Place the stems in warm water, cut the ends of the stems under water, fill up the vase with cold water and leave for several hours.

Halesia carolina
Snowdrop Tree, Silver-bell Tree

Hardy flowering tree, with small white bells. Very nice with the foliage removed, used as a background to any white flower.

Hamamelis
Witch-Hazel

Hardy deciduous shrub flowering on bare branches in January, with clusters of yellow that are a joy to behold. I love to pick a small spray or two to put in a vase of little spring bits in the very early spring. I have seen it in bloom with the snow still on the ground. *H. mollis* is scented, *H. japonica* is not. For me 'Pallida' is one of the most beautiful of all, heavily clustered with pale yellow flowers in early spring.

Conditioning Hammer ends of stems well, before giving a long drink.

Hamamelis mollis

Hare's Tail Grass *see* LAGURUS

Hawthorn *see* CRATAEGUS

Heather *see* ERICA

Hebe

Hebe armstrongii is a most useful plant with heather-like foliage which turns brown in winter, and has clusters of white flowers in summer but it is for the foliage that I use it. *H. × andersonii* 'Variegata' creates a very interesting effect planted with shrubs or ericas and again it is the foliage that stands out rather than the purple flower.

Conditioning Put the ends of the stems in boiling water and then give a long drink before arranging.

Hedera
Ivy

Hedera, with ornamental leaves green and variegated, and much better known as ivy, is one of the commonest of the hardy evergreen climbing plants. Often used these days as a house plant and in pots and troughs for house or shop window displays of all kinds. I grow many varieties to cut all the year round for their foliage. The giant ivy *Hedera colchica dentata* and its variegated form, *H. colchica dentata variegata*, *H. canariensis*, *H. helix sagittaefolia* and *H. helix conglomerata* are to name but a

From left to right: Hedera helix sagittaefolia, Hedera canariensis, Hedera helix 'Goldheart'

few; there are so many kinds. 'Goldheart' also known as 'Jubilee', and 'Golden Cloud' also known as 'Russell's Gold', are two small-leaved ivies that are extremely useful as a cut plant as well as highly decorative in the garden. You will see on page 104 a wall vase I have arranged of mixed ivy. What could be more effective on a winter's day? Lasting extremely well in water they are much sought after as cut sprays, giving any vase in which they are used a flowing line by their natural down-sweeping form.

Preserving The stems of ivy berries last very well if put in a solution of glycerine.

Hedychium gardnerianum
Ginger Lily

Greenhouse perennial. Spikes of very fragrant white and yellow flowers with handsome broad green leaves, growing wild in the Pacific Islands, where their heady scent hangs in the air. I would use them at every opportunity, though many people find the scent overpowering. Having nice long stems, they are ideal for large groups.

Conditioning Put the ends of the stems in boiling water for several minutes, before giving a long drink.

Helenium
Sneezewort

Hardy herbaceous perennials. A good plant for the back of the border, with yellow or brown daisy-like flowers that cut well and help the autumn vases. There are also dwarf summer-flowering varieties.

Conditioning Hammer ends of stems well, before putting in warm water.

Helianthemum
Rock Rose

Hardy dwarf evergreen with open rose-like red and yellow flowers. Not really suitable to cut as they do not last very long in a vase, but I sometimes slip one in to add a bit of colour just for an evening.

Conditioning The ends of the stems need putting into boiling water for a few seconds, before they are given a drink.

Helianthus
Sunflower

Hardy annual. The single annual sunflower is popular as a cut flower and lasts well in water. The bright-yellow or more unusual browny varieties are the ones I like best and they add a focal or central point to a late summer vase. They mix well with berries and autumn foliages.

Conditioning Put the ends of the stems into boiling water, and then give them a long drink.

Helichrysum
Everlasting Flower

The half-hardy annuals are grown for picking and preserving for use in winter. Their daisy-like flower heads are surrounded by papery bracts in bright orange, red and yellow. The perennials usually have grey foliage and papery-looking white or silvery flowers, which also dry very well. *Helichrysum petulatum* is not hardy so I grow it each year as an annual. It lasts very well in water and enhances every arrangement you put it into. Arching sprays of grey foliage of pairs of small, hairy grey leaves look lovely with pinks or purples. There is a variegated variety that I grew this year for the first time and find quite enchanting. This plant grows quite well outside in the summer and I use sprays of it continually. It will not stand the frost so that you need constantly to take cuttings. Use it all summer when it is at its best. The flowers are small but attractive and dry well in a daisy-like form. Useful for small dried bunches.

Conditioning Place the ends of the stems into a little boiling water, and then allow a long drink before arranging.

Preserving The perennials are best dried by having all the foliage removed and being hung upside down. The round flowers of the annuals, however, need to have thickish florist's wire pushed right down the centre of the flower into the stalk, before being bunched and hung upside down to dry. It is always better if you can do this, as the stems tend to be brittle and so often the head falls off. Remove all the leaves before hanging up.

Heliotropium peruvianum
Heliotrope, Cherry Pie

Half-hardy perennial, but usually grown as an annual, with deep-purple flowers and a delicious scent. Lovely to use tucked into any little summer vase, but is better if picked with short stems.

Conditioning Pick with short stems and put the ends in boiling water for a few minutes, before giving a long drink.

Helipterum *see* ACROLINIUM

Helleborus
Hellebore, Christmas Rose, Lenten Rose

Hardy evergreen perennial. For the flower arranger, quite one of the most useful of all the plants I can name. Starting with the Christmas rose (*H. niger*): this is a lovely flower to have; it grows well under the shade of an apple tree, or against a wall as it likes lime, and it will give you pure white open flowers in midwinter – not always at Christmas time, alas, but if it is sheltered with a pane of glass this will often bring it into flower more quickly. The green helleborus are 'musts' for any flower arranger's garden. *H. viridis* (Green Hellebore), *H. foetidus* (Stinking Hellebore) and *H. corsicus* all flower in the very early spring, which makes them specially useful; they cheer up the remains of a dried group, and mix well with all the early spring flowers. The Lenten rose *H. orientalis* hybrids, with open flowers in muted shades of whites and mauves, usually have brown spotted markings; they need careful conditioning, but for me they are a joy to have, even if they do not last very long. I have found that by allowing these stems to lie in a bowl completely submerged they really do last well. You will see this demonstrated in the picture on page 121. The wonderful 'Nigeracore', a cross between *niger* and *corsicus* hybridized by Mrs Davenport-Jones, is an outstanding new variety. The form of *corsicus* is a creamy-green clustered flowerhead.

Helleborus niger

Conditioning For the Christmas roses, it is best to take a needle and prick here and there across the stems from the flower head and especially under the water-line. For the green types, put the ends of the stems in boiling water for a few seconds and then put them in a can up to their heads in water overnight; pricking the stem is also good. Another good method is to press the point of a sharp pin against the stalk just below the flower head, and draw it down to the bottom of the stem making a fine groove along it; this should be followed by a long drink. All hellebores are much better for being in really deep water, especially the Christmas roses. If you want to arrange them for effect in a shallow container, then it is advisable to remove them at night and stand them in deep water until the next day.

Hemerocallis
Day Lily

Hardy herbaceous perennial with yellow, orange, apricot or bronze-red flowers in summer; the flowers last for only one day, but the plants go on blooming for several weeks. Some of the hybrids have lovely colours, and larger flowers, and are well worth growing.

Conditioning Cut the ends of the stems on the slant, before giving them a long drink.

Hepatica triloba
Anemone

This is the plant still often listed by nurserymen as *Anemone hepatica*, though it is now properly called *Hepatica triloba* or *H. transsilvanica*. A hardy perennial, it is a lime-loving anemone with bright-blue, cerise or white flowers, opening in February, at just the right time to put in a vase of little early spring flowers.

Heracleum mantegazzianum
Giant Hogweed

Hardy perennial. Huge flat fluffy heads, like a big cow parsley, and very serrated leaves that turn a lovely lime-green-yellow as they fade; this makes them a useful addition to any flower arrangement. However, the plant grows to an enormous size, usually reaching 3m (10ft) each year, so it should only be grown if you have plenty of space.

Conditioning Dip stems of leaves and flowers in boiling water for a few minutes, before giving a long drink.

Hesperis matronalis
Sweet Rocket

This delightful perennial is a very old-fashioned little flower – with white, pale-pink or mauve small flowers clustered on tall stems. It has a delicate appearance, that makes one imagine it would not last well, but in fact it stands extremely well in water, and adds a lovely light

Hesperis matronalis

touch to a vase of early summer flowers. It is a plant well worth growing for a little early colour in the border and has an attractive feathery green seed head.

Conditioning Lasting so well in water, it needs little special attention; but as with all flowers, it is the better for a few hours in deep water after picking.

Preserving When the seed is formed, pick the stems and hang them upside down to dry. They add a light feathery touch to any dried group.

Heuchera

Hardy perennial. Many varieties derived from *H. sanguinea*, with attractive ornamental foliage and red and pink flowers. The delicate flower-sprays are good in mixed vases, and I like to use the small leaves for putting at the base of a little group.

Conditioning I find the flowers require no special care, but the leaves are better for their stems being burnt in a little boiling water.

Hibiscus

The half-hardy tropical species are quite beautiful and have trumpet-shaped flowers in glowing rich reds and pinks, also yellow and orange, lasting only one day. They are the only flower I know that lasts as well out of water as it does in; because of this they make a lovely table decoration laid on the table-cloth, with no vase needed at all.

Himalayan Poppy *see* MECONOPSIS

Hippeastrum
Amaryllis

A greenhouse bulbous plant with enormous red, pink or white lily flower heads and very good pointed green leaves. *H. aulicum* is the one I use in big groups for weddings and special functions. The Barbados Lily, *H. puniceum*, makes a beautiful centre for an exotic group. It gives a vase of fruit a really luxurious look.

Conditioning Cut the stem, put a cane up the centre and tie firmly; this supports the head which is sometimes too heavy for the hollow stem.

Hippophae rhamnoides
Sea Buckthorn

Hardy deciduous flowering shrub yielding a rich crop of orange berries which remain on angular brown stems long after the leaves have gone. For the berries both the male and the female kind have to be grown near together.

Preserving Use the berries in the normal way, and they gradually dry off while the stems are in water; they may shrivel a little, but it is hardly noticeable in a winter group, and they are well worth while for the colour they give.

Hoheria lyallii

Half-hardy flowering shrub with single white flowers rather like philadelphus, but much later – the flowers appear in July and August. Remove some of the leaves and it is spectacular. I

Hoheria lyallii ribifolia

arranged it in a large brass bowl and stood it in our open fireplace when we opened the garden some years ago and it was a sensation. Mine took two years to bloom, from a three-year-old seedling, but was well worth waiting for.

Conditioning Scrape off some of the outside bark and plunge the ends of the stems into 2 cm (1 in) of boiling water then give a deep drink for several hours.

Hollyhock *see* ALTHAEA

Holodiscus

At long last I have identified the tree spiraea which I have admired for so many years, as *Holodiscus discolor*, a North American shrub of great value. It grows particularly well in the north of Scotland where I have used it in the autumn when the flowers are becoming seed heads and the foliage is turning a burnished bronze.

Holy Thistle *see* SILYBUM

Honesty *see* LUNARIA

Honeysuckle *see* LONICERA

Hosta
Plantain Lily, Corfu Lily, Funkia

Hardy perennials. I cannot praise them too highly. They are superb plants to grow, liking shade and moisture, but surprisingly easy. If they are grown in full sun you tend to get a better crop of their delicate lilac lily-like flowers; if they have more shade, the foliage is generally better and their striking spade-shaped leaves are very much larger. They are one of those dual-purpose plants that are a 'must' for the flower arranger. I can never have too many. I think I started growing them first of all for their leaves. These have such a wide colour range from lime yellow to deep green; they make excellent ground cover, in which no weeds can survive, and give good contrast in the front of any shrub border or by

the water-side, their broad shape a good foil to the grassy rush and iris type of bog plants. My favourite must be *H. fortunei albopicta*, which by the middle of May has unfurled a mass of bright butter-yellow spade-shaped leaves, edged with pale green; these are ideal for the centre of any foliage group and add a touch of sunlight to a vase in shades of lilac or pinks; they fade to an all-over green as the summer goes on. *H. albo-marginata*, on the other hand, has reverse markings, green centre with white edge; it is a wonderful stand-by as it retains a good colour all summer. *H. fortunei albopicta aurea* has leaves that are entirely yellow, and this makes it a valuable contribution to any small arrangement. The Sunningdale Nurseries have an attractive variety, *H. fortunei* 'Yellow Edge'; it is the reverse of *H. fortunei albopicta*, with green centre and yellow edge to the leaf. *H. undulata* is a smaller plant with twisted green leaves with a band of creamy white in the middle. The handsome large and bold leaves of *H. sieboldiana* are a real blue-grey, crinkled and deeply veined, ideal used at the base of any large group. *H. crispula*, *H. fortunei*, *H. tardiflora* and *H. plantaginea*, with its unusual white bell flowers, are all worth growing.

The latest addition to my collection and much prized is *H. sieboldiana* 'Francis Williams' (see photograph on page 175). The grey look of these large corrugated leaves is reminiscent of its parent, *sieboldiana elegans* but, added to this, it has a wide edge of superb lime-green and furthermore it keeps its colour well all summer. I have been given a small Japanese pure gold hosta and this also remains golden. It was given the unimaginative name of 'Golden Miniature' which it truly is and so is not so valuable for flower arranging as the larger forms. Netta Statham, who has a most wonderful collection of plants in Shropshire, probably better than any other I know, claims to have seventy varieties of hosta. From her I have just received *H. tokadama variegata*, strangely blue-green and interesting, but for me it seems to be a shy 'doer'.

Conditioning Soak the leaves well, either by putting them in very deep water or by submerging them completely under water for several hours. I find that, particularly in early spring, if

Hosta plantaginea

you put the leaves and a little water into a plastic bag, tie tightly and leave for two days, the leaves come out beautifully crisp.

Preserving The leaves as they fade and turn colour from green to pale yellow, are well worth pressing in sheets of newspaper placed under the carpet for several days. Always be careful to see that you pick a leaf that is perfect and also that no part of the leaf is turned under before pressing. The seed heads, once formed, are also worth picking, as soon as they are set; I try to gather them before they open. If you dry them in the house, you have a better chance of the seeds staying in the turned-back petals. I stand mine in a small amount of water and keep them in a very warm place, then store them standing in a pot out of the way until I want to use them. They are worth a great deal of care as they are so beautiful.

House plants

The popularity of house plants has increased enormously over the last twenty years, partly due, perhaps, to warmer houses where plants are happier and partly because a plant will last well with little care and attention and brings a touch of life to any room.

It is important though to present them well in a good-looking pot-holder as plants placed around the house in plastic pots can look far from attractive. Personally I enjoy plants *en masse*. This may sound extravagant but it only means putting two or three pots together in a larger container. Sometimes to make it livelier I add a small bowl with a few cut flowers in Oasis. This is the 'pot-et-fleur' idea which is becoming popular in England and in North America. In fact in the United States everyone seems to have plants because cut flowers are so expensive and die quickly in warm houses, while plants last a long time and are much better value.

For many years house plants have been an essential part of the home in Scandinavia and Holland, and now in England and the United States they are being grown in much larger quantities. It is thanks to Mr Thomas Rochford that Britain has many more interesting varieties and of a better quality than ever before.

I have found that one of the best ways of displaying house plants, and having them close together for easy maintenance, is by putting them in a trough which can be made quite easily from wood. Mine is lined with heavy polythene film, though if you can afford it zinc is the ideal. It is important to remember, when choosing the room for your trough, to have enough heating in it so that the plants won't run the risk of frost damage. You then have the fun of choosing which house plants to put in your trough. *Begonia rex* which is a particular favourite of mine is attractive all the year round and needs little or no attention except for watering and an occasional plantoid. My trough also contains maidenhair ferns, *Monstera deliciosa*, with their broad serrated leaves, tradescantia, and *Jasminum polyanthum*, whose white flowers in early spring scent the whole house. All the ivies are good value: *Hedera hibernica maculata* is very striking and with the support of a cane will grow up to 2.5m (8ft) in height: *Hedera canariensis*, the variegated ivy, is also well worth having, as are some of the smaller-leaved varieties. Sansevierias, with their dramatic pointed leaves edged with cream, last for years and provide a lively contrast in shape. These leaves are wonderful for cutting – they are most attractive in a foliage arrangement and last for several weeks in water. *Cissus antarctica*, or Kangaroo Plant or Vine, as it is sometimes called, grows quickly and climbs with little effort once you have given it an initial start on canes. The large leaves of philodendron make an excellent spreading plant, as do the fatshederas; the variegated one 'Silver Prince' I find extremely useful as a house plant and for odd leaves for cutting. The smaller plants such as peperomia and chlorophytum are useful for putting in the front of the trough.

House plants need little attention, but correct watering is most important. Press the tips of your fingers on the top of the soil. When the soil is too dry it is greyish in colour; if too wet, which can be bad for the plant, it is soggy and black. The soil should always be moist but firm. A miserable-looking plant often results from overwatering. During the summer, plants dry out more quickly and every ten days or so I take them out and submerge the entire pot in a bucket of warm water, leaving it until all the air has stopped bubbling from the pot. Then I dry it off on sheets of newspaper and return to the trough. In the late autumn and winter the growth of the plant slows, outdoor temperatures are lower and watering is therefore much reduced. About once a week I find is quite enough, and sometimes not as often as that. Forgetting to water and then suddenly remembering and overdoing it makes the lower leaves drop off. Overhead spraying keeps the leaves dust-free and cleaning the broad and shiny leaves with cotton wool dipped in a little milk and water gives them a nice gleam. Should you be using plants for a showroom or office then I suggest you try spraying them with one of the plastic plant sprays which are now sold in all garden centres. I am not very keen on them for the home as they give the leaves a rather artificial gloss, but this is a good thing if they are on display and not seen too closely as they keep a much fresher appearance. I find plantoids very good in the growing season, or one of the liquid house plant fertilizers added to a little of the plant water every now and again. All-green plants such as grape ivy (*Cissus rhomboidea*) and philodendron will live well without a great deal of good light, whereas the variegated plants, ivy and dieffenbachia, must have as much light as you can possibly give them.

Flowering pot plants Winter-flowering plants, such as primulas and cyclamen, need rather special care. The colour they bring to the trough is always a delight, but you must ensure they have sufficient warmth and are kept out of draughts. Cyclamen die more quickly from over-care than from neglect and hate both draughts and over-heating. A constant temperature, with no watering until the leaves start to wilt, is best. *Primula malacoides*, the small delicately-flowered tiered mauvish plants, should have the whole pot submerged in a bucket of warm water once a week. This is the best treatment for azaleas as well. You can quickly tell when they are very dry by tapping the pots, as they have a distinctly hollow sound. Plants in plastic pots require less watering than those in clay pots as there is no evaporation. It is quite helpful to pack damp peat or shingle round clay pots in the trough. It retains the moisture and cuts down watering. All pot plants dislike draughts and appreciate regular watering. Green plants grow well in most conditions but variegated ones need good light, so if you have a dark corner put your green plant there rather than a variegated one.

How to make an indoor tray or dish garden You will see from the photographs that the tray garden is made on a very shallow dish or tray, and surprisingly enough, it lasts extremely well and for a very long time. Many people have odd pot plants in various places about the house and it is a much better idea to put them all into one receptacle, where they can be properly cared for. Apart from avoiding the risk of some plants being forgotten about through being in some out of the way place, they look so much more attractive in a group. Any small green plant is likely to be useful and you should include some coloured flowering plants – any of them can be taken out and replaced if they should die.

Generally they last for several weeks with only the addition of a little water. I recommend a good loam for the soil or potting compost. Place the larger plants at the back, and space the others to show them off to their best advantage. Press in very firmly. A new plant must have its roots really firmly planted. Stones or bark may be added to fill some of the gaps, which makes the decorative effect even better, and a layer of moss should cover the soil. Water well and leave to drain. After that watering once a week is all that is usually necessary.

Humea elegans
Amaranth Feathers

Half-hardy biennial. Plumes of feathery red flower heads, smelling sweetly of incense. Because of this it is known to me as the Incense Plant. In the past I have used it on many occasions, arranged with lilies and heads of hydrangea. Constance Spry loved it, and for many years had it specially grown. Regrettably, one rarely sees it today, except sometimes as a bedding-out plant in parks in midsummer.

Preserving Remove the leaves and dry off for use in pot-pourri, then hang up the heads to dry for using in dried groups in winter.

Hyacinthus
Hyacinth

Hardy bulbous-rooted perennials, with fragrant spikes of pink, blue and white flowers in spring. Generally used for pot culture and forced for the house in pans and bowls. They look so nice as a cut flower, and I find that once they become straggly in their bowls it is much better to pick them and enjoy them in their last stages in a vase. Quite one of the best flowers for indoors, as their scent prevails throughout any warm room. The following varieties are a little out of the ordinary and make an excellent and unusual colour combination: 'City of Harlem' has pale yellow spikes reminiscent of Devonshire cream. 'Orange Boven' an interesting salmon orange and wonderful to mix with apricot colourings; 'Amethyst' a real purple, late flowering and a good blending colour. Lastly, one of the best

doubles 'Chestnut Flower' has large spikes with pale pink double flowers and is beautiful arranged with *Prunus* 'Pandora'. Hyacinths are rewarding to grow as they flower for many years planted out in the garden after they have been grown in the house, so you get a lot for your money!

Conditioning Cut the stems from the bulbs, leaving a piece of stem and some leaves behind for nourishment for the bulb for next year. Carefully wrap a sheet of newspaper around the bunch of flowers and put them in a jug of deep water for a few hours.

Hydrangea

Hardy or slightly tender shrubby plants. The variety that is generally grown in the garden and greenhouse is *H. macrophylla hortensis*, though *H. paniculata*, with beautifully pointed cream heads, is not one to overlook, and neither are the Lace-cap varieties. They are all very showy garden plants and excellent for cutting, lasting better if picked when they have been out on the plant for some time. They add the solidity so important to any large group of flowers if a few heads are placed centrally. With a good colour range of white, pinks and blues, they are a wonderful dual-purpose plant, used either fresh or preserved. *H. arborescens grandiflora* has slightly drooping cream heads which start life as lime-green. I try not to pick them at this stage, tempting as it is, because they last so much better when they are mature. Then they turn from cream to green before dying off, buff-coloured, and it is at this later green stage that they dry well and make a valuable bit of lime-green colour in a dried group. One of the best plants of all is *H. a. discolor* which I have used in America. It is similar to *H. arborescens grandiflora* though it has a downy underside to the leaf and the flower heads are more rounded. It is the one hydrangea variety that you may cut down as it flowers on the new wood. The oak-leaved *H. quercifolia* is well worth growing for its superb foliage autumn colour.

Conditioning Place the ends of the stems in boiling water for several minutes, then submerge the whole head and stem under water for a few hours; they can be left overnight, but no longer than that in case the heads become transparent under water. They seem to drink through their heads, so it is quite a good idea to leave these covered with damp paper to be quite certain they do not flag, if you are using them in a big group for some important occasion. I find this a helpful tip for the quick recovery of a flagging pot plant. Hydro meaning water does, of course, help one to understand why these plants do require a great deal of water. I find that the use of a plastic bag over the heads even when they are in the vase will help to keep them in good condition at least for the first night – just remember to remove it in time!

Preserving Leave the flower heads of *H. macrophylla hortensis* on the plant as long as possible, usually until the middle of September, or until the heads are fading and turning from pink to red, or blue to green. Then cut the stems, remove the leaves, stand the stems in a little water and put the vase in a very warm place – for instance high up in the kitchen so that they get as much warm air as possible, or in a linen cupboard or boiler room. The quicker they dry, the better colour they seem to keep. Having dried them, store carefully in a box or in a dry place as they quickly lose their colour. By this method you should be at least seventy-five per cent successful, but you will find that a few curl up. Do not hang them upside down; they dry much better with their 'feet' in water and their heads in the warm.

Hypericum
Rose of Sharon, St John's Wort

Evergreen and deciduous shrubs, mostly hardy, with many pet names. The Rose of Sharon (*Hypericum calycinum*) is a good evergreen ground cover plant, with single yellow flowers and, later, good sprays of small fruits; these I find most useful. The new Hidcote variety is a great improvement on the older kinds. *H. elatum* 'Elstead' is a taller variety I have come to enjoy for the lovely clusters of pointed red berries that follow the flowers. It is at this stage that I like to use them most.

Iberis
Candytuft

Hardy annual and perennial. The gay little annual *Iberis umbellata* with close flat heads of pastel pink, mauve and white, is good grown in the garden as a border plant or for edging. I like to use it in the house in a mass in a small low bowl or basket. Small pieces mix well in groups of summer flowers, picking up the soft colours. The evergreen perennial, *I. saxatilis*, which has white flowers, is a very good rockery plant as it blooms for such a long time. Suttons have the seeds of both white and pink perennials; they also have a dwarf mixed annual hybrid which should be very useful. Iberis are suitable for town gardens as they are very tolerant of dust and grime.

Preserving If the flowers are allowed to seed, they form effective open green seed heads. Wait until these are well formed before picking, and hang them upside down to dry. As the stems are quite short, they are only suitable for small groups.

Iceland Poppy *see* PAPAVER

Ice Plant *see* MESEMBRYANTHEMUM

Ilex aquifolium
Holly

Hardy evergreen trees and shrubs with deep green or variegated foliage. It is only in very recent years that I have become acquainted with the fantastic numbers of varieties of holly that there are; I would guess at least a hundred. Welcome for its bright red berries for Christmas decoration – in fact the house never seems decorated until the holly is up. Used then for decorating our churches, and hung in bunches or made into garlands for our front doors. It is so much a part of Christmas. The yellow-edged holly, *I. aquifolium* 'Aurea-marginata', was the very first tree that I planted when we came to our cottage; this was because it is slow growing, and variegated holly is a lovely tree to have in a garden.

Conditioning Holly is really better if it is kept out of water; if it is standing in water, the leaves tend to fall off very quickly. It is a good idea to spray the leaves with Polycel or a plastic leaf coating; it certainly seems to keep them on rather longer.

Impatiens
Busy Lizzie

Greenhouse perennial. Busy Lizzie, a plant so well-known to everyone, is an *I. sultanii* hybrid, a fleshy-leaved and brittle-stemmed plant that flowers continually all the summer with a mass of pink or white flowers. It is of no value as a cut flower, but I mention it all the same, as it is so very much a house plant, flourishing on many window sills. I have been fascinated by the new variegated leaf varieties that have been developed. They are simply fantastic. The American Horticultural Society has a wonderful collection and has hybridized some incredible colour combinations – apricot to cream, blotched red, lime-green and creams – well worth looking for. If you live in the United States then a visit to the American Horticultural Society at Biltmore near Washington DC is certainly rewarding for these varieties alone. They really enchanted me.

Incarvillea delavayi

Hardy perennial, with pink or rose-coloured flowers and attractive deeply-cut leaves. Not a well-known cut flower, but the few times I have had the chance to use it I was agreeably surprised how well it lasted.

Incense Plant *see* HUMEA

India-Rubber Plant *see* FICUS

Ipomoea
Morning Glory, American Bell-bind, Convolvulus

Tender perennials and half-hardy annuals. *I. rubro-caerulea* (or *Pharbitis tricolor*), the blue Morning Glory, is the best known. Growing at random in parts of Australia, it makes a glorious mass of brilliant blue, quite breathtakingly lovely. Grown here in pots as an annual, it gives very good results; the flowers start bright blue in the morning, fading to purple as the day wears on. Try as one may, they will only last an hour or so in water; I have used them only once for a lunch table, and they just survived and no more. Of the same family, the common white convolvulus, a rampant weed, can also be used as a table decoration, and looks pretty, but again, it will only last for an hour or two. The wood rose of Hawaii is the seed head of Ipomoea. It dries naturally on the plant before it is picked, and in the last few years has been sold in large quantities all over the world. I like to use them in dried groups. They need careful handling as they are very brittle.

Iris
Flag, Orris Root, Fleur de Luce

Hardy perennials, some are bulbous-rooted and some rhizomatous. The most popular are the June-flowering bearded iris, useful plants for the flower arranger's garden as the foliage is most decorative, as well as the flower. They have the most unusual dusky colours, which lend themselves to some lovely flower groups, and large heads on long stems, in soft mauve, purple, yellow, brownish and orange shades, also grey and pure white. Useful for any large flower vase.

The Reader's Digest Encyclopaedia calls the smaller bearded iris, to which I have become very attached, intermediate bearded iris. These smaller iris are most effective when cut and used in early spring, as their colour range is exciting for arranging: 'Blue Denim', pale blue, 'Green Spot', white with a green blotch, 'Golden Fair', pure yellow, and 'Scintilla', ivory, are all useful and have given me a great deal of pleasure in these last few years. So have the Californian *Iris californicae* known as the Pacific Coast iris all of which come from North America and I have enjoyed using them on my visits there. In Britain I use them in May and June and find that these mixed colours from mauve through brown have an enchanting colour range. No iris lasts all that well in water but the buds do develop eventually. Their greatest snag is that you often have a gap of a day until they open.

Iris stylosa

them actually burst open in a warm room, and as flowering continues it is possible to replace them daily. These are followed by *I. histrioides*, which is my favourite, china blue and enchanting. *Iris reticulata*, 15cm (6in), in all its blue and purple shades, is another charmer. *Iris tuberosa*, the snakeshead or widow iris, is worth a mention as it has such enchanting little green heads with black velvety petals; it is a bit difficult to grow, but comes in the spring, and is lovely with a few foliages or arranged with the striped *clusiana* tulips. Altogether, there is something from the iris world for the first six or seven months of the year.

Three irises that are worth growing just for their foliage alone: *I. foetidissima variegata* has cream striped leaves, evergreen and quite easy to manage. *I. pseudacorus*, the common yellow-flowered pond iris, has excellent tapering green leaves which last well in water and are a good background for a summer vase; like all irises they stand well in shallow water and are nice in an oriental group, with a predominance of water. The yellow-striped leaves of this form, *I. pseudacorus variegata*, are most useful, especially in early spring when the foliage is buttercup yellow before fading to plain green in late summer. *I. pallida dalmatica*, a very old plant with deliciously fragrant lavender flowers, is really most helpful as it retains its exceptionally grey foliage through the summer.

Finally, three irises that have good seed heads. *I. foetidissima* is quite one of the best: not only has it good dark-green foliage, but beautiful seed heads that burst open to display bright orange seeds. *I. ochroleuca* and *I. pseudacorus* both have excellent green seed pods that dry well.

Conditioning Cut the ends of the stems on the slant, before giving a long drink. Carefully remove each flower as it fades, so that the next one can open.

Preserving When the seed pods form, pick and hang them upside down to dry. With *I. foetidissima*, I find that it is better to stand the stems in a little water and dry them off in the warm, as sometimes the seeds fall out if they are hung upside down.

The crested iris, so called because of the resemblance to a cock's comb, are more like a delicate orchid than an iris and have an exotic look. *I. japonica* is a variety I would recommend. The Dutch, Spanish and English irises are a little shorter, growing to just 30cm (1ft) in height. These come in stronger, harder colours, blues and yellows, flowering in June and July (though they are forced under glass so that we are able to buy them in the early spring; they are more popular then, as of course there is not such a wide choice of flowers in general, and they are a good buy as they last well in water).

The genus is large and varied, with a long period of bloom, starting in January with *I. stylosa* (*I. unguicularis*); its delightful mauve blooms are greeted with open arms, being one of the very first flowers to cut. They last only a day or so and are better picked in bud. It is fun to see

Ixia
Ixia
African Corn Lily

Half-hardy bulbous plant, with clusters of star-like flowers of many different colours on very slender stems. They last well in water and are useful when you need a slender flower in a particular vase.

Jasminum
Jasmine, Jessamine

Tender and hardy climbing plants. The best known to everyone is *Jasminum nudiflorum*, which has sprays of yellow flowers in winter – a most popular visitor, bringing the spring feeling in January! Nice to use with the odd Christmas rose, or later with a few snowdrops or early iris. The white variety, *J. officinale*, has slender sprays of sweetly-scented white flowers in mid-summer; although this one does not last so well in water, it is worth picking for the fragrance it gives to any room. *J. polyanthum* is a cool-greenhouse plant with a heady scent; it is easily grown and can be treated as a house plant. The yellow *Jasminum primulinum*, scentless, is not well known, but is another cool-house plant, well worth trying for its enormous star-like yellow flowers. It lasts surprisingly well in water and it was a delight to pick its long golden sprays in California. I understand that it will grow outside in England but it would need a very sheltered position.

Conditioning The winter yellow jasmine needs little extra care, but the summer white one is better for having the ends of the stems in boiling water, before being given a long drink.

Jerusalem Sage *see* PHLOMIS

Jonquil *see* NARCISSUS

Judas Tree *see* CERCIS

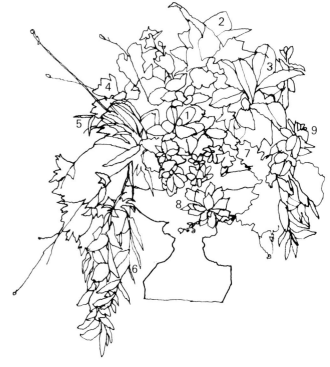

This white urn is one of a pair; it is planted up as soon as the frost is over and stands outside the front door all summer. In autumn it comes in and has one or two additions made through the winter.
1 *Echeveria gibbiflora* 'Carunculata'
2 *Dieffenbachia*
3 *Codiaeum* (Joseph's coat, Croton)
4 *Cyclamen*
5 *Chlorophytum* (Spider plant)
6 *Tradescantia albiflora*
7 *Hedera* (Ivy)
8 *Sedum*
9 *Kalanchoe*

Juglans
Walnut

This is not commonly used as a cut flower, but the catkins that precede the nuts are the most wonderful purple-pink colour, growing on such artistically-shaped branches that if you ever get the opportunity of using them, never miss it. I would sacrifice the few nuts any day for the chance of using a spray, with two or three tree peonies – an outstanding combination.

Kaffir Lily *see* CLIVIA

Kalanchoe

Until recently this succulent meant for me *Kalanchoe blossfeldiana*, a red-flowered, waxy, bright green-leafed pot plant which we often put into planted gardens in January. Having become acquainted with the tropical varieties I have really been inspired by them. *K. bebarensis* with its heart-shaped leaves like thick velvet, starting grey-green and turning grey-brown, is fascinating. I brought a leaf back from the United States and gave it to Fred Wilkinson at Winkfield Place and since then he has grown, perhaps, hundreds. I can never have enough so I grow mine on the kitchen window-sill and take off the odd leaf as I need it. They make a point of interest in any vase in which you put them, and last extremely well in water. *K. pumila* I have enjoyed in many parts of the world from Australia to Bermuda and Spain.

Kale
Brassica fimbriata

Decorative kale and cabbage I like to grow as I find them extremely useful in the winter and early spring. They have the most glorious leaves, finely cut, and good colour – green and white, and purple-red; quite beautiful as a foil for the last of the red roses or in winter with a group of fruit and flowers. In spring-time it is possible to

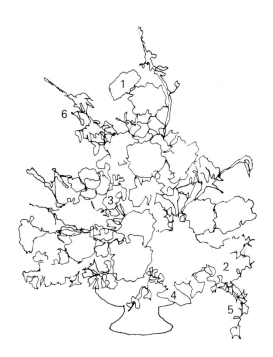

Early spring flowers surrounded by catkins.
1 *Dianthus caryophyllus* (Carnations)
2 *Hyacinthus*
3 *Freesias*
4 *Arum italicum pictum*
5 *Hedera* (Ivy)
6 Catkins of Aspen *Populus tremula*

use the whole head, and this not only fills the centre of a really large arrangement, but looks so exotic that it can fool the experts and set everyone guessing. The cabbage is more compact in growth, as one would expect, and the solid heads are often quite pink and even more effective as a single stem than the kale, but I can thoroughly recommend sowing a little of both; although they are edible vegetables, they will be really much too precious to eat! I was interested to see these plants of decorative kale used as a winter bedding plant, when I was in Long Island last year. I feel it could be an idea for British parks departments as the kale gave an excellent colour effect all winter long.

Conditioning Never use boiling water on the stems or you will never get rid of the 'cooking cabbage' smell. Pare the end of the stem to a tapering point and make cross-cuts up the stem, first one way and then the other; then push the whole point as deeply as possible into the water.

Kalmia latifolia
Calico Bush, American Laurel

Hardy evergreen shrub with good glossy foliage and delicate clusters of frilly-edged pale-pink flowers, rather like the bunches we wore on our Sunday straw hats as children. They are showy, compact shrubs and once blooming well give a lot of colour to the shrub border when the rhododendrons have finished. To keep the shrub small and a good shape, it is as well to cut short flower stems. Tuck them in low at the centre of a vase. A native of Virginia, USA, and understandably a protected plant which makes the hillsides a cloud of pink in spring.

Conditioning Well scrape the ends of the stems and give a long drink, overnight if possible.

Kerria japonica pleniflora
Jew's Mallow

Hardy deciduous shrub which produces a mass of double flowers in the very early spring. It does better in the shelter of a wall facing south or west. I like to use the sprays by removing all the leaves and so getting the full value of the yellow blossoms to mix with daffodils and other early spring flowers.

Kniphofia uvaria
Red-hot Poker, Torch Lily

Hardy perennial. A very handsome plant in any border. Tall stems that stand very erect with a mop of tiny bell-like flowers that hang in a cluster from the top of the stem, starting greenish and changing to yellow and red. They are useful

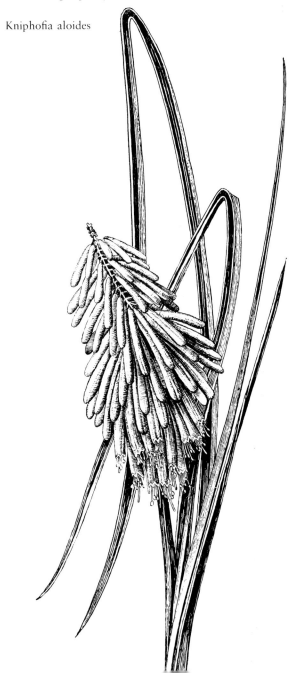

Kniphofia aloides

in late summer and autumn as they add a change of shape to a group of late flowers. Having very thick stems, they require a large vase, or of course can be arranged in a shallow dish with their stems on a pin-holder. There are many varieties in shades of coral, red and orange, 'Prince' being one of the best. Lately the hybrid yellows have become most popular, my favourite, K. *uvaria* 'Maid of Orleans', is a pale straw-colour, gradually fading to ivory white and lovely arranged with creams and browns.

Beth Chatto has been responsible for many new varieties, and her 'Jade Green' is most unusual, though it does not last quite as well in water as some of her others. 'Little Maid' is very good as a cut flower, looking like a smaller and more slender edition of 'Maid of Orleans', lovely green points, and excellent for arranging. 'Strawberries and Cream' in which the basal flowers are cream with rose-pink tips giving a pinkish glow to the flower stand really very well as cut flowers. They establish quite quickly in the garden and so make it possible to pick freely. They all have the habit of going on growing in water, which makes them twist; there is little one can do about it other than re-arrange them a little the next day. As with lupins they rarely change position again.

Conditioning Cut the stems on the slant and give a long drink of water.

Kolkwitzia amabilis
Beauty Bush

The common name for this graceful shrub is enchanting – 'Beauty Bush'. It forms a rounded bush about 2m (6ft) high, and in May and June it is covered with a mass of little soft pink, bell-shaped flowers which turn to a pretty little seed head. I find I use it in different arrangements for about four or five months. The flowers add those graceful arching sprays that look so attractive in a summer arrangement. The seed heads mix well with green and offset apricot dahlias, and late flowering roses.

Conditioning I like to place the ends of the stems into boiling water, and then allow a cold drink for as long as possible.

Preserving I find that although the seed heads do not actually dry out, they are still pretty when no longer fresh so I continue to use them.

Kumquat *see* FORTUNELLA MARGARITA

Laburnum
Golden Chain

Hardy deciduous flowering tree with racemes of yellow flowers which are such a delight in spring. *L. alpinum* (the Scottish laburnum) is better than common laburnum; but the hybrid *L. rossii* is perhaps best of all. I like to use it with the foliage removed so as to get the full benefit of the long, yellow chains of flowers shown off against the almost-black branches. It lasts very much better without the foliage.

Conditioning Scrape the bark off the ends of the stems up to about 5cm (2in) then place the stems in warm water and leave as long as possible.

Preserving When the seed head has formed, remove the foliage and hang upside down to dry.

Lachenalia
Cape Cowslip

Greenhouse bulbous flowers with bell-shaped heads on very fleshy stems. *L. bulbifera* has coral-coloured bells tipped with green, and *L. nelsonii* is a clear yellow; I think these are the two most popular and I am very happy to use either. They are charming as a pot plant and so good to cut as they last well in water; also pretty arranged with little spring flowers in a 'moss garden'.

Lagurus ovatus
Hare's Tail Grass

An attractive annual grass that seeds easily and is most useful in a summer vase, as a background for a few cornflowers or poppies. It dries so well that it becomes even more useful in the winter, as a feathery foil for more solid and heavy dried leaves.

Preserving Leave on the plant until midsummer so that the seed is well set, and then pick, remove all the green leaves, bunch and hang upside down to dry.

Lamb's Ears *see* STACHYS

Lamium
Dead Nettle

Hardy perennial. *L. galeobdolon* 'Variegatum' a plant I was given by Marjorie Fish as an excellent ground cover, as it undoubtedly is, but it has the nasty habit of not only creeping along but climbing up as well, so beware. *L.g.* 'Beacon Silver', this new variety is lovely, a truly silver carpet. It enjoys shade, gives excellent ground cover without taking over completely. I find it dries out in very hot dry conditions. *L.g.* 'Shell Pink' has close-forming frosted green and white leaves making dense ground cover, and delights everyone with its shell-pink flowers. I find that I enjoy using the trails of leaves and the small flowers. *L. maculatum aureum* has good golden foliage and gives a glow of sunlight to any dull corner. They do need careful conditioning to be of use as a cut flower, but if great care is taken it is really worth while as they last extremely well and provide nice trailing sprays that give a flowing line to a vase.

Conditioning Put the ends of the stems in boiling water for a few seconds, and leave submerged under water for twelve hours or more.

Lapageria rosea
Chilean Bellflower

Greenhouse plant. I understand that it can be grown out of doors, against a sheltered west wall in the south of England, but I have never seen it so. The transparent waxy-looking bell-shaped flowers come in red and pure white and soft rose-pink. They are superb for a bride's

bouquet, as you can imagine. I think I could count on one hand the number of times I have ever had the opportunity of using them as a cut flower: then just as a very special table decoration, with a few stephanotis and one or two leaves of delicate tradescantia and maidenhair fern.

Larix decidua
Larch

A deciduous conifer with the most graceful habit: the sweeping branches tip upwards at the ends. The trees can reach a great height and are usually grown for timber, but I love to pick branches in the spring when the new brilliant green growth is forming and you can see the young, reddish-pink cones lying along the top of the branches. Later, when the cones have formed fully on the branches, they can be picked in sprays and used as an arching background for late dahlias and then chrysanthemums; they of course dry naturally on the trees and are useful all winter, in sprays or as separate cones for Christmas and other decorations.

Conditioning Hammer the ends of stems well, before giving a long drink.

Preserving Pick the cones from the trees as soon as they are dry, and pack away in a safe place; or pick when green and hang upside down to dry off.

Larkspur *see* DELPHINIUM

Lathyrus
Everlasting Pea, Sweet Pea

Hardy annuals and herbaceous perennials. *Lathyrus* is the generic name for our favourite sweet pea, *Lathyrus odoratus*, an annual grown by expert and amateur alike. Although I love to arrange large bowls of beautifully grown long stems, with the much-coveted four, five or even six blooms per stem, I am quite happy to have a handful of shorter stemmed and not so well grown blooms, as to me the scent is of paramount importance. For this reason I think they are best put into large bowls in self-coloured

Lathyrus

bunches which as soon as you see you just long to lean over to drink in their scent. To my delight a salmon apricot sweet pea called Sheila Macqueen has been produced by Charles Unwin.

The small everlasting peas, the perennials, *L. grandiflorus*, have no smell, but last very well when cut. They have a good colour range in shades of pink, puce and apricot, softening to white.

Conditioning The annual sweet pea is better handled as little as possible; give a drink in deep water for several hours before arranging. The everlasting needs no special care.

Laurel *see* PRUNUS

Laurus nobilis
Bay Tree

Sweet bay is used as a flavouring, but sprays of the pointed green leaves look nice in the house and give off a spicy aroma.

Laurustinus *see* VIBURNUM TINUS

Lavandula
Lavender

Hardy evergreen shrub with aromatic grey foliage and spikes of purple flowers which we all know so well, if only from the old-fashioned lavender bag – a nice idea that seems to be dying out. The little dark-purple French lavender is the one I like to grow.

Preserving Gather the heads as soon as they are starting to fade, spread them out well to dry and then shake off the seeds; these retain their scent for a long time and can be a nice addition to pot-pourri.

Lavender *see* LAVANDULA

Leek
Allium porrum

Annual vegetable, but the seed heads can be of great value to use, either fresh or dried, in a vase.

They add a good solid centre to a vase of foliage, as they do equally well to a dried group.

Preserving When the seed heads are well set, pick and hang them upside down to dry. They are better tied up individually as they tend to lose their neat round shape if they press together.

Lenten Rose *see* HELLEBORUS

Leontopodium alpinum
Edelweiss

This attractive small pearly-white flower growing wild in the mountains of Switzerland is the Swiss national emblem. Although it has the appearance of being dried, it needs to stay on the plant at least a month before it is actually dry, and it is most useful at this stage. I used to grow it for many years, but it was never really happy and survived rather than thrived; but it will grow quite well in many English gardens if it has the warmth and protection of the rock garden and, as it dries so well, it can be used in winter vases of other dried flowers to great effect.

Conditioning Put the ends of the stems in warm water and allow them to have a long drink, being careful that none of the heads gets below the water, as they soak it up quickly through their hairy heads and it spoils the colour of the flowers.

Preserving Cut the heads when they have been on the plant at least a month, and bunch and hang up to dry.

Leptospermum scoparium
South Sea Myrtle

Half-hardy evergreen shrub with white flowers in June. *L. scoparium nicollsii* is not quite so well known although I have used it many times in Australia and in California, dark green small leaves on arching sprays, densely covered with tiny red and pink flowers. It lasts very well in water, and is a marvellous contribution to any red arrangement. Not often available as it is not very hardy.

Leycesteria formosa

Conditioning I find it will last very much better if the ends of the stems are placed in boiling water for a few seconds and then given a really deep drink preferably overnight.

Leucojum
Snowflake

Bulbous perennial. The spring-flowering variety, *L. vernum*, is the one I grow and find so useful, coming just after the snowdrops – although they are rather alike, the snowflake has a larger head, with green tips at the ends of the petals, and very much longer and stiffer stems which make it more useful in slightly larger vases. Later still is the Summer Snowflake, *L. aestivum*, with larger, pure white flowers in April and May.

Leycesteria formosa
Elisha's Tears, Flowering Nutmeg

Hardy deciduous flowering shrub which has clusters of pendulous dark-purple flowers with a touch of white; these are often rather obscured by their leaves, so that it is important to remove quite a lot of the foliage before putting them in a flower vase. The purple berries that follow are, if anything, even more attractive, and as they last a little longer it is sometimes better to wait for them. This shrub is a rapid grower and once established gives plenty to pick from. I love it and have used it very successfully recently with heads of mauvish hydrangeas and some bunches of hothouse purple grapes, in an elegant Japanese vase.

Conditioning Remove as many leaves as seems best, then pare the outside skin off the bottom of the stems and put them in very hot water for several minutes.

Liatris
Button Snake Root

Hardy perennial. *L. spicata* has purple flower spikes that are almost unique in that they start flowering at the very tip of their spikes and work down, unlike lupins and delphiniums that start opening at the base of the spike and work up! A nice flower to have in August when colours tend to be mostly yellows. Adds good spikes to vases of sweet peas and mauve roses, godetia and so on.

Libertia grandiflora

Libertia formosa

A plant with narrow slender green iris-type leaves, sending up spikes of white flowers, a little like an Ixia. The flowers last very well in water but if you can resist picking them, you will get the lovely spikes of brown seed heads later, which is what I love most about them. I would recommend them for this alone. *L. grandiflora* is the most beautiful but it is not so hardy.

Conditioning If the flowers when cut are given a good long drink in warm water they last extremely well for several weeks.

Preserving Leave the seed heads on the plant until they turn brown, then pick at once and hang upside down until completely dry.

Ligustrum ovalifolium
Privet

Hardy evergreen shrub with green or golden foliage; the latter (*L. ovalifolium aureo-*

marginatum) is one that I use continually, but was the first tree I took out of my cottage garden as soon as we moved in – and how I have lived to regret it! It is one of the best standbys possible as background material for large groups as it holds its leaves for weeks, even in winter, and adds a lightness to any flower arrangement. If grown as a tree and not clipped, it produces delicate branches of very good foliage and black berries in the autumn. Berries are more prolific on the common green privet *L. vulgare*, but there is little need to cultivate this as in certain areas of Great Britain and the United States it is found growing by the roadside. *L. sinense variegatum*, one of the loveliest, has grey green leaves blotched with white which will cheer up any dull corner.

Conditioning Hammer ends of stems well, before giving a long drink.

Lilac *see* SYRINGA

Lilium
Lily

Hardy and half-hardy bulbous plants. A wide and wonderful range of distinguished and elegantly beautiful flowers in all colours save blue. *Lilium candidum* (Madonna Lily) is one of the first to flower at the end of June. *L. testaceum* has heads like clotted cream. *L. henryi*, *L. davidii*, *L. tigrinum* and *L. hollandicum* (*umbellatum*) all come in varying shades of orange. *L. brownii* is one of the loveliest of all the trumpet lilies, cream with a brown back; *L. regale* is pink-backed and *L. longiflorum harrisii* pure white; the latter is forced and we can buy it for many months of the year, as we can the arum (see *Zantedeschia aethiopica*). *L. martagon* (the Turk's Cap Lilies) grow on tall stems and have small turned-back heads – and are now to be found in a wide range of colours, white, mauve, bronze and almost black. They are all lovely to use and have very good seed heads. *L. speciosum album* is fragrant and white, with such slender stems that they arch and hang most gracefully over the edge of a vase. *L. speciosum rubrum*, the pink variety, is rose-coloured with purple

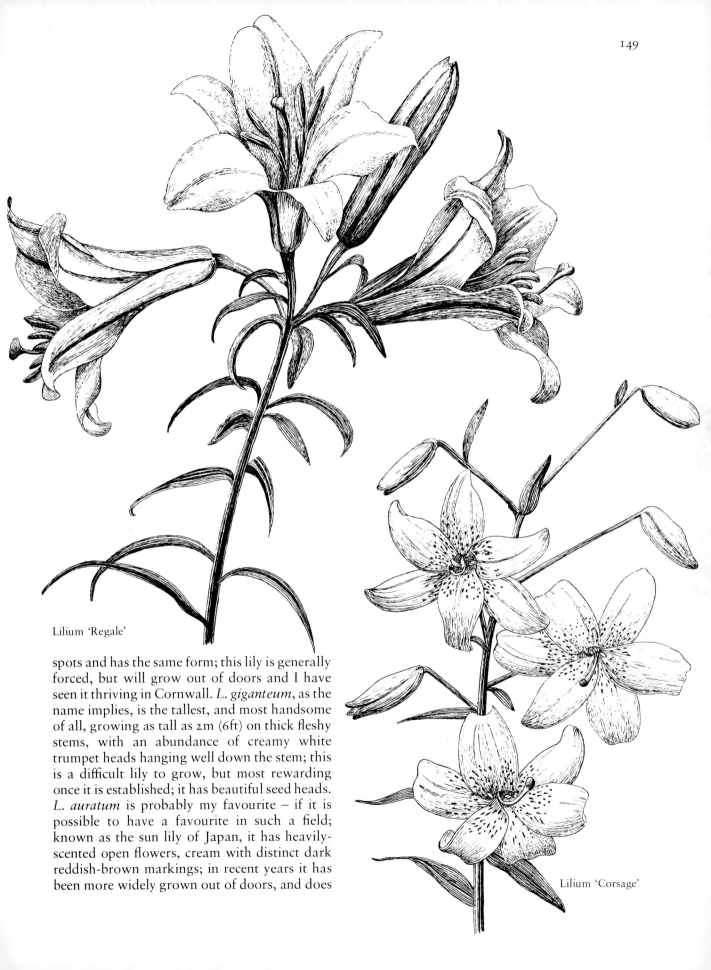

Lilium 'Regale'

spots and has the same form; this lily is generally
forced, but will grow out of doors and I have
seen it thriving in Cornwall. *L. giganteum*, as the
name implies, is the tallest, and most handsome
of all, growing as tall as 2m (6ft) on thick fleshy
stems, with an abundance of creamy white
trumpet heads hanging well down the stem; this
is a difficult lily to grow, but most rewarding
once it is established; it has beautiful seed heads.
L. auratum is probably my favourite – if it is
possible to have a favourite in such a field;
known as the sun lily of Japan, it has heavily-
scented open flowers, cream with distinct dark
reddish-brown markings; in recent years it has
been more widely grown out of doors, and does

Lilium 'Corsage'

very well, and I would thoroughly recommend it. The new American De Graaff lilies are superb; 'Limelight', one of the most beautiful, is a clear-yellow trumpet lily and I cannot begin to describe how good it can look in a vase of green and golds. The newer varieties of Mid-Century Hybrids, particularly 'Destiny' and 'Enchantment' are more robust in the garden than many, and for flower arrangers 'Corsage', pinkish with a green stripe, which I came across in the United States, is a real find.

These are but a few of this very wide range. They are a great stand-by as a cut flower and anyone who has to do many flower groups welcomes them with open arms as they have a quality and shape that makes them invaluable, they show up well from a long distance – an important asset – and also they last longer in water than almost any other flower.

Conditioning Cut the ends of the stems on the slant and give a long drink in deep cold water.

Preserving The seed heads of *L. martagon* and *L. giganteum* both dry very well. Pick when the seed head has formed, and either hang them upside down to dry or place the stems in a very small amount of water in an open-necked vase, so that the air can circulate round them; then leave them in a warm temperature.

Lily of the Valley *see* CONVALLARIA

Lime Tree *see* TILIA

Linaria
Toadflax

Hardy annuals and perennials. The annuals, in various shades, make a good splash of colour, especially the small rock varieties. The perennials are spiky and not outstanding, though they look well in a bowl of mixed sweet peas.

Linum
Flax

Hardy annuals and perennials. I advise either *L. perenne* or *L. narbonense* (both perennials),

both of which are the most lovely blue and open in a mass of colour as soon as the sun appears. Better as a garden plant, since they do not really last well in water.

Liquidambar styraciflua
Sweet Gum

Deciduous tree with the most lovely autumn colouring. Like all falling leaves, these will not last for long when standing in water, but a few branches even for a day or two give real pleasure and add colour to any autumn group.

Conditioning Hammer the stems before giving a long drink.

Liriodendron tulipifera
Tulip Tree

Hardy deciduous tree with green and yellow cup-shaped flowers on upturned branches – consequently they are best cut on fairly short stems so as to get the curved stems under water. The most suitable way of arranging them is to float them in a shallow bowl. They are lovely used in floristry; I have seen a bride's bouquet made of them and it was most unusual.

Liriope

L. muscari well describes the violet-blue flower spikes that come out of a mass of grassy leaves in late autumn. Coming so late, they add that much desired bit of blue to a small mixed vase. They seem to flower better in full sun, and thrive in the warmth of the USA where I have picked bunches of their coal-black berries as late as November for a small white and black arrangement. I have rarely been able to do this in England as they tend to get caught early by frost.

Lobelia
Cardinal Flower

Hardy perennials and half-hardy annuals. Perhaps best known to most of us as a little blue or white edging plant, *L. erinus*. The newer varieties of *L. erinus*, 'Pale Blue', 'Cambridge Blue' and 'Blue Cascade', are worthy of a

Linum narbonense

mention here as they are so popular with people making hanging baskets and they really do go on flowering for weeks and weeks. It is a plant I never thought I would ever get excited about and only now realize what good value it is. The scarlet-flowered and crimson-foliaged perennial called *L. cardinalis* or *fulgens*, which is unfortunately only half-hardy, is good as a cut flower and can look very effective if used with mixed reds or in a group of autumn colours.

Conditioning Put the ends of the stems in boiling water for a few minutes, before giving a long drink.

London Pride *see* SAXIFRAGA

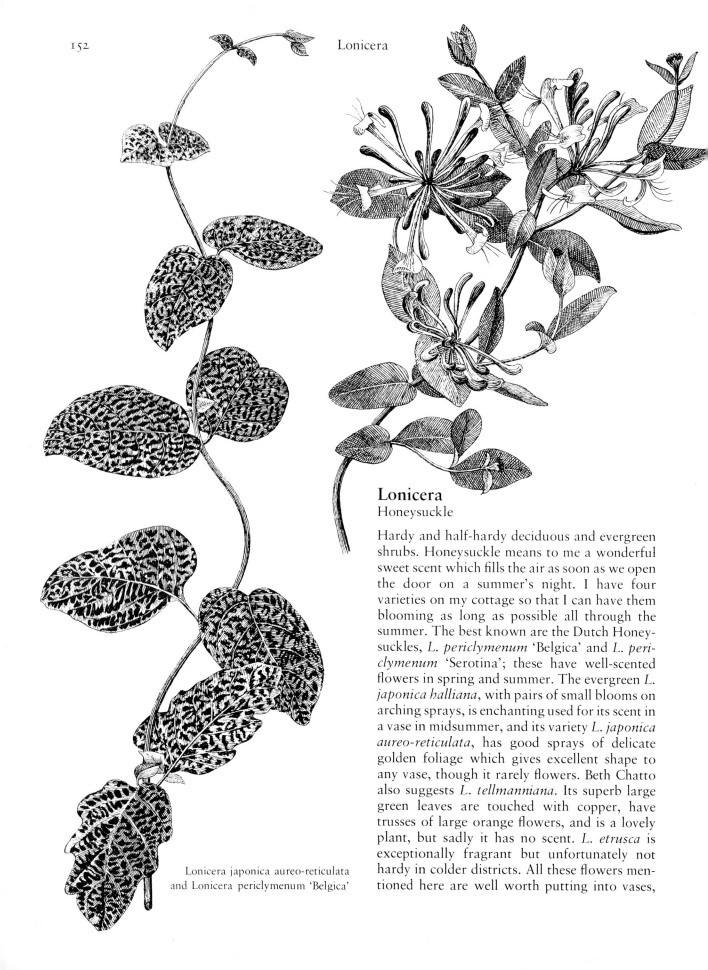

Lonicera japonica aureo-reticulata
and Lonicera periclymenum 'Belgica'

Lonicera
Honeysuckle

Hardy and half-hardy deciduous and evergreen shrubs. Honeysuckle means to me a wonderful sweet scent which fills the air as soon as we open the door on a summer's night. I have four varieties on my cottage so that I can have them blooming as long as possible all through the summer. The best known are the Dutch Honeysuckles, *L. periclymenum* 'Belgica' and *L. periclymenum* 'Serotina'; these have well-scented flowers in spring and summer. The evergreen *L. japonica halliana*, with pairs of small blooms on arching sprays, is enchanting used for its scent in a vase in midsummer, and its variety *L. japonica aureo-reticulata*, has good sprays of delicate golden foliage which gives excellent shape to any vase, though it rarely flowers. Beth Chatto also suggests *L. tellmanniana*. Its superb large green leaves are touched with copper, have trusses of large orange flowers, and is a lovely plant, but sadly it has no scent. *L. etrusca* is exceptionally fragrant but unfortunately not hardy in colder districts. All these flowers mentioned here are well worth putting into vases, even if they do not last so very well, as the scent of even a small spray will fill a room. If you grow plenty, then the nicest way of arrangement is to put a tin or bowl into an old wooden tea-caddy, or box with an open lid, and pack it tightly with stems of honeysuckle.

Lonicera nitida

A small compact-leaved evergreen shrub that is used for making a good hedge. If the bushes are left unclipped, the foliage is useful in winter. 'Baggesens Gold'. This bright golden shrub is worth a place in any garden as it adds that touch of sunlight, and is invaluable as a cut plant. It lasts extremely well in water and is an asset for any yellow toning arrangement, or added to a mixed green.

Lords and Ladies *see* ARUM

Love-in-a-Mist *see* NIGELLA

Love-Lies-Bleeding *see* AMARANTHUS

Lunaria
Common Honesty, Money Flower

Lunaria biennis (or *L. annua*) is the best-known variety, generally used as a winter decoration; the seed heads contain a satiny 'partition' that is very attractive for using with dried flowers in a winter group, or painted with gum and then

Lunaria annua flowers and seed heads

sprinkled with glitter and used with red holly berries for a Christmas decoration. Its purple flower in early spring is nice to have for the colour it gives to the garden and to mix in with a bowl of spring flowers.

Conditioning Put the stems of the flowers in very hot water as soon as they are picked, then give a long drink in cool water.

Preserving As soon as the seed has formed, hang them upside down to dry, then take each dried head between finger and thumb and slip off the outside case to reveal the satiny part. The seed heads can be left on the plant until this takes place naturally, but they so often get badly damaged in wet weather that I would really recommend doing as I suggested at first. Alternatively, you pick the seed heads as soon as they turn colour and instead of hanging them upside down, place the ends of the stems in a solution of glycerine and water; they suck it up and you have lovely cream and brown sprays. Adds quite another dimension to a dried group in winter.

Lungwort *see* PULMONARIA

Lupin *see* LUPINUS

Lupinus
Lupin

Hardy perennials and annuals. The familiar herbaceous lupins stand about 0.6–1.2 m (2–4 ft) in height, coming out in June as one of the earliest and showiest of the herbaceous plants. Thanks to Mr George Russell, who spent the greater part of his life hybridizing these plants, we have today a vastly improved strain, with multi-coloured blooms and a very wide range of colours – bluish-mauve, reds, pinks, yellow, orange and pure white. I like to use, say, a few stems of apricot colours, to add to a vase of apricot foxgloves and some early roses in this colouring, or to add lupins to any vase of really mixed summer flowers. The tree lupin, *L. arboreus*, which is a perennial, has a mass of yellow or white flowers and the most delicious

scent in late June. The annuals come from *L. hartwegii*. Although lupins tend to shed their flowers fairly quickly, I still like to use them.

Conditioning There are many different ideas about what is the best way to make these flowers last. One method is to put the ends of the stems into boiling water for a few seconds, before giving a long drink. Another is to fill the hollow stem with water and then plug the end with cotton wool; this is a lot of trouble, but worth it for some special occasion. The really old-fashioned idea of putting the stems into a weak solution of starch water has the advantage of keeping the flowers from dropping and so is quite a help. They tend to go on growing in water and so to twist their heads round when first picked, but a night in water as soon as they have been picked prevents this from taking place in an arranged vase.

Preserving Pick when the seed head has formed, remove all the foliage and hang in bunches upside down to dry. I should mention here that the Russell and good hybrid varieties should not be allowed to seed, so use your discretion.

Lychnis
Campion, German Catchfly, Scarlet Lychnis, Jerusalem Cross

Hardy perennials. A widely diverse race, varying from tiny *L. alpina* for the rock garden to *L. chalcedonica*, scarlet, and *L. coronaria*, magenta or white, both of which are tall herbaceous plants. Both the white and magenta campions are useful for small groups and have attractive grey foliage. *L. chalcedonica*, the scarlet lychnis, with flat heads of really scarlet flowers in July, is a joy to use in a mixed red group. *L. fulgens*, with a mass of vermilion double flowers, is nice to cut and a very useful edging to the border; it has the added advantage of a long flowering period.

Lysichitum
Skunk Cabbage

Hardy perennial. Water-loving plant with spathes of yellow or white in April and May, followed by a handsome crop of shiny leaves. *L. americanum* has the yellow arum-like spathes and is spectacular rather than beautiful, but is very effective if used in a flat ovenware type of bowl; impale the stems on a pin-holder and cover this with some suitable leaves. I also find the bold green centres useful for putting into a green foliage group, long after the outside of the flower has faded.

Lythrum
Purple Loosestrife

Hardy perennial. Tall stems of magenta flowers in late summer, useful to add a touch of the unusual to a vase of other shades of red. It also adds good colour to the flower border.

Conditioning Put the ends of the stems into a little boiling water, before giving a long drink.

Macleaya cordata
Bocconia, Plume Poppy

Hardy perennial. Useful for the back of the border and as a background for large groups of flowers. The fine sprays of buff flowers fade as the summer goes, forming elegant tracery for use in winter.

Conditioning Never pick until the flowers are fully open up to the tip of the stem. The stems must be boiled for a few minutes and then left to stand in deep water for twelve hours.

Preserving Cut sprays from the plant when already dry and store till required.

Madonna Lily *see* LILIUM CANDIDUM

Magnolia
Cucumber Tree, Yulan

Hardy deciduous and evergreen shrubs and trees. Of the deciduous ones a favourite is *M.*

Magnolia stellata

stellata, flowering early in spring; its white star-like flowers burst out of grey-green fur coats, on beautifully shaped branches that need little or no arranging as they look quite their best alone, in a bowl of celadon green or a glass bowl. *M. soulangeana* has large chalice-shaped white flowers flushed with purple outside, flowering on bare branches in April, but it has one of the longest flowering periods and often the flowers are still visible in June when the leaves have opened out. Again it is quite lovely alone in a vase, or it can be arranged with any other flower that picks up the colouring. *M. watsonii* has a more open flower and a very sweet scent. Of course there are many more of these deciduous varieties. Among the evergreens, *M. grandiflora* (or laurel magnolia) is usually treated as a wall plant as it needs this protection in a cold climate;

its beautiful large glossy leaves are from my point of view even more valuable than the flowers, very handsome as these are – and sweetly scented; these flowers are only suitable to use in really large groups, or perhaps floating in a bowl.

Conditioning Hammer the ends of the stems very well, before putting into really hot water, and allow this to cool off before taking out the stems to arrange.

Preserving The leaves of M. *grandiflora* take up a solution of glycerine with very worth while results. It is also possible to skeletonize the leaves in a strong solution of soda and water. As this is a very slow and rather difficult process, many people prefer to buy them ready treated – they are preserved in this form in the East. The method is a well-kept secret and I would just love to know how they do it!

Mahonia

Mahonia japonica, M. *bealei*, the hybrid mahonia 'Charity' and *Mahonia aquifolium*, related to the berberis, are winter-flowering with beautiful foliage and sprays of pale-yellow, sweet-scented flowers from January onwards; after the flowers have fallen the berries are bluish-green, turning purple on arching delicate sprays which look well in a small vase.

Conditioning Hammer the ends of the stems, or peel off some bark – up to about 5cm (2in) – to make absorption of water easier.

Maidenhair Fern *see* ADIANTUM

Maintaining *see* CONDITIONING AND MAINTAINING

Malcomia maritima
Virginia Stock

Hardy annual. Star-like flowers in various colours on stems 18cm (7in) long; useful for small mixed vases or to add a spiky background to self-coloured arrangements.

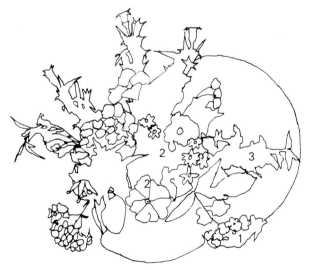

An arrangement made in a sauce boat in Spode blue and white china, blending the colours of china and flowers together.
1 *Hydrangea*
2 *Petunia*
3 *Gentian asclepiadea* (Willow gentian)

Malus
Crab Apple

Ornamental trees, spring-flowering in shades of pink, red and white. Many produce decorative fruits in autumn. One of the most popular is M. *baccata*, the red Siberian crab, with richly-coloured autumn fruits, and white flowers in April. M. *eleyi* is perhaps my favourite as it has coppery-coloured foliage, rosy when young, with red flowers and purple-red fruit, so that it is decorative all the year round; I like to use it in all its stages. It is lovely in the spring with pink tulips, and the fruits are attractive in autumn groups. It lasts better than any other blossom. M. *floribunda* has dark-green leaves and red flower buds opening to pale pink. The fruiting crabs are also well worth a mention as they are excellent for using in the autumn, 'Dartmouth', 'Golden Hornet' and others, all making trees about 6m (20ft) high.

Conditioning Hammer or scrape the stems, before giving a long drink in water.

Maranta

M. *leuconeura kerchoveana* is a good ornamental house plant which I find useful planted in miniature indoor gardens, in winter and early spring. The leaves have dark spotted markings, but although extremely decorative, they do not last well in water.

Marguerite *see* CHRYSANTHEMUM

Marigold *see* CALENDULA

Masterwort *see* ASTRANTIA

Matthiola
Ten-week, Brompton and Night-scented Stocks

Hardy and half-hardy annuals and biennials. With the exception of the sweetly scented M. *bicornis*, or night-scented stock, which is lovely in the garden but of little value as a cut flower, the stock family provides some of the best

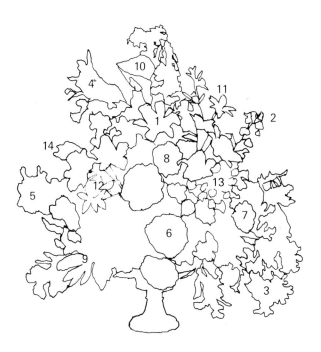

The joy of summer flowers.
1 *Lilium regale*
2 *Lilium martagon*
3 *Campanula lactiflora* 'Loddon Anna' (Bellflower)
4 Flowering branches of *tilia* (Lime)
5 *Alchemilla mollis* (Lady's mantle)
6 Rose 'Constance Spry'
7 Rose 'Chaucer'
8 Rose 'Magenta'
9 *Paeonia* foliage
10 Green *arum*
11 *Eryngium giganteum*
12 *Nicotiana affinis* 'Lime Green' (Tobacco plant)
13 *Heracleum sphondylium* (Hogweed, Cow parsnip)
14 Berries

flowers for arrangement. They are widely grown and also cultivated under glass, so that they are available for many months of the year. The ten-week stock, so named because it flowers about ten weeks after the seed has been sown in March, has a very good range of delicate off-beat colours, in pale yellow, soft pink, deep crimson, pale and deep mauve, and one called 'Antique Copper' which is just as its name suggests. These mix well in all types of arrangements, they add a useful splash of colour, and tuck well into the centre of any vase. East Lothian stocks, if sown in February, usually come into flower in July. The Bromptons, on the other hand, are hardy biennials and the seed should be sown in June to produce flowers the following summer.

Conditioning Stocks have a very woody stem that needs to be treated rather like a branch and should be hammered well; or the ends should be put into boiling water for a few minutes, before having a long drink. It is also very important to remove any leaves that go under the water-level, as they quickly make the water smelly and unpleasant.

Meadow Saffron *see* COLCHICUM

Meconopsis
Himalayan Poppy, Welsh Poppy

M. betonicifolia baileyi, the glorious blue bien-nial poppy, I have only now and again had the chance of putting into a flower arrangement, but on those few occasions they were really delight-ful. However, as they do not last very well in water, it is perhaps better to enjoy them out of doors. The yellow varieties (*M. cambrica* and *M. integrifolia*) are also attractive and have such beautiful hairy foliage that this is an added inducement for cutting. When using the flowers, it is better to cut the stems fairly short so as to see into the face of the flower, as they tend to hang their heads.

Conditioning Put the ends of the stems in boiling water, before giving a drink.

Megasea *see* BERGENIA

Melissa officinalis
Common Balm

Hardy herbaceous perennials which I like to grow for the fun of pinching the leaves as I pass to keep the delicious scent of the aromatic foliage on my hands. The yellow variegated balm *M. officinalis* 'Aurea' is one of the nicest to use in a vase, and *M.o.* 'All Gold' has really gold leaves all summer, but it is advisable to plant in partial shade as the leaves are very delicate and scorch in bright sunlight.

Conditioning The foliage does not last well, but I love it so much that I use a branch for a day or so and then replace it. It helps to put the ends of the stems into boiling water for a few seconds and then give a long drink; or better still sub-merge the whole stem in water overnight.

Melon *see* CANTALOUP MELON

Mentha
Mint, Pennyroyal

Hardy perennial with aromatic foliage, best known for its culinary use. However, there are many varieties that make it worthy of mention here. The pineapple mint *rotundifolia variegata*, is most effective as ground cover, and lovely to use in flower arrangements, as the leaves are heavily splashed with white, and often produce all-white shoots, good for foliage arrangements. Another is the golden yellow *M. gentilis aurea variegata*. They all make excellent ground cover, and are nice picked and put into small vases in late summer.

Conditioning Put ends of stems in boiling water and give a long drink before arranging.

Preserving Strip the leaves from the stems and dry in a warm place for mixing in pot-pourri.

Mesembryanthemum
Ice Plant

The half-hardy annual *M. criniflorum* is a brilliantly colourful little daisy-like flower, used as a rock plant or edging plant and at its best when enjoying hot sunshine. Not really a very good subject from the flower arranger's point of view; it can look attractive at the centre of a small vase, but has the habit of shutting up at night, which can be disappointing.

Michaelmas Daisy *see* ASTER

Michauxia campanuloides

This is a biennial so needs re-seeding if you want to have it constantly. A really dramatic plant, 1m (3ft) tall with spikes of drooping flowers rather resembling a turned-back bell, white suffused with purple outside. I have not had the opportunity to use these very often, but they need to be used almost alone or with their heads held high above any other flower in the vase. They are so effective that you want to make the most of the structure of each flower. They look splendid arranged alone with a base of deep purple *rhus cotinus* or beetroot, which carry the colour of the petals through to the base of the vase.

Conditioning Put the ends of the stems into boiling water and then allow a long drink before arranging.

Mignonette *see* RESEDA

Mimosa *see* ACACIA

Mimulus guttatus

The spotted musk, yellow and Indian red, are showy little plants which bloom for an extremely long time, and are water-loving. I find they grow well in a damp spot in partial shade. The small stems last very well in water and add a touch of yellow to a mixed flower arrangement all through the summer. 'Wisley Red' is a splendid invention, a vigorous plant with rich deep red blooms.

Conditioning Place the ends in warm water; avoid boiling as the stems are so fleshy that the hot water destroys them completely.

Miscanthus sinensis

Hardy ornamental green and creamy-yellow striped grass, decorative in the border and when used to add a spiky effect to a group of rounded and more solid leaves. More effective in its early stages in May, when the leaves are at their best.

Mistletoe *see* VISCUM

Mock Orange *see* PHILADELPHUS

Molucella laevis
Molucca Balm, Bells of Ireland

M. laevis, sometimes better known as the Shell Flower, is grown as an annual – and what a popular plant it has become! It produces spikes of shell-shaped flowers all up the stem, green to start with but a soft parchment colour when preserved. The stems take on lovely shapes, which for the flower arranger is an added

Molucella laevis

attraction. They are charming arranged alone on a pin-holder in a shallow dish, or in a dried group with pressed ferns and seed heads, to which one can add a few fresh flowers. This flower is widely used, preserved and fresh, in America and Australia.

Conditioning Remove all the leaves so that the shell flowers are shown off to their best advantage, cut the stems on the slant and give a long drink.

Preserving When the leaves have been removed, the flowers can be preserved by hanging the heads upside down and then spraying the stems with clear lacquer to prevent the flowers from falling off. Another method is to stand them in glycerine for four days and then hang them upside down to produce firm stems from top to bottom.

Monarda didyma
Sweet Bergamot

Sweet bergamot is a hardy herbaceous plant, with fragrant mint-like foliage and whorls of pink or red hooded flowers on erect stems in August. 'Croftway Pink' and 'Magnifica' are clear rose and deep rose pink respectively. 'Cambridge Scarlet' is a good clear red.

Conditioning Put the ends of the stems into boiling water, before giving a long drink.

Money Flower *see* LUNARIA

Monkshood *see* ACONITUM

Monstera deliciosa
Shingle Plant

Tender greenhouse evergreen climber with outstandingly handsome deeply-cut large leaves. The pineapple-flavoured cylindrical fruits are very good to eat, but are also excellent as the centre of a vase, especially a vase of foliage. The leaves can be used very effectively at the base of any large group. They grow to immense height in the tropics, and they make a distinctive

decoration. They are in front of the town hall in Brisbane, Australia, growing to well over 2.5m (8ft).

Conditioning The leaves need several hours in deep water once they have been cut; to maintain their glossy appearance it is a good idea to wash them in milk and water every few weeks. The fruits are best given a long drink and then placed in rather shallow water, either on a pin-holder or with the stems just under the water-level.

Montbretia *see* CROCOSMIA

Moraea
Butterfly Iris

M. *spathacea* has clear yellow iris-like flowers that last well in water and mix well in a vase to give a good colour contrast, such as green and yellow or – better still – black and yellow with near-black tulips. They also have good seed heads for winter.

Preserving Let the seed heads form, and then bunch and hang upside down.

Morina longifolia
Whorl Flower

This handsome herbaceous plant is valuable for foliage, flower and seed head. As the pet name implies, the flowers are in whorls, hooded and tubular, in white turning to pale and then deep pink with exotic green stems, lovely for green arrangements. The stems dry well for winter.

Preserving As the flowers fade, place the cut stems in a container of shallow water and leave them to dry off slowly.

Mullein *see* VERBASCUM

Muscari
Grape Hyacinth

Hardy bulbs, 15cm (6in) high, with blue heads in spikes of very close bells, suitable for small borders or the rock garden. Useful in spring to add to a moss garden in the house, taking the place of the earlier Glory of the Snow; or they can be used in a mixed vase of, say, fritillaries and some of the species tulips. The small white one, *Muscari botryoides album*, is a pet. The blues are very varied and have quite a long flowering period.

Preserving The seed heads are very effective and although it is not advisable to let too many go to seed, the delicate stems are nice to have. I think it is best to stand them in a little water, and let them gradually dry off; if they are hung bunched upside down, they shed very quickly.

Myosotis
Forget-me-not

Hardy perennial but usually grown as a biennial. Short-stemmed blue flowers in May and June, compact and good as an edging or in a small border. They add just the right touch of blue to a small vase and look childlike and pretty used with small pink and white daisies for a font decoration.

Conditioning Cut in small bunches and give a long drink before arranging. If used in small bunches for a font decoration, I would advise securing with elastic bands or tying with string for easier handling.

Myrtus communis
Myrtle

Greenhouse and half-hardy evergreen shrub with compact green leaves and small fluffy white flowers in January and February under glass, or following later outdoors in the extreme south of England. A traditional flower for a bride's bouquet. I often have the opportunity of using it in the very early spring, and it looks most attractive with white hyacinths and sprays of the indoor *Jasminum polyanthum*, arranged in a white porcelain vase or a trumpet-shaped glass vase which allows the stems to cascade.

Narcissus
Daffodil, Jonquil

Hardy bulbs. We commonly apply the name narcissus to the small-cupped varieties, though the daffodil in all its forms comes under this heading in all the botanical journals. The genus is enormous and I cannot begin to name even half of them. I personally really prefer the short trumpet types for flower arrangement, and find the very big heads of 'King Alfred' extremely difficult to do anything with. The very first narcissi to come on the market just before Christmas are Paper White, worth buying for their lovely scent alone; they arrange well in a vase of evergreen oak with some lemons, as they look so like orange or lemon blossom. The first of the trumpet type could be 'Golden Harvest', and to make the most of these I suggest arranging them in a basket, in which a baking tin or an ovenware dish is filled with wire netting and disguised by a layer of green moss; place the flowers in clumps with a branch of forsythia or catkins, and a single bunch will go a long way. A basket is always a nice container for these flowers and later on, if you can pick them freely from the garden, you can discard the moss and just have a mass of blooms. Having straight stems they do not lend themselves to complicated groups of mixed flowers; see the arrangement on page 67. The dwarf varieties of narcissus such as *N. cyclamineus*, *N. bulbocodium* and *N. triandrus albus* (the Angel's Tears daffodil) are suitable for the rock garden. Two dwarf varieties that I love are 'Silver Chimes' and 'April Tears', and I use them for small vases in the spring. Many types force very well in bowls for the house in either fibre or shingle and water. Some of my pet varieties are 'Beersheba' (a large pure-white trumpet), or any of the white-backed types, 'Geranium', 'February Gold' (as it comes so early), 'Primrose Phoenix', 'Pheasant Eye' . . . , but there are of course so many more.

Conditioning Bear in mind that the flowers last better in shallow water.

Nasturtium *see* TROPAEOLUM

Nemesia

Half-hardy annuals. The new hybrid varieties
have a good range of colour, in tones of pinks to
a lovely blue. They are generally used as edging
plants, but small pieces picked for the house and
put into little mixed vases are pretty.

Nepeta
Catmint

Hardy herbaceous perennial. *N. mussinii*, sometimes known as *N. faassenii*, is really loved by
cats and this is surely how it got its pet name. It
has feathery spikes of purple flowers in June and
July; useful as a background in a vase of summer
flowers. My earliest recollection of it is seeing it
arranged with pink or white garden pinks; my
mother always used it in this way on our dining-
room table at home. It lasts extremely well in
water and needs no special treatment.

Nephrolepsis exaltata
Ladder Fern

N. exaltata is not hardy but can be grown very
easily as a house plant. The unfurling shoots of
the new growth are enchanting and from the
moment they appear I use it all the time. It
sometimes remains green for much of the winter,
but even when it goes rather brown it nevertheless looks effective to add delicate outline to a
few flowers.

Conditioning Lasts extremely well, but the
young growth is better if it is submerged in
warm water for a few hours.

Preserving Place the stems between sheets of
newspaper and press under the carpet or some
heavy weight.

Nerine
Guernsey Lily

Greenhouse bulbous plant. *N. sarniensis* has
brilliant scarlet flowers in the autumn. They are
quite one of the most lovely of all the bulbs; their
petals have a sheen that makes them look as if
they had been painted with a touch of gold on

Nerine bowdenii

the brush. *N. bowdenii*, a semi-hardy bulb, is
grown out of doors in a mild climate; with
upright pink lily-like flowers, and flowering as it
does in the autumn, it is a great attraction to any
garden and a joy to pick. I love to use the scarlet
variety with some autumn-tinted leaves and
sprays of berries; or sometimes to stand just
three in a shallow dish with a branch of lichen.
The pink variety also looks well when arranged
like this, or can be put with a mixture of varying
shades of pink. *N. crispula* has enchanting
dainty flowers paler than *bowdenii*, petals rather
crimped and smaller so useful for delicate
arrangements. Lastly the white nerine is beautiful, but more tender and though I have managed

to keep it under a south wall for two winters I feel I have been lucky.

Conditioning Cut the ends of the stems on the slant and give a long drink.

New Zealand Flax *see* PHORMIUM

Nicotiana alata
Tobacco Plant, Sweet-scented Tobacco

Half-hardy annuals in soft mixed colours, but the green variety sometimes called 'Limelight' has become extremely popular with flower arrangers – and rightly so. Its soft lime colour blends well with almost any colour combination that you can think of. Its starry open flowers look nice in a mixed green group or with summer flowers. I see that Unwins named one 'Really Green', and it really is one of the best greens I have seen. Last year I had one with a brown back and good green flower. We saved the seed and this year have some marvellous plants true in colour. I hope to keep it going as it is quite superb.

Conditioning These flowers last better, I think, if they are placed in warm water before they are arranged.

Nigella
Love-in-a-Mist

Hardy annual with small blue flowers that are surrounded by a frill of feathery green. They produce a good seed head in autumn, useful for winter decoration. The flowers themselves are most attractive arranged with small rose-buds and garden pinks. They are so delicate that they are welcome for any posy, to put on a coffee table or in a guest's bedroom.

Preserving As soon as the seed head has set, pick carefully and remove all the foliage before hanging in bunches upside-down to dry.

Night-scented Stock *see* MATTHIOLA

Norway Maple *see* ACER PLATANOIDES

Nicotiana affinis

Nymphaea
Water Lily

Tender and hardy aquatic plants that flower on English ponds in July, and grow beautifully and in abundance in the southern states of the United States. The flowers are so lovely to use but they have one great snag, as they close up after they have been cut; there are several ways of trying to prevent this but I have never been very fortunate with them. They are most effective used for a table arrangement, and can be persuaded to last just long enough. Arrange them with the leaves of *Bergenia cordifolia*, which are as like their own as any you can find and they last so much better. I remember once using these flowers with blocks of polished glass on a large circular glass tray, giving the effect of clear water; the effect was delightful. I have also seen a bride's bouquet made of them, which looked simply lovely. It is possible to wire them so that they will keep open.

Conditioning There are several methods, but the one I would suggest is to try the Japanese idea of injecting them with pure alcohol; I understand this usually keeps them open successfully. Some people hold the flowers very near to the light, which seems to encourage them to unfold. For very important occasions we can keep them open by force, by dropping melted wax between each petal; in this way they cannot possibly close.

Odontoglossum

One of the loveliest of orchids. Very small mauve, brown and greenish flat flowers on arching sprays, unlike the lipped orchids. Some of the varieties are imported nowadays from Singapore and so we have the opportunity to buy and enjoy them.

Conditioning Cut the ends of the stems on the slant and give a good drink. Remove and recut before replacing in fresh water.

Oenothera
Evening Primrose, Tree Primrose

Hardy biennials and perennials. The most popular biennial is *O. biennis*, with pale yellow flowers, growing about 1.2–1.5m (4–5ft) tall. The perennial *O. fruticosa* has golden-yellow open cup-like flowers alternately up the stem; it lasts better in water than one would think, as every flower bud will open out, but I find it

almost more useful in the green seed head stage; this I use whenever possible, in cool green groups for a hot sunny day.

Conditioning Put the ends of the stems into boiling water for a few seconds, before giving a long drink.

Preserving When the green seed heads have formed, pick them and remove all the leaves, then bunch and hang them upside down to dry. If, however, you are using these heads in a vase, you will find that they will dry off by themselves; after that, you can store them away until you need them.

Old Man's Beard *see* CLEMATIS VITALBA

Olearia
New Zealand Daisy Bush

Hardy evergreen bush with clusters of white daisy flowers. The one I like best is *O. haastii* because it flowers in July and August and is very useful to mix with white godetia, a white lily or two, and perhaps some sweet peas.

Conditioning Scrape well up the ends of the stems and place in warm water.

Olearia scilloniensis

Oleaster *see* ELAEAGNUS ANGUSTIFOLIA

Omphalodes

Forget-me-not-like blue flowers in April–May, and will tolerate shade. Alan Bloom's variety 'Anthea Bloom' is undoubtedly one of the best. It is one of those small flowers that give the touch of blue so valuable for any mixed flower arrangement.

Conditioning Never let the flowers stand out of water for any length of time, pick into a plastic bag to shut out the air. Like forget-me-nots, once they wilt it is hard to get them to pick up again.

Onopordon acanthium
Cotton Thistle, Scots Thistle

The hardy perennial 'Scots Thistle' *O. acanthium* is an outstandingly beautiful plant. As it grows to at least 2m (6ft) it naturally needs a lot of space, but is well worth growing if you have room. It has a statuesque beauty that is excellent in silhouette. Extremely prickly, the stems are flanged with grey cotton-wool-like flounces, making a candelabra effect with the grey thistle heads, at which stage they are quite lovely before the heads burst into purple. I like to use them in all stages: the grey leaves in winter, with 'mixed greens'; then the whole branch in midsummer, beautiful either alone or in a big church group, with whites and greys or blues; the flowers of course look good in a vase of purples or mauves. They dry well and add to any collection of grey dried flowers or seed heads.

Conditioning The stems are better if they are put into boiling water for a little while before they have a long drink.

Preserving When the thistles have reached the seed head stage, pick and hang them upside down to dry.

Ophiopogon

O. planiscapus nigrescens has the appearance of tufted grass but is actually a member of the Liriope family. I have only just become acquainted with this little plant and find the very dark foliage, as near to black as you will get, a marvellous foil at the end of the border for foliage plants such as euonymus. I use a few of the spiky leaves as counterpoint in a small flower arrangement. The flowers are not very spectacular but it is a good plant for contrast.

Opium Poppy *see* PAPAVER

Orchid

I have mentioned earlier some of the best orchids for flower arrangement (see cymbidium, cypripedium, odontoglossum) but as this is such a large family, with perhaps well over five hundred genera, you may well have the opportunity of using many more. They are quite one of the best-lasting flowers in water and personally I love to use them whenever possible.

Oriental Poppy *see* PAPAVER

Ornithogalum
Chincherinchee, Star of Bethlehem

Hardy and greenhouse bulbous plant. The best-known to most of us is the South African Chincherinchee (*O. thyrsoides*), which gets its name from the funny squeaky sound the stems make as the wind blows on them across the Veldt. They are exported, arriving with a great welcome at Christmas time, and when the wax end is cut off and they are placed in warm water, they gradually open out and last in water for weeks. They look most attractive if arranged with berried holly, or with sprays of yellow jasmine just after Christmas. The hardy variety that I like to grow is *O. nutans*, which has spikes of white star-like flowers with greenish-grey centres; they flower in June and are a welcome addition to a green and white vase. *O. umbellatum*, which most of us know as Star of Bethlehem, grows wild in the west of England, and spreads almost too rapidly for the average garden. It must be picked for the house in full sunlight or when the flowers are open, as they are temperamental about opening indoors. I like

Ornithogalum nutans

their starry innocent-looking flowers massed in a shallow bowl. The chincherinchee will grow well in northern latitudes, but flowering as it does in July is not nearly as desirable then, when we already have so much to pick.

Conditioning The chincherinchees come with wax on the bottom of their stems which must be cut off. Then they need to be stood in warm water for a little while, remaining afterwards in deep water for several days to open out well, before they are arranged.

Osmanthus
Fragrant Olive, Holly-leaved Olive

Hardy and half-hardy evergreen shrubs. The spring-flowering *O. delavayi* (now also called *Siphonosmanthus delavayi*) has small white flowers and a delicious scent. *O. ilicifolius* (*O. aquifolium*), on the other hand, flowers in July. Both are good as a background for delicate flowers.

Osmunda
Royal Fern, Flowering Fern

Hardy deciduous ferns with tall handsome fronds. They are water-lovers and thrive in moist conditions. It is advisable to press them before using them, as they quickly curl if brought into a warm room. They turn very good autumn colours and make a delightful backing for autumn and winter flower arrangements. *Osmunda regalis*, the royal fern, is better known than *O. cinnamomea*, which has wide curling fronds at the tip of the stem.

Preserving Press the fronds at all stages, so that you get a wide colour range: some while green, and some when they have changed to their lovely golden and bronze tones. Spread them carefully between newspaper and place them under the carpet or under some suitable weight.

Ox-eye Daisy *see* CHRYSANTHEMUM

Oxypetalum caeruleum

This beautiful plant with its unique colour of greeny-blue is a delight but it is very difficult to obtain. Recently I did have some given me in the United States and used it with the palest pink roses – it was a mixture that would be hard to forget.

Conditioning Place the ends of the stems under a lighted match for a few seconds and then give a long drink in deep water. You *can* place them in boiling water but it is risky as the stems are so tender.

Paeonia
Paeony, Peony

Hardy herbaceous and shrubby perennials. The shrubby kinds, or the 'tree peonies', are lovely to grow and much hardier than is often supposed. Native to China and the Himalayas, they can stand quite a lot of frost in winter, but the young growth objects to cold winds and needs a little protection from a wall. They are slow-growing except for *P. lutea ludlowii*, with its single sweet-scented flowers and good seed heads. *P. delavayi* has the small single maroon blooms that are particularly nice to arrange with sprays of purple plum, and yellow-green leaves of the hosta for contrast. The Japanese, Chinese and French varieties, either double or single, but all with enormous heads that look as though the stems could not hold them, are in my opinion quite wonderful. They come in shades of pink, red, orange and white. To name a few: 'Hakugan' (single white, with golden stamens and petals like silk), 'Haruno-akebono' (white, flushed with pink), 'Elizabeth' (coral pink, double, of great beauty), 'Souvenir de Ducher' (double magenta flowers), 'Horaisan' (pink).

The herbaceous peonies are some of the loveliest subjects for flower arrangement; they are so bold that they can take the centre of any group, and are wonderful to use in any large flower vase for church or a special occasion. The delicate pinks and whites are my favourites, but I have found that the magenta red does something to a vase of mixed reds that is hard to describe. The soft shell-pinks seem more delicate than in any other flower; a vase of these with branches of lime flowers stripped of their foliage, and apricot foxgloves, is about as perfect as any arrangement I know. Good varieties are 'Messagera' (creamy white), 'Mai fleuri' (ivory), 'Phillippe Rivoire' (crimson), 'China Rose' (pink), 'Sarah Bernhardt' (deep pink). Two of the singles I would recommend are *P. lactiflora whitleyi major* (superb white with golden stamens, and with dark reddish foliage) and *P. emodii* (a smaller white flower, often bearing more than one head on a branch; it has clusters of yellow stamens, a delicious scent and a good seed head). Some of the 'Sylvia Sanders' hybrid peonies, they are all singles, are thrilling. 'Janice' is one of the first to flower, and is salmon pink. I have several others but they are not named. Any peony, whether single or double, is a superb focal point in an arrangement.

Conditioning The French peonies come over in pads, never having been in water at all, and as

Paeonia lactiflora whitleyi major

they last so well it started us thinking at Winkfield, and we have done a little experimenting. I find that if I pick peonies fresh and leave them out of water to dehydrate, as it were, this is all to the good; they can be left on a cold stone floor for some days. Or if they are cut and placed in a polythene bag, they will keep for several weeks in a cold room. Then cut the ends of the stems and finally put them in warm water for a long drink.

Pampas Grass *see* CORTADERIA

Pansy *see* VIOLA

Papaver
Poppy

There are both hardy annual and perennial poppies and I like them all, though my favourites are, I think, the Orientals and Sutton's art shades. These latter have a range of off-beat

Papaver

colours which look as if they have all been painted with a touch of grey. They have all the soft pink and mauve colours and are so muted that they blend with anything, for instance with any bluish colours, the soft pink of the Preston hybrid lilacs, muted pink and mauvey delphiniums, and of course pink roses. *P. nudicaule*, or the Iceland poppy, is a perennial, though it is often better grown as a biennial. Its flowers come in the clearest orange, apricot and yellows, and are best picked in bud and allowed to open in water. They look well when arranged in a basket or bowl with a collection of feathery grasses; or some of their subtle colours blend well with a vase in tones of cream or apricot. The Iceland poppy, Unwin's 'Champagne Bubbles', is really one of the most delightful plants I have seen in a long time, these poppies vary in shade through apricot, white, cream to rosy red, last well in water and are a joy for the house and garden. Germination is not easy, but they are really worth while. The Shirley poppy, *P. rhoeas*, is truly an annual and gives a lot of colour in the garden, and the pink and white are pretty for use in midsummer. The Opium poppy, *P. somniferum*, is worth growing for the seed heads alone.

Conditioning It is very important to burn or boil the ends of the stems, by dipping the stems into boiling water for a few minutes, before giving a long drink. The flowers tend to fall quickly; to make the most of every minute of their short lives, pick them just as they are bursting and showing colour.

Preserving The seed heads of *P. orientale* and *P. somniferum* dry very well. Remove all the foliage and bunch them, then hang them upside down to dry.

Parrot Tulips *see* TULIPA

Parrotia persica
Persian Ironwood

Hardy deciduous tree. *P. persica* makes a beautiful specimen tree with ovate green leaves in summer and rich autumn colouring. Any shrub with a good tinted foliage is well worth growing, and small pieces added to a vase in September and October give a glow that is hard to describe. However, pick with great care so as not to spoil the shape of a young tree; and remember that no foliage that has gone a good colour will last very long.

Conditioning Hammer the ends of the hard woody stems well and give a good drink in deep water before arranging.

Parthenocissus
Virginia Creeper

Climber with brilliant coloured leaves in the autumn. The leaves do not last at all well in water, but it is possible to use them for a day or so although you will find that they quickly curl up. They must be pressed.

Preserving To press the leaves when coloured, put them carefully between sheets of newspaper and place them under a weight. The stalks usually fall off when pressed, so that it is necessary to make a false stem; this can be done by putting florist's wire up the back and securing with adhesive tape. In this way the wire can be put into the vase in place of the stem.

Pasque Flower *see* PULSATILLA

Passiflora
Passion Flower

The flower gets its name from the idea that it represents features of the Crucifixion. *P. caerulea,* the almost-hardy blue passion flower, is well worth growing where the climate permits. It does better with the heat from a wall, so that the warmth ripens the wood and enables it to withstand the winter. The flowers are quite beautiful, and make a spectacular addition to a fruit and flower group in the summer. The orange fruits are also attractive for flower arrangement. The greenhouse species, *P. incarnata*, white and purple, is a fine specimen if you have the space for it. The edible variety *quadrangularis* or 'Granadilla' I have enjoyed in Australia in their famous Pavlova sweet. The flowers are most interesting. They need a lot of warmth but could be grown in a heated greenhouse.

Conditioning The flowers themselves last quite well when picked, but if you are picking a trail it is important to put the ends of the stems into boiling water, afterwards submerging the whole thing in a bath of cold water for several hours.

Passion Flower *see* PASSIFLORA

Paulownia

P. fargesii, this lovely tree that we see so rarely, does deserve a mention. Its fragrant lilac-scented flowers hang in clusters and resemble a foxglove. In full sun and sheltered from the wind it should be quite hardy. Having seen several growing in Seattle I am looking forward to planting one myself. I have never had the opportunity of using it for flower arranging but I introduce it here to make people aware of this really beautiful tree. Like so many of our lovely trees and shrubs it comes from China. It ranges in height from 4.5–9m (15–30ft).

Pearly Everlasting *see* ANAPHALIS

Passiflora caerulea

Pelargonium
Geranium

Greenhouse perennials. I always find their naming confusing, *Pelargonium* being the authentic botanical name, but then so-called 'geraniums' being so well known as such that I never think or talk of them as anything but geraniums. The scarlet 'geraniums' are all *Pelargoniums* of hybrid origin. These are now divided into several groups: Zonal, Variegated-leaved, Ivy-leaved, Scented-leaved, and Show or Regal Pelargoniums. I love all the unusual colours of the Ivy-leaved and Zonal varieties; the flowers range from petunia and scarlet to the softest pink and lavender. They are all fun to use, giving plenty of scope for ideas, and can often pick up unusual colourings in a flower arrangement. I have put them in a group of mauves with some 'Sterling Silver' roses, purple *Begonia rex* leaves, and side shoots from pink delphiniums. They are splendid arranged in a mass in a shallow bowl with some of their own

Top: Ivy-leaved pelargonium
Below from left to right:
Variegated-leaved, Zonal
and Regal pelargoniums

leaves; packed tightly like this they often seem to last better, or perhaps it is just because they are packed so closely the petals do not get a chance to fall! The Regal *Pelargoniums* have a more open flower and usually a blotch on the petals; these flowers stand very much better in water, and give a different colour range. The soft pinks look well with pink roses and, to provide a contrast, a few deep scarlet roses such as 'Crimson Glory'.

Through the years I have grown the decorative foliaged varieties and enjoyed using them for arrangements all through the summer. 'Mrs Henry Cox' and 'Mrs Burdett-Coutts' are two of the most effective quadri-coloured, the creamy gold leaves erratically marked with blotches of purple, red and green. One of the best for foliage arrangement is undoubtedly 'Golden Crampel', lime-green in colour and lovely for the garden or to cut. The flowers of these decorative foliage geraniums are insignificant. I feel I must mention the scented-leaved varieties brought to England from the Cape by early navigators during the reign of Charles the First, becoming most popular in the Victorian age. *P. capitatum* 'Constance' is used for lining a sponge cake tin, thus giving the cake a delicious flavour. *P. radens*, *P. fragrans*, nutmeg-flavoured, are useful for drying and using in pot-pourri. I love to pinch their leaves as I wander round the garden.

Conditioning By spraying some florist's gum on the backs of the petals, it is possible to prevent them from falling so quickly. It could be that hair-lacquer would be as good.

Penstemon

Hardy and half-hardy shrubby perennials. They can be grown well from seed and I would recommend some of the 'Monarch' strain with a lovely range of colour, and a long period of bloom. For one of the longest flowering you cannot beat 'Cherry' – tall spikes of red flowers about 76cm (2½ft) high. One of the best kinds for a flower vase is the little blue one called *P. heterophyllus*, which stands well in water and is hardy except in the coldest gardens. This adds a lovely bit of blue to any mixed summer vase. The

hybrids are in a magnificent colour range and are excellent in the border, but disappointing when cut as they do not last very well. This is always so sad as the colours are more than tempting to use.

Conditioning Although they do not last well, I have had a certain amount of success by burning the ends and leaving them to have a really good soak, up to their necks in cold water for two days, before arranging.

Peony *see* PAEONIA

Peperomia

A collection of good house plants with decorative leaves, some variegated and others plain, that are most useful to put into planted indoor gardens. The small leaves are individually distinctive at the base of a small mixed green group.

Periwinkle *see* VINCA

Pernettya
Prickly Heath

Low-growing evergreen shrub that has prettily coloured berries in the autumn – crimson, pink and white. Mixed with small button chrysanthemums or pink and red dahlias, they are most unusual and decorative. They are lovers of peat so are not always easy to grow, but they come on sale as cut bunches in the autumn and are deservedly popular.

Conditioning Hammer the stems well, before giving a long drink.

Petasites
Butterbur

A rampant weed, but it blooms in January and February, and so can be most welcome if you have somewhere for it to 'ramp'. *Petasites fragrans* is known as Winter Heliotrope because the vanilla scent of its pink-tinged white flowers is very like that of Cherry Pie. *P. japonicus giganteus* has a cone of lime-green flowers and a frill of leaves at the base of the stem. The flower grows straight out of the ground before the leaves appear. At this stage I use it in a vase of catkins with some of the green hellebore as a focal point. It is very unusual and despite its enormous leaves in summer I am extremely fond of it. The leaves are so large that in Japan the children use them as sunshades.

Conditioning As the flowers have very short stalks when they first appear, it is well to stand them in a teacup of water overnight, when they will grow a little and so be more easily put in a vase.

Petunia

Half-hardy annual. The three best-known kinds are the large-flowered grandiflora, the bedding or multiflora and the double-flowered. The double are, I think, the best for cutting, they last remarkably well; they are most effective alone arranged in delicate porcelain or glass. The bedding varieties, in their vivid colours, make a long-lasting show in the garden and a splash of colour in any small vase.

Conditioning Put the ends of the stems in boiling water for a few minutes, before giving a long drink.

Philadelphus
Mock Orange, 'Syringa'

Beautiful flowering shrubs with a heavy scent and a wealth of white blossom. With such a number of different kinds, you can have a succession blooming through June and July. *P. coronarius*, very early, flowering in June, has rather a twiggy habit, but a lovely scent; it is not grown so much these days. *P. microphyllus*, with small flowers, and *P. grandiflorus*, scentless, but with large flowers, are perhaps more popular. The hybrid *P. lemoinei* has given rise to many varieties with masses of fragrant flowers. Good single ones are 'Avalanche', 'Mont Blanc' and 'Belle Etoile'. 'Boule d'Argent' and 'Virginal' are lovely double varieties. For me they are all lovely, and I think they are perfect for weddings. By removing all the leaves you are left with a mass of white blossom on coal-black branches;

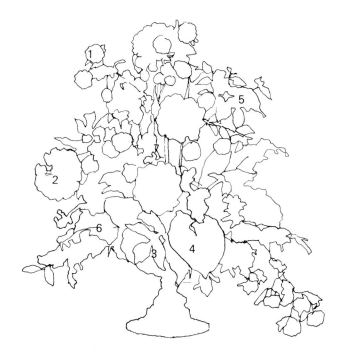

This is a large arrangement of green and white flowers suitable for a wedding or a party where a large group is important.
1 *Viburnum opulus* 'Sterile' (Snowball tree)
2 *Angelica* seed heads
3 *Angelica* foliage
4 *Hosta sieboldiana* 'Francis Williams'
5 *Philadelphus coronarius* 'Aureus' (Mock orange)
6 *Kalanchoe beharensis*
7 *Sansevieria*

Philadelphus 'Belle Etoile'

add to this some tall stems of white delphiniums, a bunch or two of white peonies, a few pink or white roses, and you have the most beautiful bridal flower group imaginable. June to July is the only time of year for a really large, completely white flower group. At any other time there is always an element of green. The small golden-leaved philadelphus, *P. coronarius aureus*, I find extremely useful; it is a compact shrub with delightful lime-green foliage – sweetly-scented, but blooms reluctantly.

Conditioning Hammer ends of stems well, or pare up the bark, and put into warm water immediately. Never leave the stems out of water for long – if they once flag it is very hard to revive them. Remove as many leaves as possible as this shrub finds it extremely difficult to take up enough water to supply both leaves and flowers at once.

Philodendron

P. scandens with its deep-green glossy leaves has become a very useful house plant and is used for many displays for showrooms, restaurants, and hotels.

An arrangement of late spring flowers.
1 *Narcissus triandrus albus* (Angel's tears)
2 *Narcissus* 'February Gold'
3 *Muscari* (Grape hyacinth)
4 *Bellis perennis* (Quilled daisy)
5 Double white primrose
6 *Scilla*
7 *Erica*
8 *Hacquetia epipactis*

Phlomis

P. samia is a perennial herbaceous plant, with heart-shaped, soft weed-smothering foliage also carrying whorls of deep yellow-hooded flowers. *P. fruticosa*, the Jerusalem sage, is a hardy evergreen shrub with whorls of yellow flowers in June. I remove some of the leaves and use these flower spikes quite often; their soft yellow colouring mixes well with a really summery group of lupins, spurges and the lime-green hosta leaves. The green rounded seed heads are nice in late summer for arranging with mixed green foliages.

Preserving Remove all the leaves and hang the seed heads upside down to dry.

Phlox

Half-hardy annuals and hardy perennials. The perennial phlox has become a great favourite of mine over the years, as they bloom for such a long time. Although they thrive on good food and plenty of moisture, they do well in my clay soil and give a wealth of colour for weeks. They are lovely to arrange with a really lavishly mixed summer group. Their vivid colours add gaiety, and the deep reds and petunia shades are excellent for a vase of mixed reds. As soon as the petals start to drop it is important to remove each one of these, or the sprays will look faded long before they are over. The variegated 'Norah Leigh', although a slow grower, is both an asset to the border and lovely in a mixed green group. The annual *Phlox drummondii* are so pretty in the border, in a wide range of colours. Small pieces used for a vase look gay and colourful and last much better than expected.

Conditioning Hammer ends of stems well and give a good drink in warm water before arranging them.

Phormium tenax
New Zealand Flax

Regrettably only half-hardy. I have used these delightful sword-shaped leaves and their strange spiky flower whenever I have had the chance, fortunately, they are imported. They are excellent used as a background for large groups in autumn and winter, and last for weeks. Besides the plain green, there is a green one with a cream stripe (*P. tenax variegatum*), and another one which has reddish leaves (*P. tenax atropurpureum*); all are most welcome.

Conditioning These leaves last extremely well in water. It is a good idea to trim the ends of the leaves to a point, so that you get the end easily into the vase; they are very square and difficult to handle, and can take up far too much room in the container unless they are trimmed in this way.

Photinia

The photinia I have is called 'Red Robin' and has the most lovely red tips to the leaves, in fact it has good colour all the year, the leaves going mahogany coloured in the autumn. As it is young I must admit I have never actually picked it to use in a flower arrangement but am looking forward to it, it is such a good coloured shrub.

Phygelius
Cape Figwort

P. capensis is a half-hardy herbaceous perennial with orange-scarlet flowers from midsummer onwards; these are nice to arrange with the orange and red dahlias and some autumn or colourful foliage.

Conditioning Put ends of stems into boiling water and then allow several hours in deep water.

Physalis franchetii
Chinese Lantern

A native of the east, China and Japan, perennial. Grown for the ornamental calix, which looks like an inflated orange balloon, these dry well for winter decoration. I love to use them in their green stage, before they turn colour. Their trails of puffy green balloons add graceful curves and outline to any green group. In the orange stage

Physalis

they give that much-desired splash of colour to any dried arrangement. *P. peruviana* is the edible variety which one enjoys so much at Christmas time as a sugared fruit.

Conditioning Place the ends of the stems into very hot water and then allow a long drink if you are going to use them in their green stage. The actual flower is nondescript, so it is better to wait until the calix develops.

Preserving As soon as the calices have turned orange then remove all the leaves and hang the stems upside down for about three days. Do not leave them too long as they may dry the wrong way round. I have found they dry off very well standing in a little water. In fact when they are still green this is the way I like to dry them.

Physocarpus *see* SPIRAEA

Physostegia virginiana
Obedient Plant, Dragon's Head

Hardy perennial, blooming in pink and carmine, 'obedient' because the individual little flowers swing round on the stem to face any way you want. These spiky flowers mix well in any group in pink and mauve colours.

Conditioning Give a long drink in warm water before arranging.

Phytolacca americana
American Poke Weed, Red-Ink Plant

Hardy perennial. Perhaps its name, Red-Ink Plant, is because it was used by the early settlers in America as a dye. It is a native of southern USA and I was particularly interested to see it growing in the gardens of the 'Shakers' in Kentucky. There they grew plants only for their use and not for their beauty, and, as a matter of fact, I never actually saw flowering plants in their gardens at all. It is a plant that I love – I think I have been partly responsible for its growing popularity in flower arrangement in recent years. I grew it from seed a long time ago, and use it continually. It is attractive in the green flower stage, but even more useful when the berries form; the heads then look like clusters of blackberries and go well with so many different things, but particularly with the red heads of the sedum 'Autumn Glory' and red or pink hydrangeas.

Conditioning When using the flower stems, place the ends of the stems in boiling water, before giving a long drink. When using the berries, remove all the leaves and give a long drink in tepid water, though as they last so well no extra care is really necessary. One point I must make here is the fact that they stain very badly, so be very careful when the seeds are really ripe as they fall easily and the stains are so difficult to remove.

Picea
Spruce, Christmas Tree

A word about the decorations for the Christmas tree. If it is possible to adopt a colour scheme, it makes just all the difference. For instance, if one year you decide to have all the decorations green and gold, or red and silver, or gold and silver, red and gold, and so on, I cannot begin to tell you what a good effect it makes. When using branches of spruce in water for a decoration, the blue-greys are the most effective. *P. pungens* is very blue and most striking for a winter group, with sprays of lichen-covered branches and some of the lovely blue-grey eucalyptus leaves.

Pieris

A plant that seems to thrive on the eastern seaboard of the United States. *P. japonica* is a hardy evergreen shrub with cascades of white flowers in the early spring like trusses of white lily of the valley. At Winkfield we get it up from Cornwall in March. It looks well in so many vases. Try one elegantly-shaped stem alone in a Chinese jar, or use it with a collection of foliage

Pieris forrestii

– eucalyptus in its various forms, forsythia branches, green guelder rose (this is of course imported into Britain as early as March), stems of green hellebores. A stem or two will transform a vase of white tulips. *P. forrestii* has the additional distinction of producing striking new growths of leaves in early spring. They are brilliant red looking at first sight rather like poinsettia flowers. The red persists until after the flowers appear so that when it is in full bloom the shrub is a magnificent sight. All pieris are peat-lovers.

Conditioning Well hammer the ends of the stems, before giving a long drink.

Pineapple Flower *see* EUCOMIS

Pinks *see* DIANTHUS

Pittorsporum tenuifolium

Evergreen, slightly tender shrub, growing in Cornwall and Ireland. It has very shiny small leaves and is in great demand by the florists in winter and early spring. It has the advantage of lasting a long time in water. I don't think I ever use it very much; I find it slightly difficult, as the stems are often clumsily laden with foliage. However, it can be a good stand-by in early spring and can be used with other foliages, but avoid crowding it into a vase so that it over-shadows the blooms of tulips or daffodils; it can hide so much of their colour. On the other hand, if you can get a delicate well-shaped branch, it is very effective alone as it has such beautiful dark stems – almost black. *P. tobira* has larger leaves and more conspicuous creamy-white flowers, sweetly scented.

I find *P. tobira variegata*, with its whorls of leathery leaves, one of the most useful plants for my demonstrations in the United States. No matter where one is, north, south, east or west, one can always buy good bunches of this invaluable plant. As the flowers fade and the berries appear I like to use these in a winter or green arrangement. It grows well in Australia and I suppose in any hot climate, but not, alas, in Britain.

Plantago
Plantain

This you may think is an odd choice, but the red-leaved and the double are very decorative and I find if I do not weed them all out by mistake (as I have a habit of doing!), they are useful to pick for any small foliage group.

Plantain Lily *see* HOSTA

Platycodon grandiflorum
Balloon Flower

Hardy herbaceous perennial. *P. grandiflorum* has blue or white flowers that are effective when cut, but it is not a plant that is very widely grown. I think it looks extremely well in a shallow bowl, with a few glass blocks to hide the wire or pin-holder; in this way you get the beauty of every flower and stem.

Conditioning Put ends of stems into boiling water for a few minutes, before giving a long drink.

Plumbago capensis
Leadwort

A charming plant, *P. capensis*, a lovely pale blue, can be trained in the cool greenhouse to cover a trellis. It can be picked from the garden in any warm climate. I found it hard to realize that it was growing in such abundance in Sydney and San Francisco, but equally well under glass in Pangbourne, Berkshire, where they seem able to make use of it as a cut flower for months. *P. ceratostigma* is a hardy shrubby related genus that has very good blue flowers in the summer.

Conditioning Put ends of stems into boiling water for a few minutes, then give a long drink.

Plume Poppy *see* MACLEAYA

Poinsettia *see* EUPHORBIA

Poke Weed *see* PHYTOLACCA

Polianthes
Tuberose

Half-hardy bulbs. As we unpacked them outside Westminster Abbey at the time of the Queen's Coronation I remember how their never-to-be-forgotten scent immediately transported us back to Kenya, Hong Kong and California. One can recall time and place more quickly by a perfume than by anything else. Added to a vase of white and cream flowers they not only look lovely, and rather exotic, but scent the whole room exquisitely.

Polyanthus *see* PRIMULA

Polygonatum multiflorum
Solomon's Seal

Hardy perennial. Has arched wands of green leaves and hanging white flowers. It is often found growing wild in the woods, and is happy growing in shade. I find that I use it a lot in the early spring, to mix in with green groups. The leaves turn a lovely shade of yellow in autumn, and I like to use it then in vases of mixed autumn colours – the stems add such good curves, giving balance to the base of a vase. There is a new one with variegated foliage which I haven't tried yet.

Preserving After flowering, the leaves absorb glycerine well: leave them in the solution for four or five days, and then hang them upside down to dry.

Polygonum
Knotweed

Hardy herbaceous perennials and climbers. The best known is *P. baldschuanicum*, the Russian Vine, which climbs rampageously and will cover an arch or wall more quickly than any plant I know. The herbaceous varieties with their pink and white flowers are very useful in the late summer. They stand well in water, and are good in small vases. *P. vacciniifolium* is more suitable for a rock garden, but its pink spiky flowers dry well and I use them in a small dried group in the winter. If you have an odd corner, *P. cuspidatum* has beautifully variegated leaves and is another asset for picking, adding as all variegated plants do a touch of sunlight to garden and vase alike. The flowers dry extremely well, and I have had the chance of using sprays in my demonstrations in America. I was interested to find how good the colour remains even when dry.

Conditioning Place the stems into boiling water before giving a long drink.

Preserving All polygonums seem to dry best if the ends of the stems are placed in a small amount of water, and allowed to dry off. They keep their colour much better this way and do not seem to become so brittle.

Polystichum setiferum divisilobum

I have become a keen collector of ferns, and as I said in the introduction to this book it is strange how one can view a plant with completely new eyes, even though one has known it for years. The slight twist to the top of the fern reminds me very much of a cat's tail. I use it frequently and find that as the fronds mature on the plant, they stand very well in water. Used with mixed greens of firmer and more solid leaves, it adds that light touch which is so rewarding.

Conditioning Submerge the whole stem in cold water, and then place in a polythene bag and leave for twelve hours. This helps prevent the fronds from curling up.

Poppy *see* PAPAVER

Portugal Laurel *see* PRUNUS LUSITANICA

Pot Plants *see* HOUSE PLANTS

Potentilla

Hardy herbaceous perennials and sub-shrubs. Starry-faced little flowers in bright red and yellows. There are many kinds and I find I have grown very fond of the shrubby varieties (*P.*

Potentilla fruticosa

fruticosa) as they give almost continuous bloom for months. I use sprays of the little yellow flowers in the summer and autumn, to add the touch of yellow that is so important in any mixed vase. Though Alan Bloom's 'Red Ace' has been a sensation, my favourite is 'Day Dawn', a soft apricot shade with a wealth of flowers that persists from June to October. I do not use the herbaceous potentilla much for flower arranging though the bright 'Yellow Queen' and scarlet 'Mrs Bradshaw' combine well in small mixed arrangements, and they last in bloom for many weeks in the garden.

Conditioning Put the ends of the stems in boiling water for a few minutes, before giving a long drink.

Poterium

P. obtusum, another easy plant, though it does like a lot of sun, has strange poker-like flowers, fluffy pink spikes obtusely angled and rather exotic looking. Leaves are glaucous and fingered. There is a white variety *P. canadensis* which flowers in the autumn. These fluffy bottle-brush spikes, are lovely mixed with pink roses or any rounded flower, and give the points to any mixed flower vase.

Preserving *see* DRYING AND PRESERVING

Prickly Heath *see* PERNETTYA

Primrose *see* PRIMULA

Primula
Auricula, Cowslip, Primrose, Polyanthus

Greenhouse and hardy perennials. This family is enormous, and I hardly know where to begin. The primrose is one of the best known of our wild flowers and I use them in posies, in 'moss gardens' and in church for the Easter festival, often in a mass to decorate the window-sills of the church. I have been trying to naturalize the common primrose ever since I came to this garden, but it has been really difficult. For those who live in an area where they grow wild I can think of nothing better than a natural woodland garden where you can grow not only the yellow but pinks and blues. But remember that these enchanting double primroses, lavender, white, deep red must be continually split up, or they die out. The Barnhaven primroses are also well worth growing.

When using primrose and polyanthus massed, you can get the best effect if you have them in bunches, surrounded by their own leaves. Never use them on very long stems as they quickly droop. Auricula I have mentioned already (see under 'A'). *P. obconica* and *P. malacoides* we know of as pot plants that give a long flowering period and are to be seen on many a window-sill. *P. denticulata*, with its rounded heads, is used as a cut flower and can be bought in bunches in spring; they are nice to use with the purple hellebore as the colourings go so well together. There are many bog varieties but these rarely come on the market, and so they are little used as a cut flower; if, however, you have them, they mix in with groups of summer flowers.

Conditioning Primroses need little special care; bunch and place in the vase. Polyanthus, how-ever, are better if the ends of the stems are put into boiling water as soon as they are picked; afterwards give a long drink. Another method which gives excellent results is to prick the stem just below the flower head to release any air bubbles. The same method can be applied to the bog varieties.

Preserving The only seed heads that dry well are those of the bog primula *P. sikkimensis*. Allow the seed heads to form on the plant, pick and bunch and hang them upside down to dry.

Privet *see* LIGUSTRUM

Protea

This national flower of South Africa has so many varieties it is hard to describe them all. And now that people know how well they adapt to climate and conditions they are grown all over the world. Australia grows so many that it is hard to realize that it is not a native. California, too, has protea farms and to my surprise they are grown on the island of Maui in the Hawaiian Islands.

They are imported all the time into the UK and though they are expensive they look so impressive in a large arrangement and last so wonderfully that they become a very good investment. *P. compacta* and *P. eximia* in soft pinks and greys, are perhaps the easiest to handle. One of my favourites is 'The Pin Cushion' with round orange heads, lovely to arrange along with apricot colourings, it adds a real touch of the exciting to a vase of fruit and flowers.

Conditioning Hammer the ends of the stems and give them a long drink.

Preserving Put the flowers into a warm oven (about 200°F, 90°C): the centres will fall out as they open, but you are left with the lovely star-shaped outer petals. To preserve the outer petals and keep the flower with the centre, press small pieces of tissue paper between the centre and outer petals to force them open, hang them upside down in a very warm place for several days. Change the paper if they do not dry well at once, to hasten the process. They should dry completely in two weeks and then you have them for ever.

Prunella

P. grandiflora is a deep purple hardy perennial, good for ground cover and excellent for cutting.

Preserving The seed heads dry well if hung upside down.

Prunus amygdalus
Almond

Almond blossom forces well to give delicate sprays of pink blossom indoors as early as February. A few sprays of this add so much to a collection of very expensive spring flowers that it cannot be valued too highly. Sprays of almond fruits are beautiful in the autumn in a mixed green or foliage group.

To force If branches are picked after Christmas, remember that they will take about five weeks to blossom. Hammer stems well, place in warm water and keep in a cold room for the first two days, then bring into warmth.

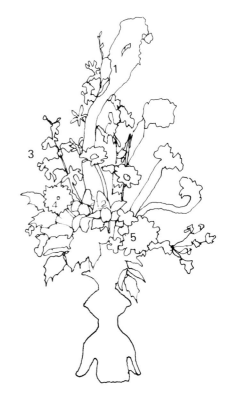

OVERLEAF
A round of wood makes a good base for a simple, long-lasting arrangement for the winter months.
1 *Ornithogalum thyrsoides* (Chincherinchee)
2 *Salix caprea* (Pussy willow)
3 *Arum italicum pictum*
4 *Tellima grandiflora*

A metal container with an oriental flavour, filled with an unusual combination of dried and fresh flowers.
1 Fasciated stems of *oenothera* (Evening primrose)
2 *Cymbidium* (Orchid)
3 'Singapore' orchids
4 *Gerbera jamesonii*
5 *Clivia miniata*

Prunus

Plum, Cherry, Apricot, Peach

A wide collection of trees and shrubs, including useful fruits and some decorative species. The peach, apricot, cherry and plum are of course edible species and although the blossom is lovely to use, it is often too precious for arrangement. This can only be managed by extremely careful pruning, and small pieces can be picked to use in a vase to great effect. Among the best flowering cherries are *P. serrulata* (Japanese Cherry); varieties include double and single blooms in pink and white. One of the best known is the variety 'Kanzan', though if I planted my garden again I don't think I would include it. While it is superb for a short time I think I really prefer the other Japanese cherries such as 'Shirotae' (*P.* 'Kojima') with its large single white flowers hanging in thick clusters from horizontal branches, and 'Shirofugen' (*P. serrulata albo-rosea*) flowers double pink in bud, changing to white with delicate bronzy young foliage. There is of course little to beat 'Sargentii' (*P. serrulata sachalinensis*) single pink flowers and brilliant red foliage in autumn, and *P. avium* 'Plena', the common gean, has given me endless pleasure. Before choosing your plants always try to see them first in blossom time. *P. subhirtella autumnalis* is one of the best for growing to pick, and flowering as it does in the winter is a joy to have. Of the doubles, the lime-green heads of *P. serrulata grandiflora* 'Ukon' are indescribably lovely. Some of the cherries have good autumn colour and although the leaves may not last very long in water, I love using a spray or two for special effect, even if only for a day or so.

A mass of subtle coloured roses chosen to blend with the alabaster vase.

PREVIOUS PAGE
This arrangement was entirely inspired by the lovely piece of fungus which I found near an old tree stump.
1 *Paeonia delavayi* 'Souvenir de Maxime Cornu'
2 *Iris* 'Canary Bird'
3 *Polyanthus*
4 The fasciated stems of *oenothera* (Evening primrose)
5 *Schizanthus* (Butterfly flower)
6 *Lonicera* (Honeysuckle)
7 *Bergenia* foliage

Prunus subhirtella autumnalis

Prunus
Portugal Laurel, Cherry Laurel

These laurels are hardy evergreens with bold shiny green leaves that are a constant stand-by for the flower arranger. Useful as a good solid background for large church-groups as they act as an excellent shield for screening light – this is very often a problem when doing flowers on church window-sills and chancel steps. Portugal laurel, *Prunus lusitanica*, has sprays of delicate pendulous white flowers, and with the leaves removed, these branches can be most decorative, having a good Chinese effect with the white blossom on dark stems. The flowers are fol-

lowed by dark purple fruits; I find these useful as well. The variegated *P. lusitanica variegata* is a plant that lights up any dark corner and I use it more and more.

The cherry laurel, *P. laurocerasus*, is an excellent evergreen for the town, with clusters of pink flowers in very early spring; these show best if some of the leaves are removed and then it can be effectively used with tulips or daffodils.

Conditioning Hammer ends of stems well, before giving a long drink.

Preserving Laurel takes glycerine very well and I find this worth applying, even though the plant is an evergreen, to have a good solidly-shaped leaf to add to a dried collection.

Pteridium aquilinum
Bracken Fern

I feel I must mention bracken as it is pressed a great deal for winter arrangements. It will not stand in a hot room without curling unless it is treated; then it is excellent used with some dried seed heads and cut chrysanthemums. A few sprays look surprisingly well with laurel leaves to help out a bunch of early daffodils; I think it is the mixture of textures that is so effective.

Preserving Cut the stems of bracken in various shades of cream, brown and green, lay them carefully between newspaper and place them under a weight. If they are to be used for Christmas decorations, it is advisable to soak them in a solution of weak starch water; this stiffens them so that they take the paint and glitter better.

Pulmonaria officinalis
Lungwort

Low-growing hardy herbaceous plant. For me its great attraction is the fact that it is often in bloom in February. It has strange little flowers that are pink and blue on the same stem. The foliage is prettily mottled, but it is a little difficult to make it last in water. The small flowers, however, look well in a 'moss garden' and add a very helpful early touch of blue.

Pulsatilla
Pasque Flower

This small hardy perennial has anemone-like flowers surrounded by soft grey serrated leaves. They are one of the joys of the spring rock garden and last well in water. They look pretty arranged by themselves, but as they are rather special it is difficult to pick a great number without spoiling the show in the garden, so I usually add one or two to a small mixed vase or to a 'moss garden'. They grow wild in Switzerland in a pale lilac colour, but some of the new hybrids are in lovely colours of pale lilac to deep reds.

Conditioning Put the ends of the stems into warm water, not allowing the fringe of fluff to touch the water.

Preserving Cut the seed heads when they are well formed and hang them up to dry. These are fluffy balls and dry very well to mix in small dried vases.

Pyracantha
Firethorn

A thorny, berried evergreen shrub. The variety I like most is the yellow-berried *P. rogersiana flava*, for arranging with dahlias and all the autumn shades. Large sprays of all these berries are very good as backing for large groups, lasting well and in churches, for instance, giving a glow of colour against a background of stone or wood. All the colours are excellent and the brilliant orange berries of *P. coccinea lalandii* last well on the bushes and give colour to the garden for many weeks.

Preserving The berries last a long time, but to avoid shrivelling it is helpful to paint them with clear varnish.

Pyrethrum

Hardy perennials with single or double daisy-like flowers in pink, white or red, properly called *Chrysanthemum coccineum*, but nearly always catalogued under Pyrethrum. They are useful for cutting as they flower at rather a sparse time of year, and as they last well in water they have become a popular cut flower. Personally I find them difficult to arrange as they have such stiff form; though they are suitable to add as a centre to a mixed garden-basket or vase in June.

Pyrus
Pear

Branches of any fruit blossom are always a joy to pick – but of course only do so if you have old and well-established trees. Gnarled and well-shaped branches are most useful in winter as a background for a few flowers. *P. salicifolia pendula* makes one of the most lovely specimen trees, with its weeping habit, silver willow-like leaves and cream flowers in spring.

Conditioning When using the branches in flower, hammer ends of stems well, before giving a long drink in warm water.

Pyracantha coccinea

Quaking Grass *see* BRIZA

Quercus
Oak

Hardy deciduous and evergreen trees with many varieties. I use the evergreen oak (*Quercus ilex*) in the winter; arranged in January with some of the very early paper white narcissi and a few lemons, it can look like the leaves of an orange tree at a quick glance. The flowers of the male oak have pendulous catkins in spring and I love to use a well-shaped branch in a shallow dish with a few tulips. Branches of really good shape are useful in winter as a background, as I have mentioned before.

Quince *see* CYDONIA

Ranunculus
Crowfoot, Buttercup

Hardy and half-hardy herbaceous and tuberous-rooted perennials. The tuberous-rooted French and Turban varieties (*R. asiaticus*), single and double, are sold in florists' shops in bunches in early spring, and there is a lovely small button red one that arrives in time to add to a candle cup for a Christmas arrangement. Just after that, a small delicate pink one arrives with a really lime-green centre; these are quite adorable in January and placed with a few sprays of forced lily of the valley make a charming group for a piece of delicate china. Any flower of subtle colouring is always of greater value for easier mixing. The later-flowering ranunculus imported from France are a great asset as they have a wide colour range and mix well with self or contrasting colours.

Conditioning The ends of the stems are best put into boiling water for a few seconds, before being given a long drink.

Reseda odorata
Mignonette

Perennial, but more often grown as an annual. It requires plenty of sun and does best in sheltered beds. A strange greenish flower that is effective with leaves and seed heads in the summer, though it is chiefly grown for its lovely scent.

Preserving If the flowers are allowed to seed, they have pretty seed heads, which should be picked, bunched and hung upside down to dry.

Rheum
Rhubarb

The ornamental-leaved species have magnificent red and coloured leaves in the spring; it is possible to use them at this time as they have not yet grown too large, though it is advisable to condition them well before you put them in a vase. They make an excellent base for a spring group of forsythia, green hellebore and a few white-backed daffodils. The flowers are tall, handsome plumes of delicate pink or white but it is better to use them when they are fully mature or even in their seed head stage, as they will then last longer. *R. alexandrae* is one of the most spectacular, and I have tried hard, unsuccessfully, to get it established since I admired it so much on Alan Bloom's stand at Chelsea some years ago. The pale green papery bracts go right up the flower stem, and stay effective for many weeks, usually flowering in May.

Rheum palmatum

Conditioning Put the ends of the leaves in boiling water for a little while, and then completely submerge the whole leaf in a bath of water overnight. This may have to be done again after the first day, as so much depends on the maturity of each leaf.

Preserving When the seed heads are drying off, pick them and finish the process by hanging them upside down. It is possible to dry them on the plant but if the weather turns wet, you will find that they quickly spoil, so it is better to be on the safe side and pick them.

Rhododendron

An enormous family of shrubs, which includes the azaleas (see p. 51). They grow from the Himalayas to the tropics in various forms. This genus, given lime-free soil, has done so much to enrich our gardens, possibly more than any other. For the flower arranger they are pure joy, and I can say no more than that. Rhododendrons, which are evergreen, have rounded heads with clusters of flowers in all the pinks, purples and reds, also white. There are endless varieties, and there has been much hybridizing through the years. They are wonderful for large groups with their nice long stems. They can also be picked with short stems, or just the flower head itself can be used. These heads give a focal point to any group, and are rewarding whichever way you decide to use them. It is often better if you remove some of the leaves, so that the flower is not obscured in any way. I use either azaleas or rhododendrons, in all their forms, to mix with other flowers or to have on their own, whenever I can get them.

R. praecox must have special mention for the flower arranger as these clusters of mauve pink flowers on leafless branches come early and are a delight to add to a small vase of early crocus, snowdrops, primroses etc.; 'Blue Diamond', 'Blue Tit', 'Blue Stone' and other small mauvish blue-flowered varieties are really useful for flower arranging though they are not so effective in the garden. It's impossible to talk about all the varieties, and again I think it is such a good idea to go to a place specialising in rhododendrons like Waterers or Wisley, see them in flower and then select. I choose to suit my house as much as, or more than, the garden. They only grow in a small area for me, so I have to be very selective. I would not be without 'Christmas Cheer' for it flowers so early, I often have a few blooms in January. 'Champagne' is another I recommend.

Conditioning As they all have particularly woody stems, it is very important to hammer the ends of the stems well and to put them into quite hot water and leave over-night or longer if necessary. Overhead spraying helps to keep the heads of some of the rhododendrons from flagging. I have been advised to use some household bleach in the water and providing the container will not suffer, have found it helps to keep them looking fresh a little longer. I expect keeping the water clear and clean is the secret.

Rhus
Sumach

R. cotinus (or Cotinus coggygria) is sometimes known as the 'Smoke Tree' because of the lovely fluffy flower and seed head that it produces. It is a deciduous tree with good autumn-coloured foliage either reddish brown or maroon in the case of R. cotinus purpureus. It does not stand well in water, and so needs special care, but it looks well in the autumn arranged with other leaves and autumn-coloured flowers in orange or red. The staghorn sumach, R. typhina. is not so good for cutting, though it is very tempting to use it in autumn as the leaves turn the most lovely colours, but they die almost as soon as they are picked. The seed heads, however, which stand up like candles on the branches and have a pretty 'red velvet' look, last well in water and are effective in a mixed fruit and flower group; as the stems curl upwards, they can only be used rather short.

Conditioning For Rhus cotinus, with its lovely but delicate foliage, the ends of the stems should be well boiled and then the whole spray submerged right under water for several hours.

Preserving The seed heads of the sumach will dry if you hang the heads upside down, but they do tend to lose their colour quickly.

Ribes sanguineum
Flowering Currant

Hardy shrub with pink or red flowers in spring.
It is useful to arrange in a vase, though it has the
disadvantage of what some people consider
rather an unpleasant smell when cut; however, I
find that this wears off very quickly as soon as
you stop handling it. It is one of the best shrubs
to force, and will come out well in water, when
brought into the house in early January. It forces
white or very pale pink, and not the strong
colour you might expect. It is then lovely to use
with a few daffodils and tulips. Also attractive
are the yellow-leaved *R. aureum* and *R. alpinum
aureum*. As I think you must already have
realized, I love plants with golden foliage! *R.
laurifolium* is another plant that I have become
familiar with and would thoroughly recommend
to any flower arranger. Its pale green leathery
leaves and racemes of green-white flowers
appear in February. *R. vicarii* proves to be the
male form of this species and seeing it for the
first time recently at Sir David Scott's garden
near Kettering I really feel it is superior, though
as a female I hate to admit it! It is best to remove
quite a few of the leaves, so you really see all
these enchanting catkin-like flowers to their best
advantage.

Conditioning Hammer ends of stems well,
before putting in water for a long drink. When
forcing it, always stand it in the cold, indoors,
for a day, before you bring it into the warm.
Allow about four weeks for it to come into full
bloom.

Ricinus communis
Castor-oil Plant

Half-hardy annual. Grown in Britain mainly
for flower arrangement, it has large palm-
shaped leaves that are good to use with foliage
groups. The one with red foliage (*R. communis
sanguineus*) is the most popular and to my mind
the most effective. I well remember being so
delighted on my arrival in Sydney, Australia, to
see it growing wild along any piece of spare
ground. I became accustomed to using the seed
heads, which are spires of nobbly, whiskered

fruits, and these were invaluable for fruit and
flower arrangements and for using with berries
and autumn flowers. Their reddish colour gave
one lots of scope for blending with gladioli and
dahlias. The perennial castor-oil plant is *Fatsia
japonica*.

Conditioning The leaves need careful treatment
by placing the ends of the stems in boiling water,
and then submerging under water for several
hours. The seed heads need the same treatment
but avoid getting the heads wet as they take on a
very drab look, and never really recover.

Preserving Hang the seed heads upside down
until dry and store in a dry place until required.

Robinia pseudoacacia
False Acacia

'Frisia' is an outstanding variety that came from
Holland, and has become one of the most
rewarding trees I know. Its leaves, rich golden
yellow from spring to autumn, add a touch of
sunlight to any area in which you plant it. It
does not stand well in water, though I have
managed to get a few pieces to take up water in
the autumn. If you find any way in which you
can condition it for flower arranging, I would
love to know.

Rodgersia

Hardy herbaceous perennials which seem to
enjoy really wet conditions. *R. podophylla*
(Rodgers' Bronze Leaf) has handsome bronze
leaves which make a decoration in themselves,
just two or three in an oriental arrangement.

Conditioning The leaves are very tender and
need careful attention, especially in the early
spring. Put the ends of the stems into boiling
water for a few minutes, and then submerge
completely in a bath overnight.

Romneya
Californian Tree Poppy

R. coulteri has enormous single white heads
with a tuft of yellow stamens in the centre of the

Romneya coulteri

flower. Quite beautiful, and superb in a white and green group, but it is a little tender and is not often available as a cut flower. *R. hybrida* is perhaps a little hardier.

Conditioning Put ends of stems into boiling water and then give at least twelve hours in a cool place in deep water.

Rosa
Rose

What flower gives more pleasure to the grower and the arranger? Roses are more widely grown these days than ever before, partly as they make for such easy gardening. The Floribundas are becoming increasingly popular, because of their long period of flowering and being so useful to pick. Of the Floribundas, to name but a few: 'Iceberg' (white), 'Magenta' (purple), 'Elizabeth of Glamis' (apricot), 'Fashion' (salmon), 'Dearest' (soft pink), 'Rosemary Rose' (cherry red) . . . though of course one could go on for ever.

The Hybrid teas are numerous; try to grow some in the newer and more unusual colours, as well as established favourites. Of all flowers I think they are the least complicated to deal with; they are excellent on their own, either just a few stems or grouped in a mass, either self-coloured or mixed. They can be arranged in almost any type of container, be it glass, china, metal, wood, or pottery. Personally, I like them best in a mass by themselves with their own foliage, but I also use them as the centre of many a large group.

The old-fashioned shrub roses have a special charm and are being widely grown, for their profusion of bloom and their exquisite scent. For arranging in the house they are not really so reliable as they do not last very well; however, they are a pleasure to cut and enjoy just for a couple of days. As they bloom so freely, it is possible to bring in a nice lot of them for a real wealth of colour, and not detract from the show in the garden. The modern shrub rose 'Constance Spry' is a 'must' for the flower or rose lover. It has large delicate-pink blooms, shading to a deeper-pink centre, with the sweetest musky scent. A word of warning – it

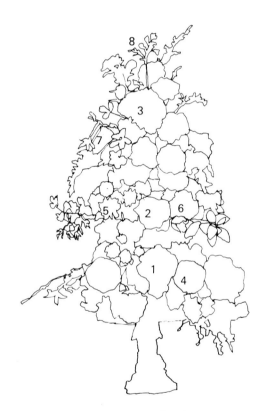

A three-tier arrangement made by placing separate alabaster vases one on top of another, suitable for some important event – a wedding, christening or special party.
1 Rose 'Elizabeth Harkness'
2 Rose 'Chaucer'
3 *Hydrangea*
4 *Dahlias*
5 *Astrantia* (Masterwort)
6 *Sedum* 'Autumn Joy'
7 *Nicotiana* (Tobacco plant)
8 *Thalictrum*

Rosa rugosa 'Scabrosa'

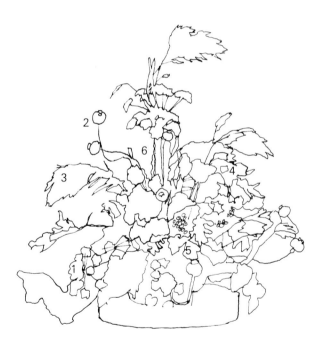

The charm of collecting from the hedgerow in high summer. On an inexpensive plastic tray a pin-holder is concealed by a branch of vine collected from the discarded prunings of a French vineyard.

1 *Heracleum sphondylium* (Hogweed, Cow parsnip)
2 Poppy seed heads
3 Grasses
4 Flowering branches of *tilia* (Lime)
5 *Lonicera* (Honeysuckle)
6 *Rumex conglomeratus* (Sharp dock)

needs space, as it does grow enormous! Now David Austin has come along with his sports from this lovely rose and one cannot pass over 'Chaucer' or 'The Prioress', the former delicate pink and the latter creamish. If I only had one to choose from then it would be 'Chaucer' for it blooms intermittently all summer, fragrant and delicious. Roses are for you to choose, but I must mention some specially for cutting, as their dusky colours are enchanting to mix with a few tinted leaves, even beetroot or carrot tops!

If you have space for a few old roses, here are six, and it's hard to choose between them. 'Fantin Latour', pale pink, 'Madame Lauriol de

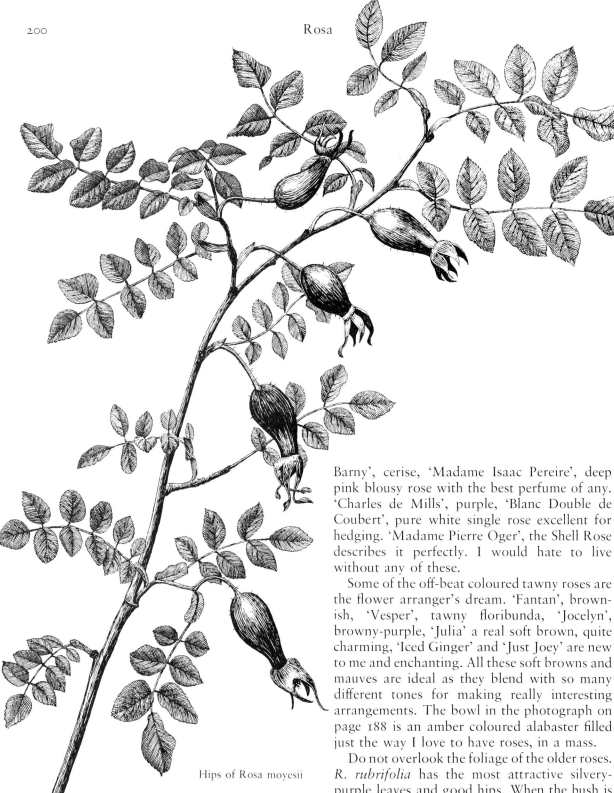

Hips of Rosa moyesii

Barny', cerise, 'Madame Isaac Pereire', deep pink blousy rose with the best perfume of any. 'Charles de Mills', purple, 'Blanc Double de Coubert', pure white single rose excellent for hedging. 'Madame Pierre Oger', the Shell Rose describes it perfectly. I would hate to live without any of these.

Some of the off-beat coloured tawny roses are the flower arranger's dream. 'Fantan', brownish, 'Vesper', tawny floribunda, 'Jocelyn', browny-purple, 'Julia' a real soft brown, quite charming, 'Iced Ginger' and 'Just Joey' are new to me and enchanting. All these soft browns and mauves are ideal as they blend with so many different tones for making really interesting arrangements. The bowl in the photograph on page 188 is an amber coloured alabaster filled just the way I love to have roses, in a mass.

Do not overlook the foliage of the older roses. *R. rubrifolia* has the most attractive silvery-purple leaves and good hips. When the bush is large enough for picking, the branches make wonderful backing for a mauve-pink vase, but in fact I find I can use it for almost any colour scheme. The species roses *R. virginiana* and *R. nitida* both have foliage with rich autumn colour. Lastly, the species rose *R. moyesii* and the *rugosa* roses 'Frau Dagmar Hastrup', *R. typica* (*rubra*) and *R.* 'Scabrosa' all have excellent hips.

Conditioning Put ends of stems in boiling water for a minute, and then give a long drink.

Rosemary *see* ROSMARINUS

Rosmarinus officinalis
Rosemary

Hardy evergreen shrub with fragrant foliage that is useful to pick and use all through the year. The flowers are delicate blue and these can be added to a mixed vase in July or August.

Royal Fern *see* OSMUNDA

Rubus
Blackberry, Raspberry, Wineberry

Hardy perennial fruits and shrubs. They can all be used in sprays as available. The wineberries (*R. phoenicolasius*) with their downy red fluffy coats are most decorative; sprays of these and blackberries are all exceedingly helpful to add interest and contrast to a vase in late summer. I have used blackberries and red roses to great effect.

Rudbeckia
Coneflower, Black-eyed Susan

Hardy annuals and herbaceous perennials. Double and single, with showy yellow, brown and orange flowers in late July and August. Their vivid colouring makes them a welcome centre for a late summer vase of browns and yellows. They last well and their daisy-like flowers with dark centres are very effective. The annuals derived from *R. hirta* are the most showy, and well worth growing. I would like to add that I have a new regard and respect for these flowers since I saw them this year after a really wet and miserable few weeks. Looking at them in Unwin's trial grounds, I was amazed

Rudbeckia

how well they had stood up; they were a mass of unblemished flower heads. The colours I particularly liked were the browns and tawnys of 'Rustic' and for a blaze of colour 'Marmalade', excellent bright yellow as the name implies.

Conditioning Put the ends of the stems into boiling water and leave for a few minutes, then allow a long drink.

Ruta graveolens
Rue

A small herb with a close crop of divided leaves that are generally grey-blue in colour, though there is a variegated green and white one. As it is evergreen, I use it often in a small vase in winter to eke out a few precious flowers. *R. graveolens* 'Jackman's Blue' is particularly good.

St John's Wort *see* HYPERICUM

Saintpaulia
African Violet

Small violet-like flowers in shades of pink and mauve; for the warm greenhouse, though they are increasingly used as house plants as well, very decorative.

Salix
Willow

Hardy deciduous trees of many varieties. The golden weeping willow, *S. vitellina pendula* (which you may find catalogued under a large variety of names, including *S. babylonica ramulis aureis*, *S. chrysocoma* or *S. alba tristis*) is one of the most decorative for the garden, and I enjoy using wands of its weeping branches for a large group in March. The pussy willows, as they are commonly known (*S. caprea*), are delightful in early spring as a background for daffodils and tulips. You can gather them from the hedgerows, and many people grow them in the garden, though as they grow rapidly and very large this is not advisable unless you have plenty of room for them.

S. *daphnoides* must be one that anyone could grow. Though it grows rapidly it can be pollarded and I find this ideal as I use those pieces for my arrangements. It has a bloom on the bark in winter and very early flowering catkins. In fact I have friends who remove the outer coat of the buds to show the silver inside and bring them into the house in time for Christmas.

S. *Wehrahnii* has just been given to me with a very good reputation, and I can hardly wait to see the long upright catkins on purple stems it is reputed to have, which glisten silver and then burst into a yellow fuzz. *S. matsudana tortuosa*, the contorted willow, I have become very fond of as it grows in superb shapes and gives a wonderful outline for an oriental type of vase; it has many uses and I should like to grow many more.

Conditioning The weeping willow needs to be very well looked after; hammer the ends of the stems or boil them in 2.5cm (1in) of boiling water, and then allow twelve hours completely submerged in cold water.

Salpiglossis

Half-hardy annual. *S. sinuata* has open cup-shaped flowers not unlike alstroemeria, except for colour; the colourings are most varied and you can often get a most unusual combination of 'dirty' brownish and reddish shades. Although they are delicate to handle, they last very well in a vase. I find that I often build up a vase in July around one particular stem, and it makes for something of great interest.

Conditioning Place the ends of the stems in very hot water and leave them until it cools. Avoid boiling water unless you shield the blooms, as they burn so easily.

Salvia
Sage, Clary

Hardy and half-hardy perennials with a wide range. Probably the ones I use most are *S. haematodes* (good clear blue) and *S. turkestanica* (tall stems of whitish flowers surrounded by pink-edged bracts). *S. turkestanica* tends to be rather short-lived and is often best treated as a biennial. Both of these flower in midsummer and are extremely pretty mixed with summer flowers, either to add a touch of blue or as a blue foil for a muted vase of mauves. *S. splendens* is not hardy and is quite different from the others, having glowing scarlet flowers and bright foliage; it adds distinction and impact to a mixed red vase of dahlias and roses, phlox, and anything else that suggests itself.

Salpiglossis sinuata

Sambucus nigra
Elder

Hardy deciduous shrub with flat round white flowers and black berries, that grows wild in the south of England. I enjoy using it both in the flower and fruit stage. The big clusters of flowers are most effective if the leaves are first removed and the sprays then put with other white flowers, such as lilies, for a large group, or the late double tulips and lilac; or just with a collection of wild cow parsley. The clusters of black fruits that follow need careful handling as they drop when ripe and stain badly, but look so good with reds, black grapes and red roses. The golden-foliaged species, *S. nigra aurea*, is very effective. *Sambucus nigra laciniata*, the cut-leaved elder, is a good hardy deciduous ornamental-leaved shrub which I like to use in a vase of foliage in late spring and early summer. It is found growing wild in parts of Scotland. The flower, in spring, is a small fluffy plume and so attractive that one is tempted to pick it, but it simply does not last, so it is better to wait for the upright clusters of bright red iridescent berries.

Conditioning If you are picking branches of elder for their leaves alone, then you will find the following method quite effective: hammer ends of stems well and then soak for several hours in warm water. Re-stand in hot water and finally allow a long cold drink. For flowers and foliage together on the stem I use a slightly different treatment: put the ends of stems into boiling water for a little while, and then allow a night in deep water.

Sanguinaria canadensis
Bloodroot

Hardy perennial flowering herb with double and single white flowers in spring. They last surprisingly well in water and are effective in small spring groups, or in a shallow dish alone.

Sansevieria
Bowstring Hemp

These plants are generally known as house plants. They have sword-like fleshy leaves, usu-ally well variegated, and are often known as Mother-in-law's Tongue. Much in demand by the flower arranger as they last for weeks and are so useful for a severe upright effect; they can look well in a shallow vase with a few rather choice yellow arum lilies.

Conditioning I have been lucky to pick these in Bermuda, Australia and California, they are a leaf that I always like to bring home if at all possible. They are one of the very few flowers whose stems I cover with adhesive tape, so as to be sure they do not actually touch the water at all. They last much better like this as the stems tend to rot if actually in water.

Santolina
Lavender Cotton

S. chamaecyparissus (or *S. incana*) is a hardy evergreen shrubby plant with aromatic small feathery green or grey leaves, and button daisy-like flowers in pale and deep yellow in late summer. I like to use small pieces of the foliage in the winter or early spring; when greenery is really scarce, they are more than useful.

Conditioning Hammer ends of stems well, before giving a long drink.

Saxifraga
Rockfoil

Hardy perennial rock and border plants. The rock saxifrages are not used very much in flower arrangement as they have such short stems, though I do occasionally use a whole cushion of the encrusted silver and green, or the yellow variegated, in a small group in early spring. *Saxifraga umbrosa* (London Pride) with its delicate stems of bell-like flowers mixes well with a vase of dianthus, candytuft and any small summer flowers. The large-leaved pink-flowering plant formerly known as a saxifrage or megasea, is now called Bergenia, q.v. *S. fortunei*, sometimes considered a variety of *S. cortusifolia*, was given to me by the late Norah Watson, and has been greatly treasured. I had grave doubts of its being hardy but now I feel I can freely include it in this book, as from experience it has thrived for years. It has enchanting broad leaves, rounded and glossy, that are reddish beneath. I use these in the autumn when the colour is best and they make a marvellous foil for a few autumn crocus. Most of the saxifrages bloom in the spring, but strangely this one flowers in October. It is for the leaves that I grow it. *S. peltiphyllum peltatum*, formerly known as peltata, with superb leaves rounded, lotus-like, is a Californian moisture-loving plant. The pale pink flowers appear before the leaves in early spring. It is known as 'Indian Rhubarb' as the Californian Indians eat the peeled stalks cooked or raw.

Scabiosa
Scabious

Hardy perennials and annuals. The most commonly used and valued flower in this family is the perennial *S. caucasica*, 'Clive Greaves', a rich clear blue, with wonderful lasting qualities, which endear it to any flower arranger. The white one is also becoming very popular. They can be arranged either alone or with a mixture of self-coloured flowers; they are lovely in a mass in a silver bowl or in delicate china. The mauves and pinks of the annual scabious are effective in small summer groups, though the perennials last a little longer and don't shed their petals.

Conditioning Cut the ends of the stems and give a long drink, preferably overnight.

Schizanthus
Butterfly-flower

A pretty annual with curiously-shaped blossoms in clustered heads of many colours on the same stem: rose-pink and orange, lilac and violet with an orange blotch – all with a strange pansy-like flower. They are usually grown in a cool greenhouse, and so it is not very often that one can use them as a cut flower, though they last extremely well and are nice in a vase on their own or mixed with summer flowers.

Conditioning Put the ends of the stems into boiling water for a few seconds, then give a long drink before arranging.

Schizostylis coccinea

Schizostylis coccinea
Kaffir Lily, Crimson Flag

Hardy perennial. Pink or red flowers, rather like a miniature gladiolus, lasting well in water and flowering in the autumn so that they make a useful change for a vase. They are very attractive arranged with a few autumn leaves.

Scilla
Squill, Bluebell

Hardy bulbous plants. The rock variety *S. sibirica* has bright blue flowers and these add just the right touch of blue to a small 'moss garden' in the early spring. The common bluebell *S. nonscripta* has a lovely scent and can be used as a cut flower (see under 'Bluebell'). The garden variety *S. hispanica* in blue, white, or a lilac pink, has large flowers and stiffer stems and therefore is really better for cutting; they arrange well and look very effective by themselves, or mixed with soft-coloured flowers.

Conditioning Cut the ends of the stems and give a long drink in cold water.

Preserving Pick in the green seed head stage and hang upside down to dry.

Scilla nonscripta

Scrophularia
Figwort

The only species which I feel is worthy of a place in the garden is *S. nodosa variegata*, a statuesque plant with strangely square stems and green leaves striped and blotched with cream. It is a delight in the border as it keeps its leaves well into the winter and is attractive in the house when cut. Unfortunately it does not last well in water, but nevertheless it is worth picking as it can easily be replaced after a day or so.

Conditioning Put the ends of the stems in 2.5cm (1in) of boiling water for a few minutes and then completely submerge the whole stem in warm water for as long as possible.

Sea Buckthorn *see* HIPPOPHAE

Sea Holly *see* ERYNGIUM

Seakale
Crambe maritima

This is of course a vegetable, but if you can get the chance of using it the blue-grey leaves are delightful, especially as a foil for a summer vase of blues and greys.

Sedum
Stonecrop

Hardy perennial rock and border plants, that are excellent for cutting. *S. spectabile* is probably the best known variety, and the hybrid 'Autumn Joy', which has slightly larger heads and a deeper colour, is one that I use continually; it gives a good focal point to a large vase in the autumn. The rich red colour is good to mix with the black heads of *Veratrum nigrum* and the berries spikes of *Phytolacca americana*. The dark maroon leaves and flower heads of *S. maximum atropurpureum* look well with any autumn group and add a touch of darker colour to a vase of dahlias, roses and others, in shades of pink. The even darker shade of maroon in 'Mahogany' is quite one of the best plants I have been given. They are most interesting plants as

Sedum spectabile

Sempervivum
House Leek

Hardy perennial succulent with rosettes of leaves that are much sought after by flower arrangers, to use as the focal point of a small group.

Senecio
Ragwort; Cineraria

Hardy and slightly-tender perennial herbs and hardy flowering shrubs. The grey-foliaged cinerarias are often tender, but are well worth growing for cutting almost all the year round. The delicate leaves of S. *maritima* I like to use complete on the chunky stem – or just the individual leaves, with garden pinks and small roses for posies in the summer. S. *laxifolius* is perhaps one of the most useful small shrubs for cutting; it has rounded grey leaves and pretty yellow daisy-like flowers in midsummer.

Senecio cruentus grandiflora, greenhouse daisy-flowered plants which have become increasingly popular as house plants. Their wide range of vivid colours, pale pink to deep petunia and purple, make them ideal for window boxes, or massed in the house in a large jardinière. They are wonderfully effective this way, much more so than in individual pots. I have only once had the fun of picking and using them as a cut flower and that was in Los Angeles where they grew in abundance in a sheltered walled garden. With no frost hazard, they also seeded themselves profusely.

Conditioning The soft-stemmed cinerarias need to have the ends of the stems put into boiling water for a few seconds, before they have a long drink. The hard woody varieties should also have a long drink and the ends of the stems should be hammered beforehand.

Shortia

Hardy perennials. Small plants with rounded leaves of good colour in the spring, with shading in red on green foliage. Enjoying shade and peaty soil, they have often been used to edge rhododendron beds. Pretty in a small vase of

they seed and cross themselves, and I now have a marvellous collection, green flowers and green foliage, light green flowers and darker foliage. Once they get established you have no idea what will appear. They last in water for weeks. They do not actually dry, but I have found that they last so well they actually take root in the Oasis. The variegated green-and-white leaved S. *spectabile variegatum* I would also recommend to the flower arranger. *Sedum rosea* (or S. *rhodiola*) has peculiarly-scented greenish-yellow flowers in spring.

Conditioning Cut the stems on the slant and allow a good drink in deep water.

Preserving The flower heads of the sedums dry well and make a useful contribution to a dried group. Pick when well matured on the plant and hang them upside down to dry. Or they can be left to dry on the plant.

Senecio laxifolius

spring flowers, with some fritillarias and a stem or two of auriculas; they add weight and interest to the base of the vase.

Sidalcea

Hardy perennial herb. Tall stems of single pink mallow-like flowers, in various shades. Useful to cut in midsummer and add to a really mixed summer vase. It lacks sufficient distinction of form for arrangement on its own.

Conditioning Put the ends of the stems into boiling water for a few minutes, before giving a long drink. This is very important as it will not stand well unless it is treated in this way.

Silene
Catchfly

The hardy perennial *S. schafta*, with a brilliant pink single flower, is the one that I like best of all to use in a flower arrangement. It adds excellent colour to a small vase in late summer.

Silk Bark Oak *see* GREVILLEA

Silybum marianum
Milk Thistle, Holy Thistle

S. marianum, an annual, is good to grow for its very decorative leaves – green, spotted with white. These are so prickly that they are hard to handle, but highly effective if used in a green or green-and-white group in July.

Conditioning The ends of the stems must be put in boiling water for a few minutes, before being given a long drink.

Sisyrinchium
Satin Flower

Hardy perennials. *S. striatum* has yellow flowers in June. I find that these flowers when cut tend to fade quickly in water, but I sometimes use them just for a touch of pale yellow in a mixed vase. I prefer their green seed heads and use these continually in vases of foliage and seed heads.

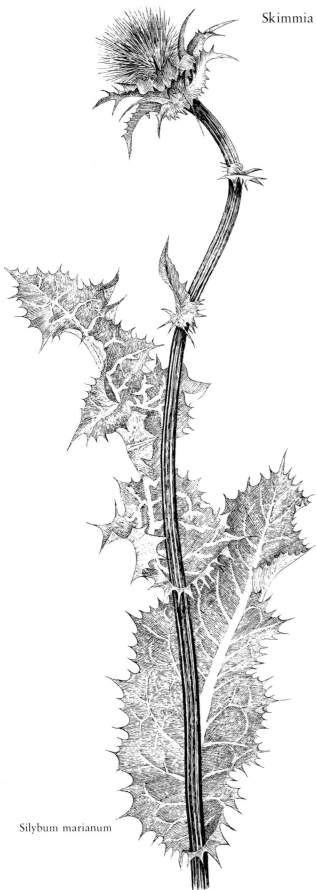

Silybum marianum

They also dry well and, turning almost black, look very effective with berries and bright autumn colours.

Conditioning Put the ends of the stems in the flower stage into boiling water and then allow a long drink.

Preserving Pick the green seed heads, remove all the foliage and hang them upside down. Recently I have tried putting the stems in glycerine and you get the most lovely coal-black seed heads, which are invaluable for a winter group, and have a glossy look which you do not get from hanging them upside down.

Skimmia japonica

Hardy evergreen shrub. Attractive, shiny foliage, pretty flowers in pointed clusters of cream, and beautiful scarlet berries, all make this a good shrub for the flower arranger. The berries form only if you grow both male and female plants. They are a good substitute for

Skimmia japonica

holly, so that if it is a bad holly year, they are a great help for the Christmas decorations. *S. foremanii* has pale-green leaves and the flower heads are more than useful in April and March.

Snapdragon *see* ANTIRRHINUM

Snowball Tree *see* VIBURNUM

Snowdrop *see* GALANTHUS

Snowflake *see* LEUCOJUM

Solanum capsicastrum
Winter Cherry

Tender berry-bearing plant that we have come to associate with Christmas. Grown under glass, and used as a house decoration at Christmas-time.

Solidago
Golden Rod

Hardy herbaceous perennials indigenous to North America, where there are literally hundreds of varieties. It has bright, showy, fluffy, yellow heads of flower in the autumn and grows readily in almost any conditions, which makes it generally popular as a herbaceous plant. It is somewhat difficult to arrange as the heads are often rather large and bulky and it is better if some of them are removed first. I think I really like it best when it is nearly over; the creamy-brown colour as it fades is more subtle and, to my mind anyway, prettier than the strong yellow in its full-blown stage. It goes well with the autumn tones of gladioli and dahlias. *Solidaster luteus*, a hybrid between an unknown solidago and *Aster ptarmicoides*, has paler yellow flowers, in narrower panicles than golden rod, and is therefore a better plant for the flower arranger. I think I undoubtedly most enjoyed arranging it in Albany, New York, picking armfuls by the wayside and massing it into large garden baskets which we put on a rustic table for a drinks party. I have never liked it so much before!

Conditioning Remove most of the leaves, before giving a long drink.

Preserving Allow the heads to dry off on the plant, and try to catch it before it reaches the fluffy stage, then pick and store. If you want to dry it to keep the yellow colour, pick in full flower and hang upside down to dry in a very warm place.

Solidaster *see* SOLIDAGO

Solomon's Seal *see* POLYGONATUM

Sorbus
Rowan, Mountain Ash, Whitebeam

Hardy deciduous trees with white flowers followed by berries of red, white or pink. The rowan or mountain ash, *S. aucuparis*, is perhaps the best known. I love to use it in autumn in a vase of colourful foliages, with a few dahlias and late roses; the clusters of shiny red berries add much interest to a group of this kind. The whitebeam, *Sorbus aria*, which grows so readily in England on the chalk hills of the Chilterns, unfurls in early spring with silver-grey tufts of leaves, which from a distance can be mistaken for flowers, on coal-black stems. These grey-leaved branches make a lovely background for a vase of white or pale pink flowers.

Conditioning Hammer ends of stems well, before giving a long drink.

Sowbread *see* CYCLAMEN

Sparmannia africana
African Hemp

S. africana is an African tree or shrub, as the name implies. It has clusters of white flowers and beautiful spade-shaped green leaves. It will only grow in Britain in a cool greenhouse, so that it is not widely used in flower arrangement; but small pieces of the white flower sprays, in June, arranged in a candle cup, give a touch of the exotic.

Conditioning Dip the ends of the stems into boiling water and give a long drink before arranging.

Spartium junceum
Spanish Broom

S. junceum is a hardy deciduous shrub with sweetly-scented yellow flowers in midsummer, giving a gay splash of colour to the shrub border. As a cut flower it is rather difficult to keep alive, so use it sparingly, but it provides the touch of strong yellow that is often so necessary to a vase of yellows and orange in July.

Conditioning Put the ends of the stems into boiling water, then give a long drink.

Spathiphyllum floribundum

A cool-greenhouse plant with shiny pointed leaves and a small spiky flower enclosed by a spathe-like white leaf. It lasts well, and I like to use both leaf and flower when possible. The flowers make an excellent centre for a mixed white vase in early spring. I was once able to use some quite large ones for a wedding in a country church, grouped with anthurium leaves and flowers and a few white lilies, but this was exceptional – the flowers are small as a rule and therefore not really suitable for anything larger than a container about 30cm (1ft) high.

Spider Flower *see* CLEOME

Spindle Tree *see* EUONYMUS

Spiraea

Hardy deciduous shrubs. The shrubby spiraea *S. arguta*, commonly known as Foam of May, has delicate sprays of white flowers which I love to use with early tulips and daffodils. *S. vanhouttei* has plumes of white flowers and these dry well in seed head form, turning a beautiful creamy brown, and this is how I really like to use them. *S. bumalda*, 'Anthony Waterer', carmine, flowers in July and this good red colour looks excellent in a vase of mixed reds, but again the seed heads are lovely, in the form of a small flat brown head which is invaluable in winter. After BBC's *Gardeners' World* did a television programme in my garden, Peter Seabrook kindly gave me a spiraea, 'Gold Flame'. It has beautiful yellow foliage in spring, in fact it keeps a good colour all the year. The flowers are red as in 'Anthony Waterer' but it is for the foliage you grow it. *S. opulifolia lutea* may be known to you as *Physocarpus opulifolius luteus*. It has leaves rather like those of a flowering currant only smaller, borne on immensely tall shoots and on shorter curving sprays, both making a useful contribution for arranging. However, it is for its lime-green colour that I have grown to like it, most vivid in spring, but useful in the autumn when the leaf ends become tinged with bronze.

Conditioning Hammer ends of stems well and put into warm water. I find that the leaves of *S. opulifolea lutea* last better if the ends of the stems are plunged into boiling water before they are given a long drink.

Preserving When in seed head form, cut and remove the foliage, stand the stems in 2.5cm (1in) of water and allow them to dry off slowly in a warm atmosphere.

For the herbaceous 'spiraeas' see Aruncus, Astilbe and Filipendula.

Spotted Laurel *see* AUCUBA

Squill *see* SCILLA

Stachyrus praecox

Half-hardy deciduous shrub growing well in Cornwall. It has hanging trails of pale yellow flowers that are a great delight as they come so early in the year – often in February – like a real breath of spring.

Stachys lanata
Lamb's Ears

Hardy herbaceous perennial, useful for borders and rough ground. Its leaves are densely covered

Stachys lanata

with silky grey hairs, and are very effective for a small group of whites and greys. The flower is pretty when picked in midsummer, but I think I prefer to save it for drying: you then get a beautiful spike of grey to add to a vase of grey dried material and pink chrysanthemums in midwinter. It is grown widely in the United States. The non-flowering ground cover stachys 'Sheila Macqueen' is a great delight to me, not only because Alan Bloom did me the honour of calling it after me, but because it is such a useful plant.

Conditioning The leaves are better if you give them a long drink before arranging, but try not to submerge them or they will lose their silvery appearance.

Preserving As soon as the seed heads have formed, pick and bunch and hang them upside down to dry.

Star of Bethlehem *see* ORNITHOGALUM

Star of the Veldt *see* DIMORPHOTHECA

Stephanotis floribunda

Clustered Wax Flower, Madagascar Jasmine

Winter evergreen climbing greenhouse shrub. The beautiful star-shaped waxen flowers have a delicate perfume. Generally used for brides' bouquets or wedding head-dresses, but a cluster just laid on a cream-coloured shell with a few of the waxy leaves makes a superb decoration for the centre of a dining-room table. We used these clusters of flowers with green grapes, on a large gold platter, as a table centre for the dinner in Lancaster House after the Queen's Coronation.

Conditioning Stretch a piece of tissue paper over a shallow bowl of water and fix with an elastic band; then make holes in the paper and insert the flower stems. This prevents the waxy flowers from touching the water, which is very important as they would quickly turn brown. Given a few hours in water like this they will stand quite well for an hour or two for bouquets or flower arrangements.

Sternbergia lutea
Winter Daffodil

Bulbous plants with yellow crocus-like flowers, blooming surprisingly enough in the autumn. Although I have grown these for many years, mine rarely flower, alas; when they do, they provide me with a touch of real spring in November, and I put them into a little green 'moss garden', with any of the little bits that I can often find at that time of year, such as a *Primula* 'Wanda' and a spray or two of *Viburnum fragrans*.

Stinking Hellebore *see* HELLEBORUS

Stonecrop *see* SEDUM

Stransvaesia

S. davidiana is such a handsome shrub, clusters of white hawthorn-like flowers in May and clusters of the brightest red berries all winter. I first became acquainted with it in Seattle, where it overhung a wall covered with white wisteria and at the base a bed of pure white evergreen azaleas. Superb, was the only way to describe it. I have never had the chance to use it for flower arranging but I feel the flowers are too precious – better to wait as the berries are so good.

Strelitzia reginae
Bird of Paradise Flower

Warm-greenhouse plants that are natives of South Africa. They have angular orange flowers with a purple tuft. They are a little awkward to arrange, and, generally speaking, are most effective alone in a shallow dish with a few of their own leaves. Constance Spry had the fun of arranging quantities of them at the time of the Queen's Coronation. We grouped them massed in large boxes in Parliament Square, with other rare flowers flown in from all parts of the Commonwealth.

Conditioning Cut the ends of the stems on the slant and give a long drink.

Summer Snowdrop *see* LEUCOJUM

Sweet Pea *see* LATHYRUS

Sweet Rocket *see* HESPERIS

Sweet-Scented Tobacco *see* NICOTIANA

Sweet Sultan *see* CENTAUREA

Sweet William *see* DIANTHUS

Sycamore *see* ACER

Symphoricarpus
Snowberry

Hardy deciduous shrub with clusters of white berries in autumn. I am always amazed how long these stay on the bushes, right into the winter. The best variety that I know of is obtainable from the Sunningdale Nurseries, and they call it 'Constance Spry' as she used and loved it so much. By removing all the leaves, you get lovely sprays of berries to cascade from the front of a small vase. Use them either with green-and-white groups or with a vase of autumn colourings.

Symphytum

The variegated *Comfrey* is the only one that interests me at all for use in the garden and for flower arranging, and I must say I think it is remarkably striking with its green leaves deeply edged with white. It keeps a good variegation all the year and when the leaves mature in the autumn it will pick and stand very well in a vase. The green variety with mauve and pink flowers is a pretty wayside wild flower, but invasive and not really suitable for cultivation. The leaves are a great asset to a mixed green arrangement in August and September.

Conditioning Put the ends of the leaf stems in 2.5cm (1in) of boiling water, and then allow a long drink. It is impossible to condition them in the early part of the year.

Syringa
Lilac

Hardy deciduous flowering shrub known to us all as Lilac, and known best for its trusses of purple flowers with a very sweet scent. Nowadays there are many lovely hybrids as well, and the pink Preston Hybrids are well worth growing; their subtle soft colourings are lovely to use in a vase of pastel flowers, with some of the Suttons art-shade poppies, and pale pink peonies. There is also a beautiful yellow one *S. vulgaris* 'Primrose' that I have refrained from growing for a long time, but have recently come to enjoy. It makes a valuable and interesting contribution to a soft-yellow and cream arrangement in May and early June.

Conditioning It is most important to remove nearly all the foliage, as the stem does not seem able to take up enough water to supply flowers and leaves. If you want to arrange a vase of just lilac alone, then you must use separate branches of leaves. Hammer the ends of the stems very well, and then give a long drink in warm water. When using forced lilac in early spring, I find it will not last well on short stems; it needs hammering and the stems should be put into really boiling water, before they have a long drink.

Tamarix
Tamarisk

Hardy evergreen and deciduous shrubs, grow-ing well near the seaside. They have plumes of feathery pink flowers in summer, which make a good background for flowers at this time.

Conditioning Hammer ends of stems well and stand them in warm water.

Teasel *see* DIPSACUS FULLONUM

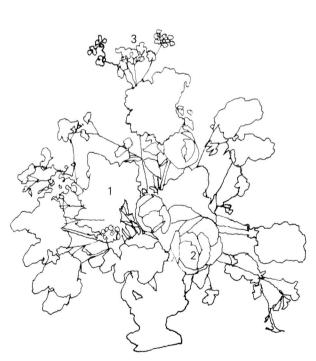

OVERLEAF
A simple white arrangement of delicacy and light.
1 Double white *syringa* (Lilac)
2 Single white *paeonia*, a Sylvia Saunders hybrid
3 *Anthriscus sylvestris* (Cow parsley, Queen Anne's Lace)

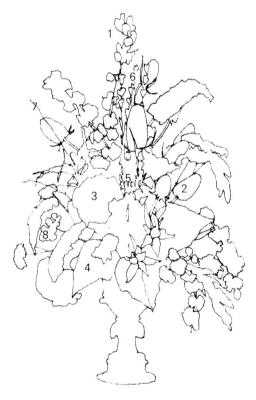

The mixture of dried and fresh flowers is perhaps one of the most interesting types of arrangement and one that lasts so well.
1 *Molucella laevis* (Bells of Ireland)
2 *Dipsacus fullonum* (Teasel)
3 *Hydrangea* heads
4 *Hedera colchica dentata* 'Variegata' (Ivy)
5 Globe artichoke
6 *Sisyrinchium striatum* (Satin flower)
7 Sweet corn seed heads and spikes
8 *Levisticum officinale* (Lovage)

Tellima grandiflora

Hardy perennial. A close relative of the *Heuchera* and *Tiarella*, this plant grows easily in woodland and makes a good ground cover. I grow it primarily for its leaves, which are heart-shaped and beautifully marked, often pinkish in their early stages and turning to a lovely bronzy colour in winter. I have used them very effect-ively at the base of a small arrangement in a candle cup with the October flowering gentian *G. sino-ornata* and a few sprays of *Viburnum fragrans*. The flowers of *T. grandiflora* are 60cm (2ft) spikes of small pink bells with a touch of green. They are a little insignificant but can nevertheless look well in contrast to bolder flower heads. *T. Americanum* is regarded by some people as a heuchera. Whatever its name it is most attractive and worth all the good treatment you can give it for the beautiful leaves it produces in early spring. It has dark maroon marking on a leaf not much darker than a *grandiflora*.

Conditioning The flowers and the leaves last better if their stems are plunged in a little boiling water before being given a long soaking.

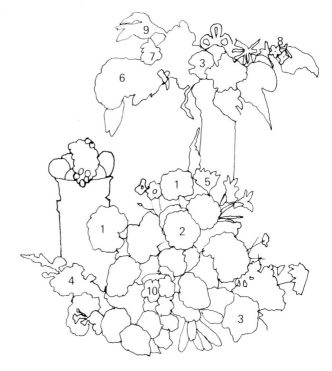

PREVIOUS PAGE
An arrangement specially designed for the celebration of a Ruby Wedding.
1 *Papaver somniferum* (Poppy)
2 *Dahlias*
3 Roses
4 *Antirrhinum* 'Bright Butterflies' (Snapdragon)
5 *Alstroemeria ligtu* hybrids (Peruvian lily)
6 *Alchemilla mollis* (Lady's mantle)
7 *Lonicera* (Honeysuckle)
8 *Nicotiana affinis* 'Lime Green' (Tobacco plant)
9 Grasses
10 *Pelargonium*

Cut flowers fade very quickly out of doors, so this mixed vegetable and herb basket might make an attractive arrangement for a barbecue.

Telopea speciosissima
Waratah

Australian bush with superb large flowers, slightly resembling a red protea. It is the New South Wales State flower, and I enjoyed using them in large arrangements in the British Pavilion at the British Fair in Sydney.

Thalictrum
Meadow Rue

Hardy herbaceous perennial with finely-cut green and grey-green leaves, and fluffy yellow and purple flowers in the summer. I find it most useful for the foliage as the flowers do not last very well in water. *T. glaucum* is my favourite as the foliage is blue-grey and I find it very good as a background in summer vases of greys and pinks. *T. dipterocarpum*, grows well in Scotland, has the loveliest flowers and I am always delighted to use it; it is so delicate with sprays of mauve flowers and looks charming arranged with a few sweet peas, or just alone in a glass vase.

Conditioning The foliage is better if given a really good soak, in deep warm water, but avoid submerging, which will diminish the grey effect of *T. glaucum*. I can recommend no special conditioning for the flowers, though a long drink is always a help.

Tiarella cordifolia
Foam Flower

Hardy perennial herb with a spreading habit which makes it suitable for ground cover. The heart-shaped leaves with dark veining are nice to use in small arrangements. It has small, white fluffy flowers in spring, which I use in small vases, but I grow it really for the leaves.

Conditioning Soak the leaves completely under water for several hours.

Tilia
Lime Tree

Hardy tree that from the flower arranger's point of view is quite wonderful. By removing the

Thalictrum dipterocarpum

Tiarella cordifolia

leaves when it is in blossom, you uncover the delightful small flowers and bracts of palest green which lend themselves as background to any summer flowers – to suggest but two, peonies and lilies. The stems, I discovered a few years ago, take up glycerine very well and you have delicate sprays of pale-brown bracts which add lightness to any dried group or make an unusual background for chrysanthemums.

Conditioning Peel off the bark up to about 5cm (2in) before giving a long drink.

Preserving Before the flower actually opens, pick the branches, remove the leaves and place the stems in a solution of glycerine and water.

Tobacco Plant *see* NICOTIANA

Tradescantia

Hardy herbaceous and tender perennials. The best known is *T. fluminensis*, a popular house plant with green and white leaves, pink-tinged if the plant is kept in a sunny position. It is most useful in bouquets and sprays, and I like to use small pieces in little vases, in winter especially. It has a sprawling, drooping form so that it is ideal to use falling from a candle cup. The hardy flowering form, *T. virginiana* (Moses in the Bulrushes), has showy blue, white or mauve flowers with three petals, and these can be used in mixed groups, but they need much of the foliage removed as the flowers are over-shadowed by the leaves.

Transvaal Daisy *see* GERBERA

Tree Primrose *see* OENOTHERA

Trillium
Wood Lily

Hardy tuberous-rooted perennial, not widely grown. They thrive in moist leaf-mould and have attractive lily-like leaves and white or mauve three-petalled flowers, which look well in a shallow bowl. Fix stems on a pin-holder, so that the full beauty of the flower is displayed.

Conditioning Put the ends of the stems into boiling water and then allow a long drink.

Triteleia
'Wisley Blue'

An attractive and useful little bulbous plant, of which I have only recently become aware and having grown it find that I use it in my moss gardens in early spring. It seems to increase freely and adds so much to a mixed bed of bulbs, with its soft lavender colour and starry flowers. It may well be known to some of you as *Ipheion*, or *Brodiaea*, for it seems to have been called all of these at one time or another.

Tritonia (Montbretia) *see* CROCOSMIA

Trollius
Globe Flower

Hardy herbaceous perennial rather like a double buttercup, with round heads in orange or yellow. *T. chinensis* is my favourite and has pale-yellow heads that I like to use with small sprays of *Acer pseudoplatanus brilliantissimum* and dark heads of auricula.

Conditioning Dip the ends of the stems into boiling water, before putting them up to their necks in cold water for a long drink.

Tropaeolum
Nasturtiums

Greenhouse and hardy perennials, dwarf and climbing. The hardy perennial creeper *T. speciosum* (Flame Flower) has scarlet flowers, and *T. polyphyllum* is a small yellow-flowered trailer. The yellow-flowered Canary Creeper, *T. peregrinum*, is best grown as an annual. The flowers of these climbers, and of the annual nasturtium, last exceedingly well when cut. The Shrewsbury Show in England always has a class for nasturtiums and it produces some lovely arrangements; this is such a good idea as it gives everyone a chance to compete. I love to arrange the flowers with their own trails (all the buds open out in water), and find them most effective arranged in wood or metals.

Conditioning Give a good long drink before arranging.

Trumpet Flower *see* DATURA

Tuberose *see* POLIANTHES

Tulip *see* TULIPA

Tulipa
Tulip

Hardy bulbs with very many varieties; it is difficult to choose which to mention. From the flower arranger's point of view, undoubtedly the delicate lily-flowered 'Moonlight' and many similar ones are lovely to work with. So, of course, are the May-flowering doubles, 'Mount Tacoma' (white), 'Eros' (pink), 'Lilac Time' (mauve), and so on, which give a good centre to any large group; grown well, they make enormous blooms that resemble a peony. 'Viridiflora' and 'Artist' are two very striking forms, and add enormous interest to any spring arrangement. And I would hate to be without the 'Apricot Beauty'. It has such a soft apricot colour, that contains a lot of pink and yellow, hence making it a marvellous colour combination for both pink and yellow arrangements. Parrot tulips are always decorative, with their feathery petals streaked with green on various colours, from almost black to shades of pink to pure white. The striped Rembrandt tulips are so typically Dutch that no modern Dutch group seems complete without them. At tulip time one can work out some beautiful colour combinations: black and apricot, pink and black, soft yellow and creams, apricot pinks . . . tulips make all these possible. The dwarf tulip species should not be overlooked. They cut well and make a striking feature for any small spring vase. As the bulbs are small and need care, it is best to grow them in a rock garden or trough so that they are not likely to be dug out during the summer. *Tulipa clusiana* is one of my favourites: its alternating pink and white petals give it a striped effect. The back of *T. hageri* is bright orange flushed with green and with the scarlet *T. linifolia* adds a vivid spot of colour. As they are very delicate, they want careful arrangement so that they are not overshadowed by larger flowers.

Conditioning Cut off the white end of the stem, wrap the bunch in newspaper with all the heads together and put in deep warm water for several hours. Tulips react well to the addition of a teaspoonful of sugar to the vase water. Just recently I have found that pricking with a pin right through the stem just under the head makes the tulips last much better.

Tulip Tree *see* LIRIODENDRON

Tulipa 'Viridiflora', 'Praecox' and 'Artist'

Turk's Cap Lily *see* LILIUM MARTAGON

Typha latifolia
'Bulrush', Reed Mace, Cat's Tail

Very useful for adding pointed shapes to a large group. *T. latifolia* is the native British bulrush and can be found in pools in many parts of the world. Invasive, so beware if you import it into your garden pond. The smaller varieties, *T. minima* and *T. gracilis* which grow so well in the lake at Winkfield Place (near Windsor), give me the opportunity to use it frequently. They last extremely well and dry off in water. I like them for background in green groups in summer, or with rushes and other water plants where you want to give that cool effect on a hot summer's day.

Preserving Try spraying the heads with hair-lacquer to prevent them from bursting indoors, as when this happens the fluff seems to travel everywhere.

Ulex
Gorse, Whin

Hardy evergreen shrub growing mainly on common land in Britain, and giving a blaze of yellow to the countryside in spring. Gorse burns easily in dry weather and therefore should not be planted near to buildings, roads or pathways. The double variety, *U. europaeus plenus*, makes a good garden shrub. Branches are effective for the house, but they need careful handling as the prickles are really quite vicious. Pick with thornproof gloves on, and strip off the lower branches, and it is then possible to handle it. I like to use the burnt stems of dried gorse for a dramatic effect in the early spring, with scarlet tulips. Of course it is important to select well-shaped branches.

Conditioning Remove the lower prickles and put into very hot water for a few hours.

Ulmus

Ulmus
Elm, Wych Elm

Hardy deciduous trees with green or variegated foliage. As a result of the vicious elm disease, the English countryside looks completely changed, sometimes for the better, though for me it brings real sadness, as I can no longer stop just to enjoy the outline of two particularly beautiful trees silhouetted against a grey winter sky because now they are gone. Fortunately the golden elms are little affected, and we have managed to keep the wych elm. Branches of the golden elms *U. procera aurea* and *U. glabra lutesceus* are glorious in a large group in springtime. The wych elm, *U. glabra*, has clusters of brilliant-green flower bracts, on slightly weeping branches, and these are interesting to use with a few tree peonies or tulips, or to add to mixed green foliages. I also like to pick the pink flowers on the ordinary elm trees in February or March and have them for a background for a vase of daffodils. The best-shaped bare branches are lovely for Christmas time; painted with gum and sprinkled with glass glitter, they look as if they were covered in frost.

Branches that have become diseased and look like cork, are effective arranged with a few chrysanthemums, as a background for some dried seed heads.

Conditioning For the flowering sprays and stems of the wych elm, it is important to hammer the ends of the stems very well, and then put them into boiling water for a minute or two before giving them a long drink.

Vallota speciosa
Scarborough Lily

Greenhouse evergreen bulbous plant. I enjoy using its brilliant scarlet lily flowers in a fruit and flower group in the early autumn. The vivid colour adds so much to a vase of late gladioli, dahlias and red roses, for a brilliant mixed red group.

Veltheimia

Tender bulbous-rooted plants for a cool greenhouse. In early spring they produce orange and reddish flowers closely resembling a red-hot poker. I have found they make an attractive show in a vase with red *Begonia rex* leaves and budding pink flowering cherry.

Venetian Sumach *see* RHUS

Veratrum
False Hellebore

Veratrum nigrum is the plant I know best. It has beautifully pleated leaves (which the slugs adore), and long slender spikes of almost-black flowers; these are a joy to use and are particularly effective with the seed heads of *Phytolacca*, some almost-black dahlias and a bunch of white 'Iceberg' floribunda roses.

Conditioning Cut the ends of the stems on the slant and give a good long drink.

Preserving In recent years I have found that one can dry these black stems with good effect, but it is important to leave them on the plant until the seed heads are set and formed, then pick and hang upside down to dry.

Verbascum
Mullein

Hardy biennial and perennial herb with yellow or pink flowers in summer. The wild yellow mullein, though quick to shed its flowers, has a good flower head and a very nice seed head. The mauve and pink spikes of *V. chaixii* are attractive in the border, but my favourite is *V. broussa*, with its 'cotton wool' leaves and stems; it is useful to put in a vase in its leaf stage and when in full flower.

Conditioning For the individual leaves, remove the fleshy part from the base of the leaf, especially the part that goes under water. If you fail to do this, you will find that the hairy leaves pick up the water and drip it off.

Preserving When the seed head has formed, remove the leaves and hang the heads upside down to dry.

Verbena

Half-hardy annual, flowering in a wide range of mauve, petunia and pinky shades. They make a good splash of colour in the garden and are effective in a small flower vase. They add gaiety to a vase of mixed annuals, and the double varieties last extremely well in water.

Conditioning Put ends of stems into boiling water, and then allow a long drink.

Veronica
Speedwell

Hardy herbaceous perennial with blue, pink or white flowers in summer. The blue varieties add a welcome touch of blue to an early summer vase of mixed flowers. This is another plant that I have recently become aware of, though I have known it for years; perhaps known to some of you as Hebe. These short bushes of dense evergreen leaves, a mass of flowers in summer, which turn violet to pinky, and white, reward one with a wealth of flower for many months. My favourites are the variegated foliage plants of *V. franciscana* 'Blue Gem Variegata', thick leaves broadly edged with creamy white, and *V. andersonii* 'Variegata'; both are superb for cut flowers and add greatly to the shrub border.

Viburnum
Guelder Rose, Snowball Tree, Wayfaring Tree

Hardy deciduous flowering shrubs with white and pink flowers, which most of all I enjoy for their lovely scent. To pick a sprig of *V. fragrans* in the late autumn or even midwinter, and put it into a small vase either alone or added to a few freesias, or into a 'moss garden' of little flowers, is a joy. They scent the whole room. *V. carlesii* or *V. carlcephalum* in April have rounded heads of sweetly-scented pinky-white flowers; these, added to a few pale-pink tulips, a spray of azaleas, and some bronzy peony foliage, make a charming arrangement. *V. carlcephalum* and *V. burkwoodii*, both crosses of *carlesii* are stronger in growth and bear larger flowers, and if you are starting from scratch I would advise *V. burkwoodii* as it is a very amenable shrub and will thrive in sunless areas and reward you with a wealth of bloom. *V. opulus sterile*, better known as the Snowball Tree, hanging with little green balls that turn white as they open, is a shrub that I love (see the arrangement on page 175), although I often use it in the green stage. It is forced in Holland and sold in long sprays in Britain during the early spring; its touch of emerald green enhances any vase. *V. tomentosum mariesii* is one of the most handsome of all viburnums, with showy white flowers in spring and lovely leaf colour in the autumn. The wild wayfarer, *V. lanata*, is lovely to pick in the flower stage, but almost more welcome for its berries in the autumn. Many of the viburnums have good autumn colour and I like to use the turning leaves. The arching sprays of the guelder rose, *V. opulus*, last better than almost any autumn foliage I know: it holds its leaves so well that they remain on the branches even when they are quite dry.

Conditioning Hammer the ends of the stems, or put the ends into boiling water for a few minutes, before giving a long drink.

Viburnum tinus
Laurustinus

Hardy evergreen with small rounded leaves and clusters of pink flowers in midwinter. Attractive used with or without its foliage. I like to remove the leaves to get the full colour from the flowers, using these in a vase of very early pink tulips and perhaps a few narcissi. A very useful shrub to grow, and excellent for picking well into the spring.

Viburnum tinus

Conditioning Hammer ends of stems well, before giving a long drink.

Vinca
Periwinkle

Hardy evergreen trailing plant used mainly as good ground cover, but the green and white variegated variety has become popular for flower arrangement. These trails, if well conditioned, are a great asset for drooping down from a tall vase of either mixed shades of green or of flowers, now that plants with naturally drooping stems are more and more in demand for arrangements.

Conditioning Put ends of stems into boiling water, then give a long drink (and in the case of variegated varieties, submerge completely) for several hours.

Viola
Pansy, Violet, Hearts-ease

Hardy perennials with a sprawling habit and of many types, including the violet. Violets are nice to have in a small vase surrounded by their own leaves; always try to leave a stem or two out of water so that you can get the benefit of the scent – in water they quickly lose it. Pansies can be arranged alone or in a mixed vase. The small viola are ideal for a small or miniature arrangement. Two that Valerie Finnis gave to me are sheer delight, 'Irish Molly' and 'Bowles Black'. These have very distinctive faces and colouring. *V. cucullata* 'Freckles', white with purple spots and *V. septentrionalis*, scentless but enchanting white with veins of blue. All these and even the little Johnnie jump up's, as they are called in America, flower for weeks as long as you can remove all the dead flower heads.

Conditioning No special treatment for pansies, but violets last better if their heads are dipped into water for a few minutes before you begin to arrange them.

Viscum album
Mistletoe

Traditionally a Christmas decoration, and connected with 'kissing under the Mistletoe', and so it has become a custom to hang up a sprig in every home at this time. I love to make a mistletoe ball with a round of Oasis; I stick in the stems until they make a rounded effect and then hang it up with scarlet ribbons. Or it is extremely pretty in small pieces arranged for a table centre and combined with Christmas roses and white candles.

Vitis coignetiae

Vitis
Vine

Hardy perennial climbing plants with brilliant autumn colouring. *V. coignetiae*, with handsome spade-shaped leaves, is one of the most valuable from my point of view. A few of these leaves at the base of an autumn group are a great asset. The purple-leaved vine has useful foliage and charming little bunches of purple grapes. I grow a small vine called the strawberry vine because the grapes are thought to taste of strawberries, but I rarely eat them as I find it so useful to cut the small bunches of fruit and let them hang from the front of a vase.

Conditioning The sprays of leaves should be put into boiling water for a few minutes, before being given a long drink. The fruit needs no special treatment.

Preserving Odd leaves of good autumn colour may be pressed between sheets of newspaper. It is then advisable to put a florist's wire right up the back of the leaf and stick it with adhesive tape to make a false stem.

Water Lily *see* NYMPHAEA

Willow *see* SALIX

Winter Aconite *see* ERANTHIS

Winter Cherry *see* SOLANUM *and* PHYSALIS

Winter Daffodil *see* STERNBERGIA

Winter Sweet *see* CHIMONANTHUS

Wisteria sinensis

Hardy deciduous climbing shrub with very sweet-scented trailing mauve or white blossom in May. It can be grown as a standard, though it is generally seen on walls or against houses. It is beautiful as a cut flower, but does not last very long in water. Used for the glory of one night it looks splendid alone in a vase, or with mauve lilac and mauve and pink tulips.

Conditioning The method used in Japan is to put the stems into pure alcohol as soon as they are cut, and then to give a long drink.

Yarrow *see* ACHILLEA

Yucca
Adam's Needle, Spanish Bayonet

Hardy and half-hardy evergreen shrubs with stiff tall spikes of creamy white bell-shaped flowers, growing out of a tuft of sword-like green leaves. Some of the finest specimens were those growing round the White House in Washington (alas, no longer there). I have used these elegant flowers for many special occasions; they are wonderful for a really large arrangement.

Conditioning It is most important to put the ends of the stems into boiling water before giving a long drink.

Yulan *see* MAGNOLIA

Zantedeschia aethiopica
Arum Lily, Calla Lily

Generally a hothouse plant. There is a good hardy variety of *Z. aethiopica*, the white arum lily, but I have only seen it flourishing in warm corners of Ireland and Cornwall. Beautiful pure white flowers and spade-shaped leaves – but too often considered funereal. It is ideal for large groups and for church flowers to be seen from a distance. *Z. elliottiana*, the yellow species, is also very handsome and bears leaves with silvery, semi-transparent spots.

All these lilies have a texture that is almost like chamois leather and they show up better from a distance than perhaps any flower I can name. For a line arrangement in early spring, three blooms and a well-shaped branch give a vase a simple beauty and outlive a bunch of daffodils by days. At last I too can grow these lilies on my south wall and even more exciting is the green one, 'Green Dragon'. I brought the seed back from Kenya and Fred Wilkinson at Winkfield Place raised them and has grown them in quantity, but I must say that my plant has excelled itself this year. For a green group they make the focal point almost better than anything else.

Conditioning Give a long drink in a bucket of warm water up to their necks after picking. The leaves can be made to last much longer, for large groups especially, if submerged in a weak solution of starch water for twenty-four hours; this gives a slightly shiny appearance, but is worth doing for church festivals, when it is helpful to have groups that last well without much attention.

Yucca

Zea mays
Maize, Indian Corn

Z. mays japonica variegata is a half-hardy annual with truly beautiful cream and green striped leaves. There is also a pink and yellow strain which when mature goes a rich reddish purple. Both of these are great assets for the flower arranger. The seed heads are good in a fruit and flower group in autumn, or in a dried group. Suttons list an ornamental sugar corn with mature cobs ranging in colour from golden to purple, and this is particularly good.

Conditioning Do not pick until the plant is mature and fully grown, as before this the foliage is very tender and will not last well. Burn the ends of the stems and then allow a long drink in really deep water for at least twelve hours.

Preserving All corn can be preserved by hanging the heads upside down in a warm place. The husks turn a lovely golden colour and can be turned back to expose the cob, and used with fruits, or mounted on a wire and put in the centre of a dried group.

Zebrina pendula
Wandering Jew

Greenhouse plant easily confused with tradescantia, but it has slightly larger leaves, about 7.5cm (3in) long, striped with silver and backed with purple. *Z. purpusii* has mid-green leaves with purple on both sides and can be seen on page 122.

Zenobia pulverulenta

Half-hardy evergreen shrub, liking peat and sandy loam and a moist sheltered position. The foliage is a delightful bluish-grey and the small bell-like flowers appear in pendulous clusters in June. The flowers will show more clearly if a very few leaves are removed, and then sprays of all lengths are of great value.

Conditioning Hammer the ends of the stems before giving a long drink.

Zinnia

Half-hardy annuals. There are many varieties that vary in both height and colour, from the really large daisy-flowered head to the dwarf doubles. They have most lovely vivid colouring and give the much desired focal point for the flower arranger. Coming in every shade of red, pink, orange and cream, also white and even green, they are in constant use in the late summer and autumn for all kinds of mixed flower groups. 'Envy', the green zinnia, is one to have. It normally needs a lot of sun for best effect. This little green delight is worth a corner of any garden.

Conditioning Cut and allow a long drink. If the blooms are exceptionally fine, it is advisable to put a thin stick up the hollow stem to prevent it from breaking.

Zenobia pulverulenta

Zinnia elegans 'Envy'

Zygocactus truncatus
Christmas Cactus

Greenhouse or house plant with cerise fuchsia-like flowers at Christmas-time. Good to use as a cut flower and effective with cerise anemones and small pieces of evergreen.

Part Three
Entertaining and special occasions

All through our lives flowers play a very special part. They are sent at the birth of a baby, and are the final tribute that you pay to anyone who has been closely associated with you all your life. They make a lovely accompaniment to a christening, a confirmation, to birthdays and weddings and all the major events of our lives. So here are some ideas for different ways of arranging flowers on these very important occasions, plus suggestions for simple party flowers and, if you are entertaining single-handed, how to get the best effect with the least amount of effort.

It is particularly important to make sure that arrangements on these occasions are seen by everybody. When you have a large number of people in a room there is no way flowers can be seen unless the arrangements are at or above eye-level. Arrangements on low tables simply won't be noticed and there is always the risk of their being disturbed in the crush. I would always aim to have a limited number of really bold arrangements with distinct colours rather than smaller more fragile arrangements which are, anyway, more appropriate for less crowded occasions.

When making large arrangements plenty of background material will be required and I suggest you should think ahead about this – you will need really large branches of foliage and they will in turn need a lot of careful conditioning. Hammer the woody stems particularly hard and cut the soft ones, putting them into deep water for at least twelve hours. Have all the vases ready in advance and tie in the wire netting with string or wire so that it is really secure. Have all your working materials ready in a basket – dust sheets, cones, scissors, extra string and florist's wire.

If you are doing flowers in a church, be sure to find out if it is free at the time you want to do the job; and if it is in a strange church, see that the vicar or clergyman is agreeable that you should do it then. It is only polite to find out if this is convenient, and may save you from clashing with a service or some other function. Nothing could be more frustrating than waiting for this to be over, and you may have a lot of worry over whether you will be ready in time. Always allow yourself plenty of time – nothing is more exhausting than doing flowers against the clock.

Christenings

Whenever possible, place some flowers actually round the top of the font itself. With the use of Oasis this presents few problems. Cut pieces of Oasis off the large bricks, making them about 4cm ($1\frac{1}{2}$in) thick and as wide as the width of the font top, and use them to make a garland. Then cover them with a layer of moss, tightly packed but with some quite large spaces in between. You then fix into the Oasis as many flowers as possible, preferably with firm stems, as they stick into the Oasis much more easily. When using bunches of primroses, or violets in early spring, make them into little bunches surrounded by their own leaves, and with your finger make a hole in the Oasis to take each bunch. Always keep one or two flowers of the same colour together even if not of the same variety, and so with a series of small clumps you continue your garland effect, with grape hyacinths, scilla polyanthus, and small pieces of blossom. Later in the year you can use daisies or narcissi, bunches of apple blossom or any child-like or simple flowers. The whole gives the impression of things growing and is one of the prettiest ways of decorating a font. Place the flowers in the Oasis so that they are well balanced since wet Oasis is very firm and you will need no additional support. A circle of plastic cut to fit the font will keep any surplus water from damaging the stone. This is just a precaution as normally the flowers are there for such a little time that it is unlikely that any harm would be done. But if you are leaving the flowers over-night then I would certainly use the ring of plastic. Small oblong bread tins painted and well weighted make excellent containers for the narrow edge of a font. As the service for a christening is not very long it is possible to lay flowers out of water round the edge of the font, but I am never very happy about this. Leave a large gap where the vicar is going to stand as it can be so uncomfortable watching him trying to keep the sleeves of his vestments out of the flowers. The effect that you are really making is a horse-shoe design. If you can do this, it is ideal, as the flowers can be seen and enjoyed by everyone. If you do not want to decorate the entire font and only want to make a spray of flowers, place one large piece of wet Oasis, wrapped in foil, on the front of the font. This can be arranged in a long low arrangement, and very effective it will look. However, if it is not possible, for some reason, to have any flowers on the font then it is a good idea to place the flowers in a vase nearby, either on a pedestal or raised in some way so that they stand at the back out of the way and yet are seen to advantage. Flowers are so often placed at the foot of the font – which is nice for the church services – but the flowers are obscured when you have a gathering of people round the font. Any florists will make a small garland if they are told exactly what is required – so if you cannot undertake to do it yourself, it can be made up on a moss frame (rather like a wreath) and the flowers wired into it. Choose delicate flowers: single American spray chrysanthemums are one of the best flowers to use for this, and as they are available nearly all the year round there should be no difficulty in getting them. Often people like to have pale pink or blue, and I think white takes a

The joy of autumn flowers and fruits arranged on a shallow brass tray, making a suitable arrangement for Thanksgiving, harvest festival or autumn party.

1   Roses 'All Gold'
2   *Achillea taygetea* 'Moonshine'
3   Variegated *hosta*
4   *Bergenia* foliage
5   *Molucella laevis* (Bells of Ireland)
6   *Kniphofia* 'Maid of Orleans' (Red-hot poker)
7   Courgette (Yellow squash)
8   Apples
9   Aubergine (Egg plant)
10   *Hypericum elatum* 'Elstead'
11   Sweet corn spikes
12   *Rosa moyesii* hips
13   *Mahonia bealei* foliage

lot of beating – it is so fresh and innocent-looking. When you are decorating the church for a christening, and are not just decorating the top of the font, try to find out where the relatives and friends are going to stand or sit, according to where the font is situated; then you can get an idea of exactly where it is best to place the flowers so that they can be well in view.

Confirmation

You may find the opportunity comes for arranging flowers at a confirmation service which may take place in a school chapel, and I have seen many impressive arrangements at these services. One of the loveliest colour schemes was in all shades of apricots and creams. White, again, always looks right, and shows up well, especially if the church is at all dark. For panelled or poorly lit, dark corners you must use light colours, either pale pink, yellow or white. Avoid blue or purple. For many confirmation services, only the altar is decorated; but if it is possible to have a large group near the steps where the candidates are to kneel, this is quite the best place.

Birthdays

Birthdays for the young may well call for a discotheque, casual wear and jeans being so much the order of the day! So perhaps flowers are not of the same importance as they were some years ago, though I still feel that a few groups or vases of flowers do help so much towards making the festive spirit, and bring life to any hall or room. It could well be that a hanging arrangement is one of the best ways of making a quick impact without too much trouble or expense. Take a shallow round basket and put in its base a piece of Oasis in a plastic bag – the bag should fit fairly tightly round the Oasis and keep it firm when you wet it. Fix two wires across the basket to hold the Oasis in place. You will find that a few heads of rhododendron, or some open roses will last well and look most effective. If flowers are very scarce then add a ribbon bow with streamer ends which will fill a large area. It is amazing how few

The delightful foliages of Christmas.
1 *Ilex aquifolium* 'Silver Queen' and berries (Holly)
2 *Elaeagnus pungens* 'Aurea Maculata'
3 *Garrya elliptica*
4 *Hedera colchica dentata* 'Variegata' (Ivy)
5 *Arum italicum pictum*

flowers you need and how much effect you can get by using hanging baskets in this way.

There are of course special birthdays, such as twenty-firsts, and naturally they call for a party. If it should be a dinner, then the table is very important. Table flowers must be kept low or really high, and should in no way detract from the easy flow of conversation; it is most distracting if you have to talk round the flowers. For a girl, especially, the flowers are best kept in soft colours, unless those of her college, or sports club, or other particular colours are chosen. We have done a table in racing colours on one occasion. Deep reds are good and suitable for a young man, and I saw a lovely twenty-first table done in pewter and shades of lilac through to deep red which looked extremely handsome for such an occasion. If the flowers are for a dance, then the surroundings should really dictate what is best and try, above all, to keep the decorations well out of the way – buffet flowers, though so nice to have, are better concentrated in perhaps just one spectacular vase.

If the party is to be held in a marquee, decorations that hang will give the best results. Tent poles are always a problem and look better covered. If you can get them just bound round with some of the lining of the marquee, they will fade gently into the background – whereas so often if they are decorated with either green or garlands, they stand out and are more of an eyesore than ever. Tins, or Oasis in foil can be fixed round the poles, and filled with flowers; in this way the pole becomes part of the decoration, which is especially effective if the flowers are so placed that they cascade gracefully downwards. Flower balls – with a base of Oasis covered in wire netting and foil, and then the stems of some tough sort of flower such as spray chrysanthemums, dahlias, hydrangeas – make a quick and easy decoration. Tie the top of the ball with ribbons and let these ends fall. It is important that the flower balls are as large as possible, as once you raise them in a big space they are quickly dwarfed. Pedestals can be used, but so often the sloping sides of the marquee prevent adequate height and they can look out of proportion. Also, the floor may have been laid on uneven ground, and this can make them unstable. Garlands hung round the walls, made out of either evergreens or suitable flowers, look most effective, but take a lot of making.

In our family we have a tradition that has gone on for many generations. We make a posy and put it on the back of their chair when the 'birthday person' comes down for breakfast. It is such a small thing, but immediately gives a feeling of it being rather a special day.

Weddings

My first feeling when a wedding is being discussed is what does the bride really want? So often it seems that everyone else in the family has ideas about what she should have, and she herself hardly gets a chance to express any ideas of her own. Of course a bride is sometimes quite happy for her mother or some other member of the family to take over the flowers and make all the decisions for her. In that case – fine, but always give her the chance to say what she would like. She may have a fixed idea from childhood that she would like to carry red roses, and it is nice that she should have her wish, despite any opposition!

Ideally, the whole wedding should be carried out as a scheme, so that the colourings for the bridesmaids and pages link up with the general effect, both in the church and at the reception. The result is so pretty if the colourings can be carried through, but of course this may not be possible for one reason or another; perhaps the difficulty in getting, say, red flowers in winter; or some unavoidably dominant colour in the church. White is always a safe choice; it looks as lovely as anything can look for either church or reception, and makes a traditional link with the bride. In any case, decide first what the bride will carry, and if this involves any colour then this may decide many other details. Then consider the colourings for the bridesmaids and their flowers. Having arranged all this, visit the church to think out what would be best. This depends so much on what the church is like, and whether it is large or small, and also the number of guests. The flowers may need to be spread out through the church if there are to be a lot of people. If, on the other hand, only half the church will be in use, then just decide to decorate the most important places: the altar, chancel steps, window-sills, and so on. I find that in a small church one large group at the side of the lectern or pulpit is quite enough. Decoration of the altar depends on whether the flowers are to be placed on the altar itself, or whether there is to be a pedestal vase on one side, or a pair of vases, one on each side. If a pair is called for, then a low bowl on a stool on either side may be all that is wanted.

Window-sills are a good place for flowers, as they help to spread the concentration of colour right to the back of the church and give it a really flowery look. I have sometimes arranged small posies on the pew ends – it is quite a lot of work, but the effect is extremely pretty and gives the feeling that the whole church is filled with flowers. I think it is only a good idea if the posies can be easily attached – you really need something like the old umbrella-stand fittings you find in some churches to attach them to. Tie the posies with a ribbon bow with long ends, and this finishes them off nicely.

There are many other ideas. For instance, you may have the opportunity of hanging something. This can be done from the screen if it allows, or occasionally from the light fittings. I had a wonderful opportunity of doing this in a recent wedding in the Inner Temple at the Inns of Court in London. The beautiful chandelier light fittings called for flowers, and, by luck, they were actually moveable, so this enabled me to lower them and attach iron baskets which were, actually, copies of Italian bird cages. These were filled with masses of white flowers and as the bride walked up the aisle under the four baskets she really looked as if she were walking under a canopy. We also had fun in giving all the 'Templars' a posy as they lay in their shrouds of stone, and I think this caused more comments from the guests than anything else!

If the church is narrow and is to hold a lot of people then something that will hang, and perhaps something for the window-sills, may be all that is required, and you can cut out the idea of a large group altogether. The flowers that you use are important, and should be as bold as possible. Choose some light background-material – branches of flowers, shrubs, or blossom in the spring, delicate sprays of beech,

or branches of stripped lime flowers. Then try four good, well-grown and solid flowers. This is the time when really large heads of delphiniums, lupins, large dahlias, chrysanthemums, hydrangeas, and lilies, all make ideal materials. Get everything collected and put into water the day before, so that it is as fresh as possible. Long sprays of berries in the autumn are excellent. Pressed bracken, branches of lichen, and preserved beech branches are very acceptable backgrounds, and much lighter and more interesting than the sombre winter foliage of, say, laurel or rhododendrons.

The reception may be in a house, hall or marquee each of which will present different problems. Many people feel the reception is the more important place to concentrate on, but I don't really think this is so. Although the reception lasts longer, everyone is busy meeting people and talking and eating, so that flowers quickly get forgotten; whereas in the church, before the bride arrives, there is time to sit and look at the flowers and so I think they are much more important there. However, the one place where they are really essential is to give a welcome at the reception. A vase to greet the guests at the entrance to the hall or marquee is in the most important place of all. The colourings here depend on the surroundings: if the hall is light or dark; if in a marquee, the colour of the lining and so on. Again, raise the flowers well up as although they may be seen by the first arrivals wherever they are placed, once you have a crowd of people they may never be seen again! The table where the cake is to stand is a good focal point, and a white cloth caught up with posies of flowers is one of the best ways of decorating it. For the cake itself the usual small silver vases are now more often replaced by a low mound of flowers that are wired into a moss pad or stuck into a mound of Oasis lined with silver foil. This is much more satisfactory from every point of view, and there is no worry about the water spilling. A garland of matching flowers around the base of the cake is the nicest way of finishing it off. The buffet is another place for flowers and here I think it should be left to the discretion of the caterers as to where they can be placed, so that they will not hamper the service.

If the cake is on a separate table, as I suggested above, then a vase in the middle of the buffet is the best place – and one really important vase is better than anything else. Candelabra, often lent by the caterers, can be fitted with candle cups, and as these are well out of the way and quite tall, they are one of the most effective and economical ways of doing a buffet table. A pyramid of roses can look very well. These pyramids can be arranged with various sorts of flowers: peonies, camellias, green grapes, gardenias . . . If you are really going to town on the buffet, a petticoat of fine material such as muslin or nylon can be made to fit the trestles, hanging loosely so that it can be caught up in loops and finished with posies of flowers. Years ago this was done with green smilax ferns. For one of the loveliest weddings I remember, we did the whole marquee in hydrangea colourings: a soft pink buffet cloth caught with posies of hydrangeas and ribbons; and round the sides large posies of hydrangeas, with ribbons looped from posy to posy all round the marquee.

Other wedding celebrations include ruby, silver, gold and diamond. All of these call for different ideas and give one plenty of scope. For a ruby wedding, the colouring must, I think, be reds; and groups of red flowers on a white or soft pink cloth can be effectively arranged in gold or silver containers. The nicest silver wedding decorations that I have arranged were done with plastic fronds of fern, sprayed with white paint and heavily glittered with a mixture of glass glitter and a little silver, and put into one of the long mirror-troughs so that the flowers stretched down the table. Then I used white full-blown roses, pure white stocks and white dahlias, having first removed all the green foliage, and added silver ribbon bows with the ends trailing down the table. This gave a glittering silvery-white effect, and on such an occasion as this I feel it is permissible to mix fresh and artificial flowers, even though it is something to be avoided generally.

Golden weddings are very special occasions. The colouring is easily decided of course, and one has a wide range with all the yellow and gold colourings. Usually it is a dinner table that one is planning for, though my parents had a garden party and I did all the flowers in the marquee in golds and creams, as well as one or two vases in the house. An inexpensive gold buffet cloth was achieved most effectively by Constance Spry at the time of the Queen's Coronation, by painting the cloths. These were plastic and painted gold, so that from the distance they looked exactly like rich gold velvet. Vases are easily sprayed with gold paint for a quick and inexpensive result, though a mixture of gold and silver is prettier.

I have only once had the fun of doing a diamond wedding. We arranged the table with large chunks of pavement glass, that looked as much like diamonds as one could get, then tucked in white gardenias, camellias, and lily of the valley, and the whole took on a sparkling, glassy and – we hoped – diamond-like shimmer.

Barbecues, cocktails and other parties

For a large number of guests a barbecue could be the answer or, to take an idea from America, a lazy Sunday Brunch. This, as the word conveys, is breakfast and lunch combined, and is served at about midday. It has become extremely popular with all ages, allowing the sports enthusiasts to have a round of golf or play tennis, before the day's festivities. Kedgeree, fish cakes, coddled eggs, home-made rolls, honey and marmalade, are the order of the day and flowers and/or foliage need to be simple. Brunch seems to call for very simple containers of wood or metal, and hessian table cloths, scrubbed pastry boards and baskets all seem to fill the bill. For colour try browns, creams and fawns, or apricots and yellows – even, perhaps, hot reds.

For a barbecue what about a basket filled with mixed vegetables? (See photograph on page 218.) It is never very satisfactory to have cut fresh flowers outside as they wilt so rapidly in the air, and wind is fatal for them. You could have a lovely lot of potted plants or the pot-et-fleur idea. But as vegetables are really so decorative I would be inclined to go for them. Root vegetables last fresh longest. Carrots, radish, turnips and onion you can rely on and heads of cauliflower, calabrese and purple sprouting broccoli are all effective. Cabbages can wilt, though I have stood them and other brassicas in a brick of wet Oasis and they were all fresh next day. Globe artichoke, peppers green or red, aubergine (egg plant), mushrooms are all superb so there is plenty of choice. Should you decide to use herbs, such as parsley or mint, you must place them in a small jar (easily concealed) filled with water.

For a cocktail or buffet party a large arrangement on the table with the food is ideal. Fruit and flowers can be arranged together on a flat plate of wood or pewter, and on to this you can pile up colourful apples, lemons, plums, peaches and bunches of grapes – in fact, almost any fruit in season, though I am never very happy about either oranges or bananas, but this is purely a personal prejudice. I find that a well pin-holder is best for putting the fresh flowers into, as it holds just enough water and is easily disguised. Place the pin-holder at the back of the plate and pile the fruit round it; then put in some coloured foliage or berries, and one or two rather special flowers, such as carnations, nerines, a stem of lilies, a spray of orchid, or a few full-blown red or orange roses – depending on the time of year. Early spring flowers never seem quite right for fruit arrangements. Late spring, summer and autumn are the most suitable times: partly because this sort of arrangement should give the feeling of plenty, as with harvest thanksgiving mixtures of fruits and flowers. A fruit and flower arrangement raised in a high vase, and not kept low on a flat plate, is also effective and can look well on the buffet table, to add height among the food and wines that you may be using.

Other flowers arranged about the rooms can be of your own choice. As with other gatherings where you have a lot of people in a small space, don't forget to raise the flowers so that they are seen by everyone. Mixed reds are always popular, and are arresting and exciting, and add to the party spirit. Bold colourings seem better than the whites and greens, but again so much will depend on what the room colourings are.

Halloween

Halloween is, perhaps, a new party idea for some of us though it has been celebrated in the United States for many years. In fact it is said to have been celebrated in Druid times, and is of Irish and Scottish origin. It is sometimes called the 'festival of the dead', being held on 31 October, the eve of All Saints' Day. Hence its association with ghosts and churchyards. The Irish brought this custom to America and it is still widely celebrated as a children's event. Children dress up as ghosts and witches and go in groups from house to house 'trick' or 'treating'. The 'tricks' can be soaping windows, or knocking on doors and running away. The 'treats' are usually sweets or biscuits.

The houses are beautifully decorated, many with decorations particularly on the front door, either with a garland or decorative corn, and gourds, dried materials, door wreaths, or carved-out pumpkins. You cut the top off a pumpkin or a large turnip or swede and hollow it out. Then carve out a face, that is, eyes, nose and mouth, and place a lighted candle in the middle, or an electric light bulb. I cut a pumpkin nearly in half, just making one piece slightly larger, hollowed it out, placed in it a half brick of wet Oasis and made a Halloween table centre, by filling it with flowers and autumn leaves. Halloween colours are black and orange, and in the States many coloured plates and napkins are sold in these colours which make a very attractive table for a tea party, followed by games like bobbing for apples.

Christmas decorations

Decorating the home for Christmas is something that nearly everyone wants to do, and for most of us it is just a matter of how much time we can give to it. With the very good electric fittings available today one can light up the Christmas tree so well that it saves greatly on the decorations. Trees are most effective, I think, when they are decorated in two colours, or perhaps three, so that all the decorations are either silver and blue, red and gold, green and red, or, adding another colour, green, red and silver, or gold, silver and blue. This is perhaps difficult, but if you bring it off it makes the most elegant and distinctive tree you can imagine. Many years ago Constance Spry did the trees for

Westminster Abbey in this way and I have never seen anything prettier.

Children love to decorate the tree, as soon as they are old enough, and it is a wonderful way of filling in an afternoon at this difficult time of year. They can make simple decorations out of silver paper, cardboard and foil. If you have a colour scheme in mind it is best simply to provide papers and bits only in the colours you want. One piece of advice I will continue to give is to establish very early on exactly where the tree is to stand and to make it a convenient place! (It is so often tricky to move the tree around once it is decorated.) I think most children are sticklers for convention and tradition, and like to see it thereafter in the same place every year.

Garlands are extremely decorative, and can be made out of most evergreen – box, yew, any conifer, and holly, either variegated or berried – but avoid bay and ivy as both of these die easily when out of water. Make the garland on string, and bind with fine reel wire. Cut all the pieces in lengths of about 7.5cm (3in) and for easy working have these laid out in piles ready for use. Bind each piece on to the string with a figure-of-eight movement, once over the stem and once under. In this way they stay firm. I find wire holds the stems better than string.

If you are making garlands for your church those made on rolled newspaper stick well on stone pillars. Garlands do take quite a lot of time but they are most effective, and can be used in so many situations, round the picture frames, lintels of the doors or wound round the staircase.

The Christmas table is always a place for flowers or some decoration. I find one of the easiest and most successful ideas for quick effect is just to place a wide strip of red felt, right along the length of the table – mine is about 18cm (7in) wide. On this you can place mixed fruits and crackers even if you do nothing else. Candle cups can be used with any candlesticks, and look splendid filled with fresh holly, red candles, and some of that very pretty glitter added. Plasticised

ferns and red ribbon bows all add a further Christmassy look.

One of the most dramatic table arrangements is to put a large white church candle into an Oasis holder, and surround it with fresh green foliage or plastic ferns and flowers in colourings suited to your room. Dried materials sprayed with gold or silver aerosol sprays, and sprinkled with a little gold glitter when the paint is still tacky, add a pretty touch to a very economical and effective decoration.

The North American custom of hanging a wreath on the front door to give a welcome is one of the most charming ideas. Even if you don't want to make a wreath, just a bunch of evergreens tied with a ribbon bow is sufficient. You can use a metal coat-hanger made into a round; or buy a lamp-shade ring, bind it with ribbon and put clusters of evergreens attached with wire round the circle. The traditional form is a circular evergreen wreath with a bow of red ribbon at the top, with the ends hanging down. However, it can be varied in any way you like.

Paper flowers are easily made once you know how to do it, and with a wide range of shiny stretch paper you have a chance of making lovely decorations. There are many classes, and you should have no difficulty in getting help and instruction from one of the many Flower Clubs should you want to learn.

Finally, a brief word about church flowers at Christmas. I find with delight that many churches have now gone in for having a Christmas tree, which immediately gives the right feeling. You can add to this best by making a simple arrangement for the altar. I have used some curved branches of willow, or alder with the catkins just showing, and with a paint brush have put some clear glue on the branches, and sprinkled them with glitter which picks up the light. I have then added variegated holly, and either arum lilies or white chrysanthemums, or, when possible, sprays of red berries, holly or cotoneaster.

Suppliers' names and addresses

BULBS
Walter Bloom & Sons Ltd., Coombelands
Nurseries, Leavesden, Watford, Herts
Broadleigh Gardens, Bishop's Hull, Taunton,
Somerset
Van Tubergen Ltd., Willowbank Wharf, Ranelagh
Gardens, Fulham, London, SW6

FERNS
Reginald Kaye Ltd., Waithman Nurseries,
Silverdale, Carnforth, Lancs.

ROSES
E. B. Le Grice (Roses) Ltd., Roseland Nurseries,
North Walsham, Norfolk
John Mattock Ltd., Nuneham Courtney, Oxford
David Austin Roses, Bowling Green Lane,
Albrighton, Wolverhampton, WV7 3HB (Constance
Spry Roses and hybrids)

SEEDS
Sutton & Sons Ltd., Torquay, Devon
Unwin & Sons, Histon, Cambridgeshire
Thompson & Morgan Ltd., London Road,
Ipswich, Suffolk

SHRUBS
Hillier & Sons, Winchester, Hampshire
Notcutt's Nurseries Ltd., Woodbridge, Suffolk
John Scott & Co., The Royal Nurseries, Merriott,
Somerset

UNUSUAL PLANTS
Beth Chatto, White Barn House, Elmstead Market,
Colchester, Essex
Margery Fish Nursery, East Lambrook Manor,
South Petherton, Somerset
Treasures of Tenbury Ltd., Tenbury Wells,
Worcestershire
Mrs Desmond Underwood, Colchester, Essex.
(Specializes in grey foliages)

Index